CATHERINE BOOTH
From Timidity to Boldness

David Malcolm Bennett

To Mary Bennett

From David Bennett

Christmas 2020

MORNING STAR PUBLISHING

Published by Morning Star Publishing
An imprint of Bible Society Australia
GPO Box 4161
Sydney NSW 2001
Australia

ISBN 9780647530726

Cataloguing-in-Publication entry is available from the National Library
of Australia http://catalogue.nla.gov.au.

This edition first published in 2020

Cover design and typesetting by John Healy

CONTENTS

PERMISSIONS

Thanks go to the British Library, The Salvation Army and the Booth family for permission to quote from the Booth Papers, ref: 64799–64806. Thanks also go to the International Heritage Centre of The Salvation Army for permission to quote from Catherine Booth's Reminiscences, ref: CBB/8/2/1.

ACKNOWLEDGEMENTS

A special thank you goes to Garth Hentzschel who dropped a few hints that I should write this book and gave practical support and encouragement once I had started it. Thanks also go to the following who helped in various ways: Julia Archer, Phil Case, Angela Egan, Ruth Macdonald, Trevor Sketcher, Sue Ellen Smith, Gordon Taylor, Alison Tough, Paula Vince, Margaret Wilkie, and my ever-tolerant wife, Claire.

Libraries and other institutions that helped and major websites used include: the Ashbourne Methodist Society website; The Bodleian Library; British Online Archives; findmypast website; the Heritage Centre of The Salvation Army, Australia; the International Heritage Centre of The Salvation Army, London; the Methodist Heritage Website; My Wesleyan Methodists website; the Our Ashbourne website; and the Tyne & Wear Archives & Museums, Newcastle upon Tyne.

ABBREVIATIONS

AJSAH: *The Australasian Journal of Salvation Army History.*
'CBLP': 'Catherine Booth's Letters to her Parents' PDF.
CMM: *The Christian Mission Magazine.*
DMBI: *The Dictionary of Methodism in Britain and Ireland.*

MNCM: *The Methodist New Connexion Magazine.*
WRU: Wesleyan Reform Union.

INTRODUCTION

This is the first volume of a two volume biography of Catherine (Mumford) Booth. It examines her early life up until January 1866 when William and Catherine Booth had settled in London and the mission that would become The Salvation Army had been commenced. I have had the unique experience and privilege of transcribing, editing and publishing the letters that William and Catherine wrote to each other (mainly pre-1865), the letters that Catherine wrote to her parents (the last of which was written in January 1865), Catherine's diary (1847–48 and 1852), and Catherine's Reminiscences. This all gives me a great familiarity with her early life and an understanding of her complex personality. This book, therefore, is not only about what Catherine Booth did during the first 37 years of her life; it is an exploration of who she was.

It needs to be noted that there appear to have been two versions of Catherine's Reminiscences. Only the second half of one edition now exists, and the other version can only now be found in fragmentary form in the early biographies. (For details about the problems with the Reminiscences, see the appendix.)

These transcriptions and other contemporary sources such as newspapers and Christian magazines are the main sources for this part of her story. In addition, the earlier biographies of Catherine and William Booth have been used. However, it must be noted that some of the biographies, most notably those by Frederick Booth-Tucker (1892), W. T. Stead (1900) and Catherine Bramwell-Booth (1970), tend to be a little too 'adoring' and often hide the real woman. They, therefore, have been used with caution. Yet, it must be noted that Booth-Tucker is the primary source of some of the early events, so in such instances there is usually no place that is more reliable. It is, in fact, probable that he copied a few stories from the early pages of Catherine Booth's Reminiscences before they were lost (see the appendix), though with his usual string of amendments. Where possible the original record of a particular event in Catherine's life has been consulted, though on occasions that is untraceable or uncertain. Later accounts, when available and relevant, have also been compared and considered.

This book is written with the hope that Catherine (Mumford) Booth will shine through its pages.

David Malcolm Bennett (2019)

PRELUDE

W.T. Stead, a leading nineteenth century journalist, called Catherine Booth 'one of the most remarkable women' of the Victorian age and 'one of the Makers of Modern England.'[1] While Stead was an ardent admirer of Catherine Booth, those words still carry weight, coming, as they do, from a man who knew so many leading figures of his time, both male and female.

In October 1855, soon after she was married, Catherine Booth told her parents 'at best I am but a frail thing, soon ex[h]austed.'[2] Catherine Booth, in her own words, 'a frail thing!' And she was. Her health throughout her life was poor. She had curvature of the spine, which caused her considerable pain and she often referred to it in her letters, she had a nervous disposition, at times she had piles, she had long term problems with her bowels (she frequently had diarrhoea), she had angina, with heart palpitations, and she later died of cancer.

However, this 'frail thing' married, had eight children, all raised to adulthood, plus one (or was it two?) adopted, she preached, wrote, organised, campaigned for the rights of the poor and marginalised, and played a major role in establishing an Army. That is a remarkable catalogue of achievement for a 'frail thing'.

So, who was this Catherine Booth? How did she become 'one of the Makers' of late nineteenth century England?

---

1 Stead, *Catherine Booth*, pp. v., 3.
2 Bennett, 'Catherine Booth's Letters to her Parents' PDF (hereafter 'CBLP'), Letter P18, 22 October 1855, p. 33.

CHAPTER 1

The Mumford Family

Catherine Mumford was born in Ashbourne, a small market town in the English county of Derbyshire, on 17 January 1829. William Booth, the man who was to become her husband, was not born until 10 April that same year. This book is about Catherine Mumford Booth, but, inevitably, her life becomes entwined with William Booth's from 1852 when they formally met.

What was Catherine's background? Who were her parents? In answering those questions, it is difficult at times to separate myth from reality. It is easy, of course, to name her parents, John and Sarah Mumford, but to establish what they were like and what they did is much harder. Researching their lives is also only carried out with difficulty. The reason for this is that the Mumfords were not famous, so their lives were not written up in the newspapers of the day. Nor were they well-educated, so they did not leave prolific writings of their experiences. Indeed, it is probable that writing anything of a lengthy and detailed nature was alien to them. Genealogical information about the Mumford family exists, but it is limited.

Some details about their lives and origins can be gleaned from, newspaper and census websites; the biography of Catherine by Frederick Booth-Tucker, one of her sons-in-law; the letters and recollections of Catherine herself, who, though she often protested that she 'hated' writing, wrote prolifically and often vividly about an array of subjects, including family life; and the obituary of Sarah Mumford that appeared in the *Christian Mission Magazine (CMM)* in February 1870.

Yet there are problems with these sources. Firstly, some of the genealogical information is unclear or contradictory. Secondly, though Booth-Tucker is the major source for the early years, he is not always reliable. He will be used with care. Thirdly, while Catherine's record appears generally more dependable, a child born about four years after her parents' marriage, as Catherine was, usually has only a limited understanding of her parents'

1

lives before she reached an age for her own memories to form. This also applies to the obituary in the *CMM*, as Catherine Booth was presumably the source behind it. Fourthly, Catherine's spelling in her letters was often poor and her limited punctuation was so bizarre that it tends to confuse rather than clarify her meaning. Booth-Tucker's information presumably came from either his wife Emma, who was the Booths' second daughter, or from William Booth, or both. Indeed, both were on hand when Booth-Tucker was writing his book.[1]

While Booth-Tucker is known at times to have rewritten and twisted the sources he consulted, he had less reason to change the story of Sarah Mumford than he did of her daughter. So, we will accept what he says about Mrs Mumford as generally correct, though at times elaborated. Sadly, Sarah's *CMM* obituary says nothing about her husband John who was still alive when that obituary was published.

In September 1799, Edward Milward married Martha Ballinton in Ashbourne in Derbyshire. They were Catherine Booth's maternal grandparents. Edward came from Ashbourne, but Martha came from Mayfield (aka Mathfield), a village in the neighbouring county of Staffordshire. Though the two places are in different counties they are only a few kilometres apart. Edward and Martha were both aged 21, and Edward was 'a joiner'[2] and cabinet maker by trade. They may have had a son in 1801 and did have a daughter, Sarah, in 1802, probably on 17 February. The 1851 Census gives Sarah's age as 49, and her obituary in *CMM* dates her entering 'into rest' as 'December 16th 1869, aged 67.[3] Sarah was to become the mother of Catherine Booth. (Martha Milward's maiden name, Ballinton, probably Ballington, presumably would be why William and Catherine Booth called their second son Ballington.)

Booth-Tucker tells us that when Sarah was a child her mother died. She was then brought up by her father, who does not appear to have been particularly affectionate, and a 'harsh, unsympathetic' aunt.[4] Little has been recorded about Sarah's parents and this aunt, though some information in contemporary newspapers may shed some light on the family.

---

1 I have seen nothing more than hints in Catherine's letters about her parents' early lives.

2 See 'Staffordshire, Dioceses of Lichfield & Coventry Marriage Allegations And Bonds.'

3 '1851 England, Wales & Scotland Census: 7 Russell Street, Lambeth, London'; *The Christian Mission Magazine (CMM)*, 1 Feb. 1870, p. 30. The *CMM* has 'Ashbourn', but it should be Ashbourne; for the birth date see letter P45, possibly 14 Feb. 1856, 'CBLP', p. 76.

4 Booth-Tucker, *Catherine Booth*, vol. 1, p. 3.

According to advertisements in the *Derby Mercury* and *Staffordshire Advertiser* in November 1805 and August and December 1808, a 'Mrs Milward' of 'Ashborne' [sic] ran a 'Ladies Seminary', also called a 'Ladies Academy' and 'H.S. Milward's Academy.' The advertisements indicate that the academy took boarders at 'Eighteen Guineas per annum' and day pupils at 'Eight Guineas per annum.' The first *Mercury* advertisement says that Mrs Milward had 'taken a desirable House for the Reception of Pupils,' which suggests that she, seemingly acting without a husband, may have been a widow, which would rule out her being Sarah's mother. Therefore, this Mrs Milward may have been Sarah's aunt.

It would be a mistake to suppose that the terms 'Seminary' and 'Academy' suggest a high standard of education. What was offered was probably rather basic. The first advertisement says that the curriculum included 'English Grammar with Works', 'Respectable Manners', and 'French'.[5] It is known that Sarah Milward could read and write reasonably well as an adult, so she may have been one of the pupils of this 'Academy', although she does not seem to have had a high level of literacy. It is also known that, as an adult, Sarah did not trust schools, suggesting that she may have attended one she did not like. She also had a horror of her daughter learning French, which suggests a degree of exposure to that language and the writings of some of the French authors.

If all that is correct, it would have been a difficult environment for Sarah. It would be easy to imagine that it was a situation from which she desired to escape. Booth-Tucker says that when she was a young woman an escape-route appeared. Sarah Milward 'had become engaged to a gentleman of good position… The prospects were brilliant, and the wedding day had been fixed.' However, shortly before that grand day 'certain circumstances came to her knowledge, which proved conclusively that her lover was not the high-souled, noble character she had supposed him to be.' What that means one can only guess, but on hearing about those 'circumstances' Sarah immediately broke off the engagement.

The man then called on her to try to get her to change her mind. Sarah, clearly a determined young woman, refused to relent. At this point the

---

5 'Ladies Seminary,' 'Wanted,' 'H. S. Milward's Academy,' *Derby Mercury*; 'Mrs Milward's Seminary,' *Staffordshire Advertiser*. Late in August 1805, a 'Mr Milward' of 'Ashburne' sold some property, see 'To be sold by auction,' the *Derby Mercury*, 29 Aug. 1805, p. 2, col. 4. This may or may not be the property purchased by Mrs Milward. Note that Ashbourne is spelled in a variety of ways in these documents.

story becomes melodramatic. Booth-Tucker tells us that the man 'seized with despair … turned his horse's head from the door and galloped away, he knew not, cared not, whither–galloped till the horse was covered with foam–galloped till it staggered and fell, dying, beneath him, while he rose to his feet a hopeless maniac,' and he was taken to an asylum.[6]

It is impossible to know how much of Booth-Tucker's account is true, but elements in it do sound imagined. It was common in Victorian times to record that men who were thwarted in love went mad and those who jilted their fiancées already were mad. Catherine Mumford Booth, who later took a keen interest in the love affairs of her friends, told one such story, when one of her friends was jilted by the villainous 'Mr. Crow,' who had 'something the matter with his brain.'[7]

However, this must have been a time of deep anguish for Sarah Milward. Booth-Tucker says, 'She was overwhelmed by the catastrophe, and, shutting herself into her room, lay for sixteen weeks hovering between life and death.'[8] While again these words may be an exaggeration, it is known that later Sarah's daughter Catherine was highly emotional, and sometimes made herself sick with worry and stress. It is therefore believable that her mother, who seems to have had a similar temperament, became ill under these distressing circumstances. The *CMM* obituary says nothing about this romance, but it does say that she suffered 'a severe affliction' when she was 19, which seems to refer to this event.[9] That would then date it to, presumably, 1821.

Enter the Methodists

The Milward family belonged to the Church of England, but it is unclear to what extent they had embraced the Christian faith. From what little we know about them, they do not seem to have had a deep experience of Christ. But Sarah must have been aware of the basic Christian beliefs and she appears to have had a deep sense of guilt at this time, no doubt because of the events associated with her breaking the engagement. So, she turned to God, specifically through *The Book of Common Prayer*, with which she

---

6 Booth-Tucker, *Catherine*, vol. 1 pp. 3–4.
7 Bennett, *The Letters of William and Catherine Booth*, Letters CM53, 22 or 29 Aug. 1853, and CM56, possibly 16 Sept. 1853, pp. 143, 150; Booth, *Letters CD*, pp. 146, 152.
8 Booth-Tucker, *Catherine*, vol. 1, pp. 4–5.
9 *CMM*, 1 Feb. 1870, p. 30.

seems to have been familiar. Her eyes settled particularly on the words 'I believe … in the forgiveness of sins.'[10] For someone experiencing the ravages of guilt, that offered hope and the words forced their way into her mind, but she appears to have been unsure how those words might be applied to her.

Then, in the providence of God, Edward Milward sold a block of land to a group of Methodists. They soon began to build a chapel and a Methodist preacher visited Sarah. Through this and, perhaps, subsequent visits, she came to faith in Christ. Now she believed that *her* sins were forgiven. The words in the prayer book took on a whole new meaning and she joined the Methodists.[11]

John Wesley, a Church of England minister in the eighteenth century, had been the founder of Methodism, though he had never established a Methodist denomination. He did, though, establish a Methodist Society in Ashbourne as early as 1755.[12] After Wesley's death in 1791, the Methodists in Britain emerged slowly and unevenly from the Church of England. By the time of Sarah Milward's conversion (the early 1820s) the Methodists had established a separate identity, indeed several identities, because there was by that time more than one Methodist denomination.

Booth-Tucker says that 'special preachers' often came to take services for the Ashbourne Methodists. One of these was John Mumford.[13] Mumford was probably never a fulltime preacher and it is known that he was a coachbuilder and wheelwright during his early married life, and before. He also may have only been a preacher for a few years.[14] He seems to have come from Boston in Lincolnshire; he returned to Boston with his own family late in 1833 and his mother still resided there in the late 1850s.[15] However, according to the 1851 Census, he was born in Derbyshire, not Lincolnshire.[16]

But to which Methodist denomination did John Mumford and the

---

10 'A Catechism' in *The Book of Common Prayer*, p. 290.

11 Booth-Tucker, *Catherine*, vol. 1, pp. 5–6; *CMM*, 1 Feb. 1870, p. 30.

12 Wesley, *The Works of John Wesley*, vol. 2, pp. 325–26; 'Ashbourne Methodist Society.'

13 Booth-Tucker, *Catherine*, vol. 1, p. 7.

14 Ibid., vol. 1, p. 15; Bramwell-Booth, *Catherine Booth: the story of her loves*, p. 22. I have been unable to find John Mumford's name in any Methodist publication of the 1820s and 1830s, Wesleyan or Primitive.

15 Booth-Tucker, *Catherine*, vol. 1, p. 16; 'CBLP', Letters, P132, 22 or 23 July 1858; P133, 8 or 15 Aug. 1858; P183, 17 Sept. 1860, pp. 183, 185, 243.

16 '1851 England, Wales & Scotland Census: 7 Russell Street, Lambeth, London.'

Methodists of Ashbourne belong? Was it to the Wesleyan Methodists (the major body), the Methodist New Connexion, the Primitive Methodists, or one of the fringe groups? According to the Ashbourne Methodist Society, a 'Primitive Methodist Chapel' was built in Ashbourne 'around 1820.' The Wesleyans do not seem to have built a chapel until later.[17] If this is correct, then the Methodists who built a chapel on the block of land that Mr Milward sold in about 1821 were the Primitive Methodists, not the Wesleyans. The Primitive Methodists were an energetically evangelistic, quickly-growing group formed in 1811.

Primitive Methodism had been at the centre of a revival in Belper in mid-Derbyshire in 1819. It continued into the spring of 1821 and spread to other parts of that county.[18] According to H.B. Kendall, the Primitive Methodists had 'missioned' Ashbourne early, for Ashbourne was on the Tunstall preachers' plan as far back as 1819.[19] However, this does not mean that there was a chapel there then. Meetings were probably held in the open air and in homes. A Primitive Methodist missionary meeting, held at Turnditch and Belper on 8 July 1821, decided to evangelise 'the benighted villages in the Peak of Derbyshire,' which included Ashbourne.[20] This timing fits well with the apparent building of a Primitive chapel in the early 1820s, on the block sold by Mr Milward. While this does not prove that John Mumford was a preacher for the Primitive Methodists, it does suggest it.

John Mumford quickly became rather popular in the town; it would appear, at least, that he was the most favoured of the Methodist preachers. He inevitably met Sarah Milward and they became attracted to each other. While Sarah's father and aunt had accepted her allegiance to the Methodists, they were not favourably disposed to her developing relationship with John Mumford. According to Booth-Tucker, when the preacher asked for Sarah's hand in marriage, Mr Milward ordered him out of the house and locked the door behind him.[21]

Milward then gave his daughter an ultimatum: either she should end the relationship with John Mumford, or she should leave the family home. So, she left home. At some stage she seems to have moved to Manchester, though this may not have been immediately. Booth-Tucker informs us that 'a

---

17 'Ashbourne's Chapels and Ministers.'
18 Werner, *The Primitive Methodist Connexion: Its Background and Early History*, p. 81.
19 Kendall, *The Origin and History of the Primitive Methodist Church*, vol. 1, p. 534.
20 Ibid., vol. 1, p. 184.
21 Booth-Tucker, *Catherine*, vol. 1, p. 7.

few months' later (though it was probably longer) Mr Milward relented and allowed the two lovers to marry.[22] However, as by this time she was over 21, he could have done little to stop it. The *CMM* tells us 'at the age of 23' Sarah Milward 'married in the Lord.' It is striking that the *CMM* says nothing else about whom she married.[23] In fact, she was married on 14 February 1825, which seems to have been just before her twenty-third birthday. John and Sarah appear to have been married in the parsonage of St Mary's Church of England in Manchester. That they were married there and not in Ashbourne, might suggest that Sarah's relatives still did not fully approve of the union, though it might be because she was living in that town.[24]

John Mumford was a little younger than his wife. However, there is contradictory information about his date of birth. The 1851 Census says that he was born in 1804 and aged 47 at his last birthday before the Census, which was taken on 31 March 1851.[25] As his birthday seems to have been at the end of August, if he was 47 when the Census was taken then he must have been born in 1803. This is confirmed in a letter that Catherine Mumford wrote to her fiancé probably on 23 or 30 August 1853, in which she said, 'It is my Father's birth day tomorrow. He is fifty.'[26]

The Mumford children

The Mumfords settled in Ashbourne and lived, though not necessarily immediately, at 13 Sturston Lane (now Road) in Ashbourne.[27] Sarah gave birth to three boys, who sadly all died young[28], and Catherine was born on 17 January 1829. She was baptised on 16 February by the Reverend John Brandreth in King Street Wesleyan Chapel in Derby.[29] Sarah's father, Edward

---

22 Ibid., vol. 1, pp. 7–9.

23 *CMM*, 1 Feb. 1870, p. 31.

24 'Record Transcriptions, England Marriages 1538–1973, John Mumford and Sarah Milward.' This record clearly states that they were married in 'Manchester, St Mary's Parsonage.'

25 'Age at last birthday.' A Search Ancestry article on the 1851 Census says that one piece of information taken was the 'Age at last birthday', which for John Mumford would have been late August 1850.

26 Booth, *Letters*, Letter CM53, probably 23 or 30 Aug. 1853, p. 143; *Letters* CD, p. 146. The dating of this letter has been rechecked (in December 2018) and it appears to be correct.

27 'Catherine Booth', in 'Experience Ashbourne History.'

28 Bramwell-Booth, *Catherine*, p. 17.

29 Page from Church Register, England & Wales Non-conformist births and baptisms.

Milward, died on 5 September the year Catherine was born,[30] which must have made that a year of mixed emotions for Sarah.

One of Catherine's earliest and most vivid memories was, at the age of two, being taken into a room to view the dead body of one of her little brothers. Much later, Catherine recalled, 'But I can remember to this day the feelings of awe and solemnity with which the sight of death impressed my baby-mind. Indeed, the effect produced on that occasion has lasted to this very hour.'[31] This baby seems to have been named John, as there was an infant John Mumford buried in Ashbourne on 21 December 1831. He was not yet a year old, so he was born after Catherine.[32]

Late in 1833 Sarah gave birth to a fourth son, and they called him John Valentine. This John was baptised at St Botolph's Church of England in Boston on Christmas Day that year.[33] Why they chose to have him baptised in an Anglican church is unclear.

---

30 'Deaths', *Derby Mercury*, 9 Sept. 1829, p. 3, col. 1.

31 Booth-Tucker, *Catherine*, vol. 1, p. 10.

32 John Mumford, Derbyshire Burial Index 1538–1910.

33 Baptismal Register, St Botolph's Church of England, Boston.

CHAPTER 2

Catherine: A sick yet gifted child

'The instinct of Motherhood … must have exercised a profound
influence on Catherine Mumford from her earliest years',

(William) Bramwell Booth.[1]

The family moved to Boston in Lincolnshire probably late in 1833, so about the
time John Valentine Mumford was born. It would have been a homecoming
for the senior John Mumford.[2] If he had been a preacher for the Primitive
Methodists, as earlier suggested, one would have expected them to have
attended a Primitive Methodist chapel in Boston. The Primitive Methodists
had been active in that town since the early 1820s,[3] and it was presumably
that group with which John Mumford had been associated before moving
to Ashbourne. The Primitives were still very active in Boston at the time the
Mumfords moved, for they had three preachers in the town in 1834.[4]

However, the Mumfords seem to have joined the Wesleyans, probably
soon after their arrival there.[5] This is confirmed by a comment Catherine
made in a letter to her parents late in 1857. She said, 'If I had been fortunate
enough to have been brought up amongst the Primitives, I believe I
should have been preaching now.'[6] So, clearly, in the years that she could
remember, the family did not belong to the Primitives. However, this does
not necessarily mean that John and Sarah Mumford were not originally
Primitive Methodists. In a letter that William Booth wrote to Catherine

---

1 Bramwell Booth, *These Fifty Years*, p. 20.
2 Some give the year as 1834, but as John junior was baptised in Boston on Christmas Day
1833, it was presumably before that; Booth-Tucker *Catherine*, vol. 1, p. 16; Bramwell-
Booth, *Catherine*, p. 22.
3 Petty, *The History of the Primitive Methodist Connexion*, pp. 119–20, 149.
4 *Primitive Methodist Magazine*, 1834, New Series, vol. IV, p. 359.
5 Booth-Tucker, *Catherine*, vol. 1, p. 30; Green, *Catherine Booth*, p. 27.
6 'CBLP', Letter P106, 7 Dec 1857, p. 146.

late in 1852 he spoke of some of her Boston friends who belong to 'the Conference party',[7] which was a pseudonym given to the Wesleyans during the troubled times in Methodism in that era. This again suggests that Catherine and her family had been attending a Wesleyan church at least for the later part of the Mumfords' time in Boston.

According to Booth-Tucker, at this time John Mumford began to take a keen interest in the temperance movement and held temperance meetings in their home. Little Catherine sat in on those gatherings and, thus, was early exposed to the arguments against alcohol, even though early on her understanding of the issues must have been limited. Yet, at the age of 12 she became the secretary of the local juvenile temperance society.[8]

In Catherine Bramwell-Booth's opinion, Catherine Mumford was much closer to her father than she was to her mother in her childhood[9], though others view those relationships differently. For example, Booth-Tucker said, 'From an incredibly early age, Catherine became her mother's companion and *confidante*.'[10] However, whatever was true about Catherine's childhood years, by the time she had become an adult she was much closer to her mother, as her letters to her parents clearly demonstrate. Indeed, this is even evident in the first period of her diary, written when she was 18.[11]

Catherine and her father

One reason that Catherine was not close to her father was because of another disaster that struck the Mumford family. John Mumford became an alcoholic and turned from the Christian faith. This must have been a startling fall for the family when one considers that he had been a preacher and a keen promoter of temperance. In some of Catherine's letters to her parents after her marriage (the late 1850s and early 1860s), she asked her father to advise her on giving temperance lectures and to get her some old copies of the *Temperance Intelligencer*[12], which he must have read in his

---

7 Booth, *Letters*, Letter WB16, 6 Dec. 1852, p. 23; *Letters* CD, p. 27.

8 Booth-Tucker, *Catherine*, vol. 1, p. 16.

9 Bramwell-Booth, *Catherine*, p. 24.

10 Booth-Tucker, *Catherine*, vol. 1, p. 11.

11 See for example diary entries 13, 15, 21, 22 & 24 May 1847, Booth, *The Diary and Reminiscences of Catherine Booth*, pp. 1, 2, 5–6; *Diary*, in *Letters CD*, pp. 6–7, 10–12. These two editions of the Diary are the printed academic edition and the PDF version in the Booth, *Letters CD*. References to both editions will be given in these notes.

12 See for example, 'CBLP', letters P105, probably 22 or 29 Nov. 1857; P106, 7 Dec. 1857;

younger days. But from an unknown time in Catherine's childhood until his death, John Mumford had a struggle with alcohol, and alcohol was usually the winner.

This must have cast a dark cloud over their family life. There is no evidence of any brutality, but in one letter just after Christmas 1852 Catherine told her fiancé, 'My dear father seemed kinder and more comfortable than usual; he is still a teetotaller & is abstaining altogether from the *pipe*; there is a change for the better in many respects.'[13] Clearly, there must have been other times when, influenced by drink, he had been unkind and difficult to live with. Sadly, his 'dry' period did not last.

It comes as no surprise that Catherine Mumford became strongly anti-alcohol and was not afraid to let people know it. Another result of her father's addiction was that it bound mother and daughter together, and as time progressed Sarah Mumford seemed as dependent upon Catherine as Catherine was upon her.

Catherine and her mother

It was common in the Victorian era for the mothers to have charge of the children, sometimes with the help of servants, while the fathers spent long hours at work. This seems to have been the case with the Mumfords. In other words, Sarah Mumford had much more direct influence over Catherine than John did. Sarah was a devout and dedicated Methodist, so she inevitably imparted her beliefs to her daughter.

Years later Catherine spoke of her mother in these terms:

> The longer I live the more I appreciate my mother's character. She was of the Puritan type. I have often heard my husband remark that she was a woman of the sternest principle he had ever met, and yet the very embodiment of tenderness. To her right was right, no matter what it might entail… She had an intense realisation of spiritual things. Heaven seemed quite near.

Sarah was also greatly concerned about the dangers of damaging outside influences. Booth-Tucker states that Sarah allowed Catherine no playmates except for her brother John, and, in the early years, no school.[14]

---

and P240, 11 Apr. 1863, pp. 145, 147, 328.

13 Booth, *Letters*, Letter CM11, 27 Dec. 1852, p. 47; *Letters CD*, p. 47.

14 Booth-Tucker, *Catherine*, vol.1, pp. 11–12.

However, Sarah did not neglect her daughter's education. She took on the role of teacher herself. There must have been an element of the blind leading the blind in this, for the evidence suggests that Sarah's education had been limited. It appears that soon after Catherine had reached the age of three she knew the alphabet and could read small words, but this type of education did leave gaps in Catherine's knowledge, especially with her spelling and punctuation.

A major part of that education included Bible stories and the essential elements of the Christian faith. This resulted in Catherine's early search for the God behind and within the Bible. She later said, 'I cannot remember the time when I had not intense yearnings after God.' As the years passed, reading fiction was forbidden and learning French banned. If Sarah had learned some French, as suggested above, she knew enough to realise that some of the great French authors taught things that she thought no decent Christian girl should read. If her only daughter did not understand French, then it reduced the likelihood of her reading their works. The ban on French was something that Catherine came to regret.[15] Harold Begbie said that 'there was no element of submission' in Catherine's response to her mother's strict training, for Catherine, in his opinion, was 'a born puritan'[16], so she accepted it readily.

Later, at times, Catherine succumbed to the lure of fiction; at least, she seems to have read some of the works of Harriet Beecher Stowe, including *Uncle Tom's Cabin* (1852)[17] and Susan Warner's *Wide, Wide, World* (1850). *Uncle Tom* is said to have quickly sold more than a million copies in Britain and had a powerful impact upon its people.[18] Warner's book was a Christian story, typical of the Victorian age, but was sufficiently strong on gender equality to be republished by the Feminist Press late in the twentieth century.[19] Perhaps Warner played a part in Catherine's developing feminist

---

15 Ibid., vol. 1, pp. 12–13.

16 Begbie, *Life of William Booth*, vol. 1, p. 122.

17 Booth, *Letters*, Letter CM8, 16 Dec. 1852; pp. 32–33, fns. 72 & 77; *Letters CD*, pp. 36–37, fns. 106 & 111; and 'CBLP', letter P171, 14 Nov. 1859, p. 227, fn. 427; Booth, *Fifty*, p. 27.

18 Wilson, *The Victorians*, p. 268.

19 See Walker, *Pulling the Devil's Kingdom Down: The Salvation Army in Victorian Britain*, pp. 10–11; there is a hint about Warner's book in Booth, *Letters*, Letter CM34, 26 Apr. 1853, p. 100; Booth, *Letters CD*, p. 104. Warner wrote under the name Elizabeth Wetherell. https://en.wikipedia.org/wiki/The_Wide,_Wide_World.

ideas. Catherine had earlier also read John Bunyan's *Pilgrim's Progress.*[20]

She loved reading from an early age. She later recalled, 'I cannot myself remember a time when I did not find pleasure and consolation in reading, or hearing others read, either the Bible or some religious book.' Even in her early years she read the Bible right through. One suspects that the reading of Christian books was all Catherine was allowed in her younger childhood, but as a teenager she also loved to read secular history.[21]

Catherine did have some regrets later about the limits of her education. In 1853 she told her fiancé, 'I have often repined & murmured at the permissions of providence with reference to my education, & bitterly wept for the loss of advantages, but I thank God for what no education could have given me & for what thousands who have poss[ess]ed all its advantages have not.'[22] Without question, she went on to achieve far more than most who had a superior education.

She also recalled, 'I was a very highly nervous and delicate child from the beginning, and the fact that I was not strong enough to occupy my energies and time like other children doubtless had something to do with' her early love of books.[23] The phrase 'very highly nervous' in this passage stands out. Assuming it is recorded accurately, Catherine is saying that she was not just a nervous child, nor even just a highly nervous child, but that her nervousness went beyond that into another even more emotional category. Catherine's nervous condition plays an important part in our story. Her nerves troubled her violently, physically and emotionally, but they also compelled her to act.

Catherine does not seem to have had any childhood friends, except her younger brother. This was partly because her mother did not want outside influences contaminating her daughter and partly because she was often unwell. However, she did play. Indeed, she later became a great advocate of play, and her own children benefitted greatly from that. In her own lonely childhood, Catherine's friends were her dolls. She dressed them, 'fed' them, put them to bed, and even made clothes for them.[24] They seem to have been

---

20 Booth-Tucker, *Catherine*, vol. 1, p. 28.

21 Ibid., vol. 1, p. 27.

22 Booth, *Letters*, Letter CM71, 23 Nov. 1853, p. 182; Booth, *Letters CD*, p. 184.

23 Booth-Tucker, *Catherine*, vol. 1, p. 13.

24 Ibid., vol. 1, p. 14. Catherine Booth also encouraged her children to play with toys, and toys have become common in Salvation Army ministry, see Youssef (with Garth Hentzschel), 'An Overview and History of Toys Relating to The Salvation Army,' *AJSAH,*

the prototype of the family she was later to have.

Catherine's early social awareness

Two dramatic incidents in her childhood portray her character well. Booth-Tucker tells us that one day while still quite young she was out and saw a drunkard being 'dragged to the lock-up by a constable.' Behind them was 'a jeering mob … hooting' at the captive. Catherine immediately felt intensely sorry for him, rushed to his side and walked with him to their destination.[25] If John Mumford was already well down the path of alcoholism at that time, Catherine would have known how devastating drunkenness could be, which could easily have given her a negative attitude to this man. But someone in trouble, whatever the cause, stirred her heart, so she acted in sympathy.

The other event directly concerned her father. Catherine loved animals and the family had a pet retriever named Waterford. One day she went to visit her father where he worked, taking Waterford with her. She said that upon arriving at the place of business, she entered and 'closed the door, leaving the dog outside.' Unfortunately, inside she stubbed her toe and cried out in pain. The dog hearing his mistress's cry of distress, rushed to her aid, 'crashing through the large glass window.' Her father was furious and had the dog shot. Catherine was inconsolable. Her beloved companion had been killed, and that because he loved her. She was unable to speak to her father for several days, even though he soon regretted his action, and much later she remembered, 'For months I suffered intolerably… The fact that I had no childhood companions doubtless made me miss my speechless one the more.'[26] The young Catherine Mumford was already a highly emotional and compassionate person. Though no mention is made of it, one wonders whether the dog was injured in the incident, and that that was a contributory factor in having it shot.

Catherine developed a keen social awareness while still a child, and this appears to have been fostered by her father, who was involved in political and social affairs. 'By the time I was twelve,' she said, 'I had my own ideas in politics and could fight my father across the table.' One matter they debated

---

vol. 3, iss. 1, pp. 21–44.

25 Booth-Tucker, *Catherine*, vol. 1, pp. 17–18.

26 Ibid., vol. 1, p. 19.

vivacity. My soul found some repose in Christ, which, alass [sic], soon became disturbed & was ultimately lost.[40]

Booth-Tucker tells us 'that it was not until she was *sixteen* that she believed herself to have been truly converted' (emphasis added). He then quoted Catherine, saying,

About this time [presumably 1845], I passed through a great controversy of soul. Although I was conscious of having given myself up fully to God from my earliest years, and although I was anxious to serve Him and often realised deep enjoyment in prayer, nevertheless I had not the positive assurance that my sins were forgiven, and that I had experienced the actual change of heart about which I had read and heard so much. I was determined to leave the question no longer in doubt, but to get it definitely settled... For six weeks I prayed and struggled on, but obtained no satisfaction... Both in public and private I had made use of the means of grace, and up to the very limit of my strength... Still, so far as this was concerned, I realised the truth of the words:

> Could my zeal no respite know,
> Could my tears forever flow–
> These for sin could not atone.

I knew, moreover, that 'the heart is deceitful above all things and desperately wicked.' I was terribly afraid of being self-deceived... Neither could I call to mind any particular place or time when I had definitely stepped out upon the promises, and had claimed the immediate forgiveness of my sins, receiving the witness of the Holy Spirit that I had become a child of God and an heir of heaven.

It seemed to me unreasonable to suppose that I could be saved and yet not know it. At any rate I could not permit myself to remain in doubt regarding the matter...

I can never forget the agony I passed through. I used to pace my room till two o'clock in the morning, and when, utterly exhausted, I lay down at length to sleep, I would place my Bible and hymn-book under my pillow, praying that I might wake up with the assurance of salvation. One morning as I opened my hymn-book, my eyes fell upon the words:

> My God, I am Thine!

---

40 Booth, *Letters*, Letter CM16, 16 Jan. 1853, p. 57; Booth, *Letters* CD, p. 61.

> What a comfort divine,
> What a blessing to know that my Jesus is mine.

Scores of times I had read and sung these words, but now they came home to my inmost soul with a force and illumination they had never before possessed. It was as impossible for me to doubt as it had before been to exercise faith. Previously not all the promises in the Bible could induce me to believe; now not all the devils in hell could persuade me to doubt. I no longer hoped that I was saved, I was certain of it... I jumped out of bed, and, without waiting to dress ran into my mother's room and told her what had happened...

For the next six months I was so happy that I felt as if I was walking on air. I used to tremble, and even long to die, lest I should backslide or lose the consciousness of God's smile and favour...[41]

So, according to this account, at the age of 16 Catherine Mumford had doubts about her salvation, but then had a spiritual experience that removed those doubts, giving her assurance and joy. Yet, according to her diary, which she kept later for two short periods, Catherine believed that she became a Christian on Monday 15 June 1846, at the age of 17. Her entry for the first day of June 1847 says,

'Praise the Lord, O my soul, and all that is within me praise His holy name.' I see the month[42] return that fixed my happy choice. Twelve months this month I became a child of God, an heir of heaven, but I do not know the day of that month. But it was on the Monday morning before coming down, I think in the middle of June.[43]

In a diary entry two weeks later, on the anniversary of that event, she writes,

I believe it is 12 months today since I received the blessing of pardon, thrice blessed day that fixed my happy choice. That awesome hour of God made me heir of heaven, a joint heir with Christ. O my loving

---

41 Booth-Tucker, *Catherine*, vol. 1, pp. 32–34. Attempts have been made to trace the origin of this account without success. It is possible that it comes from the Reminiscences that Catherine Booth dictated on her death bed, but as the first 600 pages of that manuscript were lost in June 1891 and, apparently, never found, it is impossible to check. See the appendix to this book and Bennett, 'Catherine Booth's *Reminiscences* and the Lost Pages', *AJSAH*, vol. 2, iss. 2, pp. 154–55. Booth-Tucker may have copied some of the early pages before they were lost.

42 Bramwell-Booth, *Catherine*, p. 41, has 'month's'. The word is very hard to decipher, but it is probably 'month'.

43 Booth, *Diary*, 1 June 1847, p. 9; Booth, *Diary CD*, p. 14.

Lord, on looking back over the past year what cause I see to praise thee; what infinite cares, temptations and snares thy hand hath conducted me through. Thou hast been with me in the furnace of affliction; thou hast raised me up kind friends, and provided for my temporal wants, and blessed me with numberless spiritual blessings… How have I often greived [sic] thy holy Spirit and provoked thee by a thousand falls, but still thou lovest me. After all my sinfulness, all my unworthyness, [sic] Jesus lives and loves me,[44] and now I come afresh to thy attoning [sic] blood by Jesus.

> I take the blessing from above,
> And wonder at thy boundless love.[45]
>
> O, take me body, soul and spirit,
> Only thou possess the whole.[46]

O cleanse me this day from all sin, wash me in thy own blood, make me quite ready for glory. Perhaps next June I shall be engaged in praising the[e] in nobler strains above. Even so Lord, thy will be done, only let me press[47] triumphant home, but keep me. W[h]ether I live or die, let it be to thy glory… Take me for another year, let me bear abundantly more fruit, let the sun of Righteousness shine in ful[l] luster [sic] on my soul, and make me spotless and pure. 'Praise the Lord, O my soul, and forget not all his benefits.'[48]

According to these diary entries, Catherine had an experience that sounds very much like the one recorded by Booth-Tucker. But there are differences, most notably her age at the time. Did it occur in 1846 when she was 17 (as in the diary) or 1845 when she was 16 (as in Booth-Tucker)? The diary accounts seem more likely to be correct, as they were written soon after the event, so 1846 is probably right. The record in Booth-Tucker seems to have been recalled years later.[49]

---

44 The wording of these two sentences is heavily influenced by Charles Wesley's hymn, 'Depth of mercy! Can there be…?'

45 This is from Charles Wesley's hymn, 'What am I, O Thou glorious God!'

46 This is from Charles Wesley's hymn, 'Jesus, all-atoning Lamb.' Catherine has reversed the order of 'spirit' and 'soul'.

47 This is probably 'press' but could be 'pass'.

48 Booth, *Diary*, 15 June 1847, pp. 18–19; Booth, *Diary CD*, p. 24.

49 In one of her addresses delivered in 1880 she says that she was converted 'between 15 and 16', Booth, *Papers on Aggressive Christianity*, p. 91. However, that address was delivered more than 30 years after the event.

But was this 1846 experience her conversion or not? Here we are entering John Wesley territory. On 24 May 1738 John Wesley had his heart 'strangely warmed'. That is usually regarded as his conversion. But even he had doubts about whether it was or not. He later wondered if he was converted on an earlier occasion, and the 1738 experience was his being assured of his salvation.[50] It seems that we have a similar situation with Catherine Booth.

Perhaps Christian conversions are often a process rather than an instantaneous experience. The conversion of Saul of Tarsus is often regarded as the classic example of an instantaneous conversion, but was he converted on the road to Damascus or when Ananias came to him three days later and his blind eyes were opened (Acts 9:1-19)? Or was it a process that lasted three days or more?

Whatever is true here, one thing is certain. By her mid-teens, Catherine Mumford was a dedicated Christian with strong views about how to live the Christian life.

---

50 Wesley, *Journal*, 24 May 1738, in *Works*, vol. 1, pp. 103–104. For a discussion about Wesley's conversion experience see Arnett, 'What Happened to Wesley at Aldersgate?'

CHAPTER 3

Recovery in Brighton

'Last night I went to class and felt blessed, but my mind is so
excited at these times that it is a great exertion to speak.
I am most blessed when alone in my own room.
Quietness and solitude best suit my nerves',

Catherine Mumford.[1]

From early October 1846 and through the following winter, Catherine was
very ill with consumption. She was confined to her room for most of that
time, but gradually recovered.[2] In the late spring of 1847 John and Sarah
Mumford sent their daughter to stay with some relatives in Brighton in
Sussex on the south-eastern coast of England, in the hope of aiding her
recovery. Brighton was a highly popular holiday resort in Victorian England,
especially with invalids hoping for a cure for their ailments. While this was
still the early years of the railways, five different companies had built lines
to Brighton by about this time[3], which demonstrates its popularity.

The diary

While in Brighton Catherine kept a diary[4], which she continued to write
into 1848, and she added a few entries in 1852. Her diary is a remarkable
document and it tells us much about her. It is a diary, but it is also a prayer
journal. It shows that she had a great love for Christ, which often rises to
considerable heights of spirituality. Though it was written when she was
young, it frequently shows great maturity. Yet in some of the entries, as a

---

1 Booth, *Diary*, 19 May 1847, p. 4; *Diary CD*, p. 9.
2 Booth-Tucker, *Catherine*, vol. 1, p. 38; Booth, *Diary*, 4 Oct. 1847, p. 30; *Diary CD*, p. 35.
3 Wilson, *Victorians*, p. 72.
4 Catherine wrote three letters to her parents from Brighton, which are often thought to have
been written in 1847. However, they were almost certainly all written in 1851. Therefore,
her diary shall be the main source for her 1847 visit.

teenager ill and away from home, she writes much like any other teenager in similar circumstances, feeling a desperate need of her mother's care. Her deep relationship with her mother emerges in this diary. That closeness is also apparent in the letters she wrote years later to her parents. As has been seen, it appears that John Mumford's drunkenness had welded Sarah and Catherine in an extremely close bond, seemingly closer than most mothers and daughters experienced. One gets the impression from these sources that Sarah was greatly dependent upon her only daughter for companionship and support.

Catherine arrived in Brighton on 11 May. The next day she wrote,

I arrived here safe yesterday, but very much fatig[u]ed. I felt very ill in the train but could lay down when I felt faint. My mind was kept calm, and while passing through some tunnels I thought should any accident hap[p]en amidst this darkness and hurry me into eternity, shall I find myself in Glory? And I fe[l]t I could say even here, 'Lord, if it were thy will to take me, I could come.' But how unworthy I am of heavenly rest, but

> This is all my plea,
> I the chief of sinners am,
> But Jesus died for me![5]

> Glory be to His dear name.[6]

They are gloomy thoughts, perhaps, for an eighteen-year-old, but, no doubt, her suffering had caused her to take a pessimistic view of life on earth. Yet through the gloom shines a hope, a hope of eternity.

But she soon missed her mother. Two days after her arrival she wrote, 'Felt much cast down at the thoughts of being from home when I so much need its comforts, and away from My Dear Mother. I who can[']t tell the value of a Mother's attention and care till deprived of it.'[7] Indeed, during this time away she felt 'deprived of earthly happiness more than us[u]al,'[8] which almost certainly referred to being away from her mother. Ten days after her arrival in Brighton she wrote,

> This morning I was much blessed in prayer for my Dearest Mother... O, how I long to see her. I know she is very lonely, but it will soon be over. O, my Lord, enable her to lay her child upon the altar at thy cross, and

---

5 This is from the hymn 'Let the world their virtue boast', by Charles Wesley.
6 Booth, *Diary*, 11 May 1847, p. 1; *Diary CD*, p. 6.
7 Ibid., 13 May 1847, p. 1; ibid., p. 6.
8 Ibid., 14 May 1847, p. 2; ibid., p. 7.

say, thy will be done. I greatly need a Mother's care and attention, but now I am deprived of these streams of happiness I draw more from the fountain. What should I do without Jesus?[9]

Catherine believed that Sarah Mumford was 'very lonely', so the mother was also missing her daughter.

Mrs Mumford's spirits may have been lifted a little later. In a diary entry late in May, Catherine praised God, saying, 'Blessed be thy name! Thou hast enabled her [Catherine's mother] to give me entirely into thy hands and say, "thy will be done."'[10]

In June Catherine prayed, 'Lord, bless my Dearest Mother to night. O, bless her, answer prayer in her behalf, fill her soul unut[t]erably ful[l] of glory and of God. Give unto her perfect resignation, help her at all times to offer me, her unworthy child, upon the altar that sanctifyeth [sic] the gift…'[11] It is apparent from what Catherine says in these diary entries that her mother had had considerable difficulty letting her daughter leave home even for a few weeks.

Catherine's hosts in Brighton were probably Richard and Jane Burt. She refers to one member of the household as her 'dear Aunt' (which Jane was), and Catherine indicates that they had more than one child (the Burts had two in 1847), though beyond that there is no identifying information in Catherine's Diary.[12] But by Catherine's understanding, at least, they do not seem to have been Christians. She prayed for them[13], and in one early diary entry Catherine said,

> O, that I may be made useful in this family. Lord, they know the[e] not, neither do they seek thee. Have mercy upon them and help me to set an exa[m]ple at all times and in all places worthy of immitation [sic]. Help me to display the Christian Character and adawn [sic] the gospel of God my saviour in all things. I find much need of watchfulness and prayer, and I have this day taken up my cross in reproving sin. Lord, follow with the conviction of thy spirit all I have said.[14]

---

9 Ibid., 21 May 1847, p. 5; ibid., p. 10.

10 Ibid., 24 May 1847, pp. 6–7; ibid., pp. 11–12.

11 Ibid., 6 June 1847, p. 14; ibid., p. 19.

12 Ibid., 16 May 1847, p. 3; ibid., p. 8. On Catherine's return visit to Brighton in 1851, she did stay with the Burt family. The 1851 Census says that they then had four children, one of whom was born in 1845 and a second in 1847; '1851 England, Wales & Scotland Census Image, 35 Duke Street, Brighton, Sussex, England.'

13 Ibid., 16 May 1847, p. 3; ibid., p. 8.

14 Ibid., 14 May 1847, pp. 1–2; ibid., pp. 6–7.

It sounds as though the one Catherine had reproved was a member of that household. If so, she may not have been the easiest of guests to host.

It comes as no surprise that a few days later she wrote, 'I have this day learnt a lesson, which I hope I shall never forget. That is, to be more watchful what I say and who I say it too [sic], for what is said with the greatest innocency [sic] is often turned or reppresented [sic] as evil.'[15] However, Catherine did forget, for it seems to have been a lesson that she never learned. She lacked tact and could often speak or write inappropriately, as shall be seen.

Catherine's struggles

During the early part of her stay in Brighton she read Elizabeth (Singer) Rowe's *Devout Exercises of the Heart*. Elizabeth Rowe (1674–1737) was an artist and poet among the dissenters, and her book contains prose and poetry. Her *Devout Exercises* also had a dedication by Isaac Watts, in which he called the book's contents 'pious Meditations of so sublime a Genius.'[16] Rowe's writings had deeply impressed Isaac Watts; a hundred years later they also deeply moved Catherine Mumford. Through reading it she 'was much blessed and enabled to give [herself] affresh [sic] into the hands of God'[17], and on another occasion as she read it she 'felt a sweet calm overspread' her mind.[18] It is easy to imagine that she took note of the fact that this remarkable book had been written by a woman, and while Catherine had probably not yet arrived at her belief in women's equality with men, it may have been part of the inspiration for that.

She attended a class meeting in Brighton on 1 June. (Class meetings were small fellowship gatherings under a designated leader, introduced into Methodism by John Wesley.) She recorded in her diary that day,

> I have been to my class tonight. There was only two beside Mr Wells. He asked me to pray but I did not and I do not feel right about it. I was just going to begin and he began. I made the cross bigger than it really was, but I have made my mind up tonight that I will never do so again. I will pray if I can at all.[19]

Presumably, what she did 'not feel right about' was that she did not pray,

---

15 Ibid., 17 May 1847, p. 3; ibid., p. 8.
16 Rowe, *Devout Exercises of the Heart*, pp. 37–38.
17 Booth, *Diary*, 14 May 1847, p. 1; *Diary CD*, p. 6.
18 Ibid., 3 June 1847, p. 12; ibid., p. 17.
19 Ibid., 1 June 1847, p. 10; ibid., p. 15.

not that Mr Wells had asked her to do so. Seven days later in her class she 'Pleaded with God for the evidence of a full salvation'[20], which she probably did out loud. Then she recorded that the next day in a prayer meeting 'I engaged in prayer. The cross was great and so was the reward. My heart beat violently but I felt some liberty.' On that same day she visited the sick and tried to lead a 'young girl to Jesus.'[21] Perhaps Elizabeth Rowe had inspired these actions.

Catherine had doubts but had assurance too. The two seeming opposites jostled in her mind and heart. Through her diary she prayed,

> reveal thy self to my longing soul and let me be satisfied with beholding thy beauty. Drive back Satan and his temptations. If I love thee not, why these fears of offending thee? Why these restless longings after thee? O let me love thee more; never let me greive [sic] the[e] again. Give now a ful[l] salvation from all sin. Let me gloryfy [sic] the[e] with my every bre[a]th. Preach thee to all and cry in death, 'Behold, behold the Lamb.'[22]

She described 'sin and self' as her 'two greatest enemies' and it would seem that 'pride' was not too far behind.[23]

A little later, in a similar mood, she said,

> I feel very poorly to day, so excessively low and very much inclined to fret, but I find great relief in pouring out my soul to God in prayer. I am much tempted to fear my own state… O, I feel as if I should like to leave this world of sin and sorrow and go w[h]ere I could not possably [sic] greive [sic] my Lord again. O, for more patience and resignation! Lord, thy will be done, only let me feel that all I do is right, according to thy will and word, well pleasing in thy sight. This alone can constitute me happy. Without the assurance of thy favour I am truly miserable. I feel I am unworthy of the least of thy mercies, for thou alone knowest the depths of inbred corruption that lurk within. Every moment, Lord, I need the merit of thy death, but though 'I the chief of sinners am, Yet Jesus died for me', His blood attones [sic] for me. I will hold fast on Jesus, and I now come afresh through him and accept what thou hast promised to impart: pardon, holiness and heaven.[24]

---

20 Ibid., 8 June 1847, p. 15; ibid., p. 20.
21 Ibid., 9 June 1847, p. 15; ibid., pp. 20–21.
22 Ibid., 14 May 1847, p. 2; ibid., p. 7. The last two sentences in this quotation are a paraphrase of the last verse of Charles Wesley's hymn, 'Jesus! The name high over all.'
23 Ibid., 16 May 1847, p. 3; ibid., p. 8.
24 Ibid., 18 May 1847, pp. 3–4; ibid., pp. 8–9.

A few days later she took a slightly different tack, saying,

> What should I do without Jesus? Though I love earthly friends dearly, I could leave them all to go to Jesus. He is the chief among ten thousand & the alltogether [sic] lovely one. O Lord, ashamed I feel that I love him so little and serve him so unfaithfully, and give place to my doubts and fears when I have his promises to rely upon.[25]

Four days later she said, 'I do not feel what I want to feel. I do not abide in Christ every moment as I ought. O, for more faith and love, Lord. Impart unto me a more watchful spirit. Give me true sincerity and meekness, all the mind that was in Christ.'[26]

Just before the anniversary of her conversion, if such it was, in June, she prayed,

> when I look back at my own unfaithfulness and backsliding of heart, I feel ashamed before thee. O, the numerous instances in which I have brought condemnation into my soul and grieved thy Holy Spirit by yeilding [sic] to the tempter, the many times my heard[27] heart has been unbelieving and been ready to doubt of thy faithfulness, the numberless temptations thou hast brought me through and has caused me to praise thee and rejoice in thy salvation, and now thou hast by the dispensations of thy providence brought me here and raised me up kind friends and temporal associates. Glory be to thy name. I will praise the[e]. I will be more than ever devoted to thy service.
>
> > O, take my body, spirit, soul;
> > Only thou pos[s]es[s] the whole.[28]
>
> ... Help me to love the[e] with all my soul and strength, "the cheif [sic] among ten thousand", thou 'alltogether [sic] lovely'. If it is thy will to restore me, O, keep me. Do not suffer me to recover if I should leave the[e] now, my God... O, thy will be done, only let me be thine, w[h]ether suffering or enjoying health, w[h]ether living or dieing [sic]. Let me ever be thine in time and eternity and all shall be well. Direct me in every future step of life... I will acknowledge thee in all my ways, and thou hast promised to direct my steps.[29]

---

25 Ibid., 21 May 1847, p. 5; ibid., p. 10.
26 Ibid., 25 May 1847, p. 7; ibid., p. 12.
27 This should be 'hard'.
28 This is from Charles Wesley's hymn, 'Jesus, all-atoning lamb'.
29 Booth, *Diary*, 1 June 1847, pp. 9–10; *Diary CD*, pp. 14–15.

Later that month she wrote,

> 'Bless the Lord, O my soul, and all that is within me bless His holy name'
> [Ps 103:1]. O Lord, my Lord, thou art good and thy mercy endureth
> forever. This day thou hast been by my right hand and on my left. I
> have seen the[e] in thy works. I have held sweet communion with thee.
> I have been crying, 'There is nothing in heaven or earth I desire beside
> thee.' Thou art my God and my all. O cleans[e] me. Let me feel the full
> assurance that I am pure… I feel I am ut[t]erly unworthy. My heart is
> pol[l]uted and not fit to entertain thee, and so it must remain till thou
> cleanses it. 'Come, thou fount of every blessing', and if thou enterest, all
> sin shall flee away before thee, as clouds before the noon day sun.
>
> I am going to meet with thy dear children. O let me find it good to be
> there. Let the heavens drop fatness. Let me feel[30] thy sacred presence
> from all entanglements.[31]

Her father's low spiritual condition was also clearly a great concern to her.
She prayed with great passion for him. In one diary entry she recorded,

> I was much blessed in the morning at private prayer, particularly in
> commending my dear parents into the hands of God. I sometimes
> get into an agony of feeling while praying for my dear father. O my
> Lord, answer prayer; and bring him back to thyself. Never let that
> tongue, which once delighted in praising the[e] and showing others
> thy willingness to save, be engaged in uttering the Blasphemies of the
> lost. O awful thought! Lord, have mercy. Save, O, save him in any way
> thou see'st best, if it be ever so painful, if by removing me, thou canst
> do this. Cut short thy work and take me home. Let me be bold to speak
> in thy name. O give me true Christian courage and lively zeal, and if
> I write to him from this place, bless what I may say to the good of his
> soul. O, guide me, teach me what I shall say, and make it a blessing to
> him. I feel my own insufficiency, my own ignorance. Help me to trust
> in the[e] for strength and wash all my poor works in the attoning [sic]
> blood of Jesus, amen.[32]

Two weeks later, on 29 May, she sent a letter to her father and she prayed,
'O, my Lord, bless it to his soul; accompany it with the … influences of
thy Spirit and I will praise thee.'[33] Three days later she seems to have sent

---

30 This appears to be 'feel' in the original, though 'free' is possible and may make better sense.
31 Booth, *Diary*, 11 June 1847, pp. 16–17; *Diary CD*, pp. 21–22.
32 Ibid., 15 May 1847, p. 2; ibid., pp. 7–8.
33 Ibid., 29 May 1847, p. 8; ibid., pp. 13–14.

another. She described it as 'a really encouraging letter' and prayed,

> Lord, accompany it with the influence of thy Spirit; without this it will
> be as water spilled upon the ground. But if thou deign to bless this
> unworthy instrument, I will praise thee to all eternity. O save him at last
> and my Dear Brother too.[34] O, it will be a happy day when we all meet
> in heaven.[35]

Yet her father did not neglect her, nor did she neglect him. Early in June
she recorded,

> Received a letter from my Dearest Mother and one from my Dear
> father that did me good, telling me of some good resolutions he had
> half formed. I wrote a long letter to him and fe[e]l[36] much blessed, in so
> doing. I believe I had the assistance of the spirit. O, my Lord, bless it to
> the good of his immortal soul. Amen.[37]

What those 'half formed' resolutions were and whether they developed into
long-term decisions we do not know. However, if one of them was to stop
drinking, then, sadly, it did not produce the desired result.

But it was not only John Mumford who was considering resolutions.
Catherine was too. A few days later she wrote in her diary,

> This day I have been framing fresh resolutions to be more than ever
> devoted to God. My soul has been drawn out anew to Him. This
> morning, while on the sea beach, admiring the wonderful work of my
> heavenly father, who has set the barriers of the sea so that it cannot pass,
> and said, 'Hitherto shalt thou come but no further', I lifted up my heart
> to God and asked him to let me bathe in the full ocean of his love when
> I bathed. The language of my heart was, 'Lord, wash my soul in thy all
> cleansing blood and it matters not w[h]ether this is good for the body or
> not, for I have a building of God, a house not made with hands, eternal
> in the heavens.'[38]

For much of the early part of her time in Brighton she had had a toothache.
She finally plucked up courage to go to the dentist on 12 June. However,
the dentist said that 'he feared [Catherine] was too weak to undergo' the
procedure. He said that her pulse 'was feeble as an infant's, and he thought

---

34 This would be her brother John Valentine Mumford.
35 Booth, *Diary*, 1 June 1847, p. 10; *Diary CD*, p. 15.
36 This could be 'feel' or 'felt'. Booth-Tucker, *Catherine*, vol. 1, p. 42, has 'feel'.
37 Booth, *Diary*, 7 June 1847, p. 15; *Diary CD*, p. 20.
38 Ibid., 10 June 1847, p. 16; ibid., p. 21.

the shock' of the extraction might do her harm. She said, 'He was very kind in giving me his advice, and said he whould [sic] try to make me something' to relieve the pain 'if it got no better.'

That same day she also had a pain in her chest with 'difficulty of breathing'. This caused her to reflect 'I think I may perhaps arrive at home sooner than I have been thinking', and it seems home in this case was not Brixton, for she immediately continued, 'O, how sweet will heaven be to me.'

But the following day was Sunday. She continued Saturday's diary entry, 'I think of receiving the Lord's supper tomorrow. O my Lord, infuse thy love into the bread, thy life into the wine. Let me feel thee eminently present. Let it be an antepast of that time when I shall drink it new with thee in my father's kingdom.'[39]

However, Sunday did not turn out as she had hoped. She wrote in her diary, 'I went to Chappel [sic] in the morning, but felt very poorly with raised heart and palpitations. The afternoon I spent in my bed in reading and contemplation. In the evening I went again and stopped to receive the sacrament but was so ill I could scarcely walk up to the communion rail.' When she got to the rail she held onto something to retain her balance. Fortunately, one of the men saw that she 'was ill and held the cup for' her. She went back to her lodgings, with two gentlemen assisting her. On the walk 'The pain was so violent, [she] had to keep stop[p]ing in the street. The cold sweat stood on' her. One of the gentlemen wanted to get a carriage for her, but she 'managed to walk home.' When she arrived, she went to lie on the bed, and one of her helpers 'came in and read a chapter' of the Bible, 'and prayed with' her. Despite the prayer she became pessimistic, and wrote in her diary, 'I thought perhaps I am going to be worse here. Perhaps I am going to die here. But,' she continued, 'even these thoughts could not disturb my peace. I felt a quiet acquiescence in the will of my heavenly father. I know if [I] do not reach my earthly home, I shall get to my heavenly, and that will be sweeter still… Lord, protect me safe home to the fond embrace of my Dearest Mother.'[40]

It seems extraordinary that a teenager should have been so concerned that she did not have long to live, and to feel that as often as Catherine did, but short lives were common in nineteenth century England. In addition, her poor health and the death of three of her brothers would have made her

---

39 Ibid., 12 June 1847, pp. 17–18; ibid., pp. 22–23.
40 Ibid., 13 June 1847, p. 18; ibid., p. 23.

even more aware of how short life could be.

On Friday 18 June she took the 9 a.m. train to return to London and arrived safely. As she closed her diary entry for that day, she prayed, 'O my Lord, continue to bless me with thy sacred presence now I am come home. O bless me and make me a blessing.'[41]

---

41 Ibid., 18 June 1847, p. 22; ibid., p. 27.

CHAPTER 4

Her early preparation

'Oh, I love to feel my soul swell with unutterable feeling for all mankind… I love to feel a deep & thrilling & intense interest in what concerns the good of my species',

Catherine Mumford.[1]

There are two main sources for details of Catherine Mumford's life from the time she returned to London in June 1847 until she met William Booth in 1852. They are her diary, which she continued to write, though spasmodically, until March 1848, and three letters that she sent to her parents on her return visit to Brighton in 1851. During those years she developed spiritually, began to gain confidence in her God-given abilities and was forced to take a step that was crucial to her future.

Her visit to Brighton in 1847 had been meant to improve her health but it seems to have been only partly successful. Four days after arriving home she said, 'I feel better in many respects for my visit. What I suffer most from is pain in my bre[a]st and shoulders, difficulty of breathing at times and a general fever with a craving for food which I cannot satisfy.' Inevitably she wondered whether she would ever enjoy good health. 'Sometimes,' she said, I think perhaps (God) will restore me to perfect he[a]lth, though I never feel led to pray for this, but rather that I may glorify him in death.'[2]

A further three days later she said that despite still feeling 'much pain,' she enjoyed 'the light of [God's] countenance and his favour, which is better than life.' She added,

I think I never felt a greater desire to be fully devoted to God than now. I never fel[t] more trust and confidence in him than now, and though tempted to murmur sometimes, I feel I cannot murmur. O no, my Jesus has done all things well, and he will do all things well. I know it is because he loves me he afflicts me, and if he spares me, it is to prepare

1 Booth, *Letters*, Letter CM71, 23 Nov. 1853, p. 182; Booth, *Letters CD*, p. 184.
2 Booth, *Diary*, 22 June 1847, p. 22; *Diary CD*, p. 27.

me fully for glory. O, I long to die sometimes. I am ready to cry, 'Come, Lord Jesus, and take me home', for this is a wilderness of sorrow, but blessed be God this is not my home. I seek a city out of sight.[3]

Thus, the thought of death still hovered over her.

Death was never far away in Victorian England. In August she wrote in her diary,

Since last week we have been deeply affected by a circumstance of a very affecting nature. My Dear cousin has been here at times lately. She was expecting to be married next Thursday, and I was thinking of going down to Southampton with them, w[h]ere they had a house prepared for their reception. But, allas, [sic] how soon the cup of happiness is dashed and all our dreams vanish. The young man was taken sud[d]enly ill on the friday and died on the Tuesday morning, but, blessed be God, he died in peace and I doubt not is now in heaven. He is to be buried on Thursday next, his intended wedding day. O, what need there is to [be] constantly ready. O, that I may be found watching when my Lord shall come. I am thinking of going down after the funeral, as I think the change may be beneficial, but I would say in all things, 'Thy will be done'.[4]

Does Catherine show a lack of empathy here? It is true that she said that 'we have been deeply affected' and she was glad that the young man had 'died in peace', but there is little evidence of sympathy for her 'Dear cousin' in this diary entry. It is unknown whether Catherine went to Southampton or not.

On the second Saturday in July Catherine was badly cast down. The next day she wrote, 'I felt very poorly indeed and so nervous that I could scarcely bear any thing. The enemy thrusted sore at me and greatly distressed me by enjecting [sic] wicked and rebel[l]ious thoughts of God and his ways, tempting me to think him a hard marster [sic].' But by Sunday she had vastly improved. 'To day [h]as been a better day to my soul,' she recorded, for

I have been reading in [Richard] Baxter's *Saints' [Everlasting] Rest*.[5] O, it is a blessed book. O, the importance of leading a heavenly life upon earth. I am determined to try this rest. My Lord, help me. I went to Southvill[e Chapel] tonight and heard a delightful sermon by Mr Felvus on the suffering of Christ. O my Jesus, what hast thou suffered for me,

---

3 Ibid., 25 June 1847, p. 23; ibid., p. 28.

4 Ibid., 22 Aug. 1847, p. 29; ibid., pp. 33–34.

5 Richard Baxter (1615–91) was a Puritan preacher and writer who was deprived of his living by the Act of Uniformity (1662), and when he continued to preach was imprisoned. *The Saints' Everlasting Rest* was probably his most popular book.

and shall I have rebel[l]ious thoughts after all thy love? O, deliver me from this, I beseech thee, and I will praise thee.[6]

Teaching in a school

Soon after her return to London, she began teaching in a weekday school. The full nature of that endeavour and the frequency of her efforts are not clear, though at least some of her teaching was of a spiritual nature. She appears to have been teaching her scholars on Friday 9 and Wednesday 14 July and on other days. She found that the duties of the school tried her patience and exhausted her feeble body. Indeed, they were 'a great exertion'.[7] On a Tuesday near the end of August she wrote,

> To night my spirit doth rejoice in God my Sav[i]our. Blessed be His name, he is answering prayer and smiling on my endeavours in a temporal sense. I have reason to expect an increase in my school, but, O, what a need I feel of an increase of patience and love to guide and govern every action and word. I feel the responsability [sic] of my undertaking. I feel I am working for eternity as well as time. O Lord, teach me; strengthen me in body and soul, as long as it is thy will I should keep it, and at last receive me home. I feel very poorly. I suffer much with pain in my left bre[a]st and difficulty in breathing, with almost constant ir[r]itation in my throat. This tryes [sic] me in having to talk, but blessed be God he does strengthen me.[8]

Early in October she was unwell but was still 'able to attend *my* school ... which increases fast. O, that I may be able to sow some seed to the honour and glory of God. I feel my responsibility is great and the prevailing desire of my heart is to live and die for the glory of God' (emphasis added).[9] Note that it was 'my school', though how literally one is to take that is unclear. One would assume that it was connected with her church in some way. Eleven days later she found her duties at the school 'almost too much for' her.[10] She had a holiday from school over the Christmas/New Year period, after which she hoped to 'reopen my school'.[11] On the first Sunday of 1848,

---

6 Booth, *Diary*, 11 July 1847, pp. 24–25; *Diary CD*, p. 29.
7 Ibid., 9 & 14 July 1847, pp. 24–25; ibid., pp. 29–30.
8 Ibid., 24 Aug. 1847, p. 29; ibid., p. 34.
9 Ibid., 4 Oct. 1847, p. 30; ibid., p. 35.
10 Ibid., 15 Oct. 1847, pp. 30–31; ibid., p. 35.
11 Ibid., 26 Dec. 1847, p. 34; ibid., p. 39.

she recorded in her diary, 'Tomorrow I reopen my school. I have been enabled to continue it Longer than I expected when I began.'[12] For the third time it was 'my school', and she appears to have had sufficient control over it to decide when to close and reopen it. It also needs to be borne in mind at this point, that Catherine was not quite 19 and, though very intelligent, had had a very limited education herself.

More struggles

Not all went smoothly in Catherine's life. On the last Sunday in July 1847 she wrote,

> I have not written in my journal the past week. It has been one of spiritual conflict and bodily weakness. The temptations of Satan have been numerous and powerful and the feelings of my mind very distressing. I never felt in such a state before. I have felt as though I could not pray at times. Such rebel[l]ious thoughts and feelings have arisen in my mind, as I cannot express, and ir[r]itability of temper. My warring passions have refused to be calmed. I have experienced a spiritual deadness, though at times I have felt a true hungering and thirsting after righteousness. I fear I have greived [sic] the spirit of God by giving way in some measure to temptations, but, blessed be His name, this has been a better day to my soul...
>
> This morning I went with my dearest Mother to Southvill[e] and heard young Mr Thompson preach a bea[u]tiful sermon[13], and am going tonight. Lord, bless me more abundantly. O quicken thou me, according to thy word. Thou knowest I would not willingly grieve thee and the thought of thou being angry with me fills me with greif [sic]. I long to be all thou wouldst have me to be. Lord, cleanse me from sin and, O, bruise Satan under my feet. Suffer him not to inject such distressing thoughts into my mind, and if I have given way or lodged one unkind thought of thee in my bre[a]st, now forgive me through Jesus, thy only son. O keep me to the end. Save [me] weather [sic] by suffering or health, life or death, only let me be fully thine and all will be well.[14]

Yet, that did not bring her spiritual struggle to an end. At the end of the first

---

12 Ibid, 2 Jan. 1848, p. 35; ibid., p. 40.

13 Bramwell-Booth, *Catherine*, p. 45, assumed that this was Rev. David Thomas preaching at Stockwell New Chapel (a Congregational Church). However, Catherine has written 'Southvill' and 'Thompson', not Stockwell and Thomas.

14 Booth, *Diary*, 25 July 1847, p. 26; *Diary CD*, pp. 30–31.

week in August she wrote,

> The past forghtnight [sic] [h]as been one of spiritual conflict and distress. My mind has been much harrassed [sic] and cast down by a vewe [sic] of my past unfaithfulness and present inbred corruption. I have been powerfully tempted to give up my confidence and yeild [sic] to dispare [sic] and in some measure [have] given way, so as to bring doubts and fears. My cry [h]as been, 'Lord, quicken me,' but I often felt as though I could not pray. I have been looking too much at myself and too little at Jesus, but, blessed be God, last night he did bless me with more peace, in fact, than I have had lately. I went too [sic] my class and was blessed.
>
> I have been reading *The Memoirs of Mrs Little*, which speakes [sic] much about the finished work of Christ as the only ground of the sinner's hope, I feel it is and wants constantly to dwell on the mind to keep it alive. O my Lord, thou knowest I desire to love and serve thee with all my heart, and on Jesus are all my hopes rested for eternity. O forgive all fresh incur[r]ed guilt, all broken promises and rebel[l]ious thoughts.
>
> Today I have been blessed in private prayer and contemplation. I have been striving to think of the rest which is prepared for the children of God, and, glory be to his name, I feel still through Jesus it is for me, but, O, how unworthy.[15]

It is clear that for the young Catherine Mumford living the Christian life had its ups and downs. It was not a continual flow of triumphant spiritual experiences. In this case, too, the doubts and struggles recorded above went on for at least a few more days. Part of the cure was a return to Richard Baxter's *The Saints' Everlasting Rest*, and she began to try 'heavenly contemplation at stated times.' She prayed,

> Lord help me to think much of the rest thou has[t] prepared for them that love thee… Whosoever will may come and drink of the water of life freely. O, infinite love, boundless compassion!

> Jesus, thy blood and righteousness
> My beauty are, my glorious dress;
> Midst flaming worlds, in these arrayed,
> With joy shall I lift up my head.[16]

---

15 Ibid., 7 Aug. 1847, pp. 26–27; ibid., p. 31.
16 This is the opening verse of the great hymn by Count Zinzendorf, in the translation by John Wesley. In her original Catherine had written 'falming' instead of 'flaming'.

It is on the finished work of Christ that all my hopes for eternity are founded. He alone can attone [sic] for sin and His blood alone can cleanse from all sin. Nothing I have done or can do can enhance the value of that sacrifice.[17]

Her diary entries are much less frequent after August. There is only one entry in September and three each in October, November and December, and most are brief. Mid-September she said, 'We have had some trying circumstances to contend with of a provoking character,' but she did not describe them. She continued,

my soul has not enjoyed that spiritual life it did some time since. I have seen more than ever the inbred depravity of my heart, and at times I have been almost overwhelemed [sic] and ready to think instead [of] living to the glory of God, I dishonour his cause by my conduct. These thoughts have humbled me in the dust at my sav[i]our's feet, and I feel astonished at the goodness of God to such an unloving, disobedient child. I feel without the influences of His Spirit I nothing good can do or think. O Lord, bless me again with the light of thy countenance and let me again walk by faith.[18]

In the period immediately following, matters continued their up and down course. Early in October she said,

Since I last wrote I have past [sic] through many Temptations and much heaviness of Spirits. I feel ashamed of my barrenness and backslidings of Heart. I have been living at too great a distance from God and therefore have deservedly suffered loss. But blessed be God, I have had some seasons of refreshing from His presence, and when tempted to think He had forgotten to be gracious He has favoured me with the influences of His spirit. But, O, I feel myself so unproffitable [sic] and disobedient that I am astonished at the goodness of God in continuing to send the gracious visitations of His Spirit.

But yesterday was a better day with me. I heard our new minister twice at Walworth. In the morning on Elijah's Temptation; at night from 'Exceeding great and precious Promises' [2 Pet. 1:4]. He is a delightful preacher and his words were blessed to my soul. I stop[p]ed [for] Sacrament. It was a proffitable [sic] time, but my mind will wander at times, though I strive to stay it upon God.[19]

---

17 Booth, *Diary*, 9 Aug. 1847, pp. 27–28; *Diary CD*, pp. 32–33.
18 Ibid., 12 Sept. 1847, p. 30; ibid., p. 34.
19 Ibid., 4 Oct. 1847, p. 30; ibid., p. 35.

Later in October her spirit seems to have been at a higher level, even though she was unwell. She wrote,

I desire to praise the Lord. My soul is in a more comfortable state than it has been. I have been reading a little in Mrs Fletcher's life and have been blessed, particularly one part, her observations on the acceptance of the soul after any fall is by simply beleiving [sic] Christ has allowed for that sin. I feel this is a blessed way of salvation and shows the infinite mercy of God in receiving me again after greiving [sic] Him, but, O, I want a conscience tender as the apple of an eye, the slightest touch of sin to feel. I believe it is possable [sic] to live, by the grace of God, without greiving [sic] the Spirit of God in any thing, though I see this to be a very high state of grace. It seems impossable [sic] for me to attain to it, but all things are possable [sic] with Jesus.[20]

But highs do not always last long in the Christian life. In the following period she 'suffered much from Temptation,' though she still 'experienced some gracious seasons at the throne of grace.'

As was noted before, Catherine could speak inappropriately. It was a fault of which she was well aware. In a November diary entry she confessed, 'I often bring condemnation into my soul by unwatchfulness in words. When I speak, I don't feel as if it was [w]rong. I don't do it with a [w]rong motive, but afterwards when examining it I find sin mingled with all I think or do.'[21]

Yearning after holiness

It comes as no surprise that she yearned after holiness. In nineteenth-century Methodist circles, following and developing the teaching of John Wesley, holiness was regarded as a post-conversion experience that could be received through faith.

At the end of November, as her desire to live closer to God increased, she said,

This [h]as been an especial[ly] good day to my soul. I have been reading the life of Mr William Carvosso. O, what a man of faith and prayer was he. My expectations were raised when I began the Book. I prayed for the divine blessing on it, and it has been granted. My desires after holiness have been much increased. This day I have sometimes seemed

---

20 Ibid., 21 Oct. 1847, p. 31; ibid., p. 35.
21 Ibid., 12 Nov. 1847, pp. 31–32; ibid., p. 36.

on the virge [sic] of the good land. O, for mighty faith! I beleive [sic] the Lord [is] willing and able to save me to the uttermost. I beleive [sic] the blood of Jesus cleans from all sin, and yet there seems something in the way to prevent me fully entering in. But I beleive [sic] to day at times I have had tastes of perfect love. O, that these may be a drop before an overw[h]elming shower of saving grace. My cheif [sic] desire is holiness of heart. This is the prevailing cry of my soul to night is [sic] 'Sanctify me through thy truth; thy word is truth' [Jn 17:17]. Lord, answer my Redeemer's Prayer.[22]

One striking and oft repeated feature of her diary is that she gained great help from reading books by and about the great Christians of the past. This time the subject was William Carvosso, who was a Methodist itinerant evangelist from the county of Cornwall at the end of the eighteenth century and the beginning of the next. Carvosso's book seems to have been an encouragement to her to live a holy life.

On Christmas Day she looked back in her diary over the past year. In a lengthy entry she again painfully acknowledged her sinfulness, and once more she recognised that her tongue was often at fault. Yet there was hope. She wrote,

On Faithfully examining myself and looking back over the past year, I beleive [sic] and solomy [sic] acknowledge that my heart has on various occasions been in some measure drawn from God. I mean experienced a deadness & dul[l]ness in Spiritual things which must have been displeasing in His sight. My battles with the Enemy have been distressing, my temptations numerous and powerfull, [sic] and the thoughts of my heart at times awful, such as I would not refer, but I beleive [sic] these have been injected by the Enemy, for I would not have had them. I have tried to put them off, but sometimes they have almost distracted me. I have been accused in many things I have said. Often have I spoken unadvisadly [sic] with my lips and brought condemnation into my soul. In fact, the Lord only knows my unfaithfulness, and indeed depravity. I have not been so constant over private prayer as I ought to have been, though I have not neglected it so much as I have been insensible to proper feelings while engaged in this sacred duty.

But amidst all this I will not forget the every kindness of my God. He has often heard my groanings and appeared to my releif, [sic] as the

---

22 Ibid., 28 Nov. 1847, p. 32; ibid., pp. 36–37.

past Journal testifies. Many times have I rejoiced with 'joy unspeakable & full of glory', and often experienced blessed seasons in prayer. My expectations and anticipations of heaven have at times been animating & encouraging. My longings after purity have often been very ardent, and I have breathed out, 'Come to thy temple, come.'

The experience I have here set down more particularly relates to the time since I came from Brighton. There I enjoyed much of the Love of God, I think more than ever I did before or since. O, for a return of some such precious seasons. I am often strongly tempted to burn this journal and to think I have been deceived, but I hope to gain encouragement by looking at the past goodness of my God. Perhaps no eye may ever see it but my own, but if it answers this end it will accomplish that for which I commenced it.

I feel an earnest desire now I am entering another year to be more devoted to God, to live fully to His glory, or I earnestly pray that if He sees my heart will be estranged from Him by sparing me, to cut short His work this year and take me to Himself. O, I feel willing to do anything, to suffer anything, so that my soul may prosper, and yet my heart seems hard and unbelieving [sic]. O my Lord, let me enter on the next year with a new heart total[l]y cleansed from sin.[23]

The new year

There was no great celebration on New Year's Eve. Catherine was ill again, and she and her mother saw the new year in quietly together. There was no mention of her father.[24] On the second day of 1848, a Sunday, Catherine went to church and later, in her diary, she wrote, 'I have been writing a few daily rules for the coming year, which I hope will prove a blessing to me by the grace of God. I have got a printed paper of rules also, which I intend to read once a week.' (A little less than two years later her future husband also made a list of rules to live by, but that was before they had met. He vowed to read his rules 'every day or at least twice a week.')[25] She continued,

May the Lord help me to ad[h]ere to them all, but above all I am determined to search the Scriptures more attentively, for in them I have eternal life. I have read my Bible through twice in 16 months, but I must

23 Ibid., 25 Dec. 1847, pp. 33–34; ibid. p. 38.
24 Ibid., 1 Jan. 1848, p. 34; ibid., p. 39.
25 William Booth's 'Resolutions' were written on 6 December 1849, Begbie, *William*, vol. 1, pp. 105–106.

read it with more prayer for light and understanding. I intend it to be the first thing and last most days. O, may it be my meet [sic] and drink, may I meditate in it day and night, and then I shall 'bring forth fruit in season, my leaf shall not wither, and whatsoever I do shall prosper' [a paraphrase of Ps 1:3]. O, precious [sic] promises contained in the word of God! Lord, help me to claim them now through Christ. I feel I want more faith. I want to walk more by faith and not by feeling. I want to beleive [sic] more, then I should love more and serve better. O, for firm and lasting faith to credit all the Almighty saith. I do beleive [sic] all the Lord has said, but I want faith to ap[p]reciate[26] the blessings promised to myself through Christ. O, when shall I learn to abide In Christ? Haste happy day![27]

On the second Sunday of January she regretted that she had been unable to go to church. It was very cold, and she was not sufficiently well to walk the necessary distance. That day she wrote in her diary,

Next Sunday will be the last day of another year of my unworthy life. On Monday, if spared, I am 19 years old. O Lord, I pray thee, let the next be a better year to my soul, let me bring forth fruit to thy glory. I expect my Dear [class] Leader and 2 or 3 more to spend the evening. Oh Jesus, be in our midst. Baptise us affresh [sic] with thy Spirit. Oh, let me experience a new birth unto Righteousness and a death unto all sin. Amen.[28]

On her birthday her entry was brief. She looked back and looked forward: '19 years this day I have lived in this world of sin and sorrow, but, Oh, I have had many sweets mingled with the bitter. I have very much to p[r]aise my God for, more than I can conceive, but, Oh, may I for the future live to praise Him and bring glory to His blessed name. Amen.'[29] Sadly, the expected birthday visitors failed to come.[30]

As the winter proceeded, Catherine's attendances at chapel were not as frequent as she would have liked. On the first Sunday in February she reflected,

This morning I went to Chapel and felt the Hallowing influences of the living Holy Ghost. I believe if I get to the means [of grace] oftener, my

---

26 One might expect 'appropriate' here, but the original reads 'apreciate'.
27 Booth, *Diary*, 2 Jan. 1848, p. 35; *Diary CD*, pp. 39–40.
28 Ibid., 9 Jan. 1848, p. 36; ibid., p. 40.
29 Ibid., 17 Jan. 1848, p. 36; ibid., p. 40.
30 Ibid., 21 Jan. 1848, p. 36; ibid., p. 40.

soul would prosper better. I know I might be blessed more at Home, if I lived in the Spirit of Prayer and earnest expectation. I see in reading some of the past pages, I live too much by feeling instead of Faith, for it is faith that Conquers all Spiritual Enemies. I want constantly to look to Jesus, who is the author and finisher of my Faith. Oh, may the Lord help me to be more in earnest. I can say it is my longing desire to glorify Him, to be more fully devoted to His service. I will in the strength of grace deny myself more, take up my cross and follow Christ.

Catherine then added, 'I have renewed my practice of Abstaining from dinner on a friday and butter in a morning, as I had discontinued it for some time. Oh my Lord, Help me to be fully decided in all things...'.[31] It is unknown when Catherine had first adopted these practices. She had clearly begun them, and then 'had discontinued [them] for some time,' so it seems likely that she had first abstained at least a year earlier. It is also unknown what or who had influenced her to do this.

But life was still a spiritual struggle. Three days later she said,

Oh, I cannot express what sights I have of my self. I cannot tell what I often feel. Oh, if ever I reach heaven, what a miracle of mercy I shall be. Lord help me to strive to enter in. Give me true earnestness of Spirit. I see great cause to be decided in every thing that relates to my soul.[32]

Later that February her spirits had risen. She wrote,

Blessed be God, my soul prospers better than it has done. I feel more access to a throne of grace and more comfort in reading the Scriptures. I feel my Chief desire is to be all the Lord would have me [be], but I want more faith constantly to hang on a crucified God. Oh, what love has the Lord bestowed upon me after all my unfaithfulness. May He enable me by His grace to seek His Glory in return.'[33]

That month she also received a visit from her 'Dear Cousin Ann', who was probably Ann Milward, aged 19 or 20. Catherine tried to impress upon Ann 'the importance of giving her Heart to God in her youth'. However, Catherine does not seem to have been comfortable with face-to-face evangelism at this stage. Rather, she felt 'most at liberty in writing' and she did write to this cousin.[34]

---

31 Ibid., 6 Feb. 1848, p. 37; ibid., p. 41.

32 Ibid., 9 Feb.1848, p. 38; ibid., p. 42.

33 Ibid., 25 Feb. 1848, p. 38; ibid., p. 42.

34 Ibid., 25 Feb. 1848, p. 38; ibid., p. 42. Ann was probably the eldest daughter of John and

In fact, she also wrote 'long letters to' another cousin 'on spiritual subjects', though in this case the circumstances were different. This cousin had three young children and her health seems to have been 'in a deep decline… But,' said Catherine, 'the Lord graciously supports her and often fills her with His love.' Catherine believed that the Lord owned these 'weak endeavours for His glory by blessing them to her good.'[35]

The first stage of her diary ended on 24 March 1848. The second, briefer section did not begin until 1852 after she had met William Booth. But this earlier part of the diary closed positively. She wrote, 'Blessed be God I have felt better in my soul this last few days than I have done for some time. I have been more blessed in Prayer and enjoyed a stronger confidence in God. Oh, when I look at my own unfaithfulness, I feel grieved, but Jesus ever lives… What a mercy! Lord, help me to be more faithful.' But if well in spirit, she was still 'poorly' in body.[36] But in that sense Catherine was nearly always poorly.

Another visit to Brighton

Next to nothing is known about Catherine's life between March 1848 and September 1851. John Read calls it 'an intriguing gap'[37], and so it is, though it probably can be assumed that her life continued much the same as in the earlier pages of this chapter.

It was almost certainly in September 1851 that she made another visit to Brighton. The evidence for this is in three letters that she wrote to her parents whilst she was at that south-eastern coastal town. These letters have been traditionally dated to 1847 and it has been assumed that they were written on her visit to Brighton that year.[38] However, overwhelming evidence indicates that they were written from Brighton in September and October 1851.[39] In other words, she went to stay in Brighton on a second occasion.

Mary Milward. John appears to have been the brother of Catherine's mother.

35 Ibid., 17 Mar. 1848, p. 39; ibid., p. 43.

36 Ibid., 24 Mar. 1848, p. 40; ibid., p. 44.

37 Read, *Catherine*, Kindle loc. 197.

38 Booth-Tucker, *Catherine*, vol. 1, pp. 40–41; Bramwell-Booth, *Catherine*, pp. 43–44; Green, *Catherine*, pp. 32–33, 301, fns. 39–40.

39 See Catherine's letters 'CBLP', P1–P3, pp. 11–12 & 14–15, and fns. 5, 8, 11–12, 20, 24 & 26–27; and Bennett, 'Catherine Booth's Letters to her Parents, John and Sarah Mumford', *AJSAH*.

The most significant piece of evidence for the 1851 dating is in the third of these letters, in which Catherine wrote,

I hope you will get this on monday morning, & I will write again on monday, so that you may get it before you go to the glorious Exhibition. Oh, I should like to see it again so much. It seems a pity for such magnificence to be disturbed. I hope the closing ceremony will be worthy of its history.

There is one thing I trust will not be forgotten: that is to give God thanks for having so signally disappointed our enemies, & made the fears of friends groundless. This unparalleled production of art & science was born in good will, has lived in universal popularity, & will, no doubt, expire with majestic grandeur, lamented by all the nations of the earth.[40]

That 'glorious Exhibition' must be the Great Exhibition held in London in 1851.

The 1851 Exhibition was the major social event in the mid-nineteenth century. It was a wonderful display of 100,000 exhibits of the arts, sciences, and the commercial world, all held in a vast building of glass and cast iron, designed by Joseph Paxton. Its opening in May was said to have attracted half a million people, and the crowds continued to flood in until it closed in mid-October.[41] Catherine had clearly visited it and sounds as though she had been overwhelmed by its magnificence. One might even dare to say it made her feel proud to be British.

So, Catherine Mumford went again to Brighton in 1851, probably in the middle of September, and stayed until early October. On this occasion she definitely stayed with her uncle and aunt, Richard and Jane Burt, who had probably also hosted her in 1847. According to the Census of 1851, the Burt family had a lodger by the name of 'Maria Numford.' It is easy to imagine that that spelling was an error and that the young woman's name was in fact Mumford.[42]

Catherine made numerous references to a young woman named Maria in the three 1851 letters. Catherine said, 'I do pray and read the scriptures

---

40 'CBLP', Letter P3, late September or early October 1851, pp. 15–16.
41 Wilson, *Victorians*, pp. 128–30, 136–37.
42 'Richard Burt's Household Members' and 'Maria Numford's Household Members', 1851 England, Wales & Scotland Census, Duke Street, Brighton, Sussex, England; and 1851 England, Wales & Scotland Census Image, 35 Duke Street, Brighton, Sussex, England. (This link to the 1851 Census was kindly provided by Gordon Taylor.)

with Maria,' who was probably also a Christian. Catherine seems to have had doubt about that, but it was not uncommon for Catherine to have doubts about the spiritual status of others. Maria was not a Methodist and had a Calvinistic background, which may have been the cause of Catherine's uncertainty about her salvation. In the first letter Catherine said that Maria had 'prayed in my presence once, *the first time* she ever attempted it, except alone. I hope the work is begun; if not, I tremble for her.'

She added, 'I have had a deal of talk to her about election & christian perfection, the last of which she would not admit possible.' But whatever Maria thought, Catherine 'never felt clearer light on these points than now'[43], and one can be sure that Catherine did think that perfection was possible for the Christian, even a desired goal, and she presumably rejected election.

Catherine, however, admitted that Maria had a quality that she lacked.

Maria's living & mine is a perfect contrast, poor girl. She has not many comforts, but she seems very content. Her disposition is so even. It is not a little thing that will move her. I wish I had a little more of that evenness of temper. But alas, you know I am very irattable [sic]. Well, the Lord says, 'My grace is sufficient.' Oh, that I had a sufficiency.[44]

There may also have been another letter from Catherine to her parents written before the three we still have. Booth-Tucker quotes a letter from Sarah Mumford to Catherine in Brighton, presumably written in 1851, though with Booth-Tucker's combining of Catherine's two visits to Brighton that is not certain. In that missive Sarah Mumford indicates that her daughter had sent an earlier letter. It will be helpful to quote Sarah's letter, as practically all we know about her comes from her daughter's pen, and thus her daughter's perspective.

Sarah Mumford said,

Oh, may the Lord help me to hang on his faithfulness alone, and when all seems gloomy without, 'still to endure as seeing Him who is invisible.' The enemy tempts me to doubt, because I do not *feel* as I did before. But I say to myself, 'Thou knowst,

Other refuge have I none,
Hangs my helpless soul on Thee.'

May He help me to believe for a clearer manifestation of His love and favour.

---

43 'CBLP', Letter P1, about 22 Sept. 1851, p. 11.
44 Ibid, Letter P2, probably 25 Sept. 1851, p. 13.

> I would not my soul deceive,
> Without the inward witness live.

I am glad you are getting on so well. Live close to Jesus and He will help you to the end. Oh, may He bless you with all his fullness. You say I must pray for you. Do you think I could approach the Throne of Grace without doing so? Oh, no! You are ever in my mind as an offering to the Lord. May He sanctify you wholly to Himself, is the prayer of

> Your ever-loving Mother,
> Sarah Mumford.[45]

Gloom and doubt hang over Sarah Mumford, but her faith in God still shines through, and her Catherine is 'an offering to the Lord.'

In what appears to be Catherine's response to this, she says, 'Pray for me, my dear Mother. I wish we knew each other better and have grace to deal with each other in *wisdom*. It would save us much sorrow. Perhaps the Lord will teach us more than we ever knew before.'[46] Clearly, mother and daughter did not always see eye to eye.

In a letter probably written a few days later, Catherine says,

> I have been here a week to day. It has been a pleasant week, & I hope by another week to feel much better. The weather has been lovely till to day, when we had a little rain with cold wind, which, as I am not strong enough to walk for to get myself heat, won't suit me, and I could not stop long on the beach. But it seems clear and promising this evening, so I hope it will be fine tomorrow.

Catherine's love of nature comes through in that letter, when she says,

> I have just returned from the beach. It is a lovely morning but very rough and cold. The sea looks sublime. I never saw it so troubled. Its 'waters cast up mire and dirt' [Is 57:20] and lash the shore with great violence. The sun shines with full splendour, which makes the scene truly enchanting. It only wants good health & plenty of strength to walk about to keep me warm, for it is too cold to sit.

Then later in the same, by then, lengthy letter, she responds to what she sees

---

45 Booth-Tucker, *Catherine*, 1:39–40. We have quoted all Booth-Tucker has of this letter, but as Catherine calls what is presumably this a 'long letter' ('CBLP', P1, about 22 Sept. 1851, p. 11), we can assume this is only part of it. It is possible that P1 was written *before* this specific letter from Mrs Mumford, i.e. Catherine says, 'Pray for me'; Sarah says, 'You say I must pray for you.' However, these two letters give contradictory signals concerning dating.

46 'CBLP', Letter P1, about 22 Sept. 1851, p. 11.

in a slightly different way. She writes,

> There is nothing on earth more pleasing and profitable to me than the meditations and emotions excited by such scenes as I witness here. I only want them I love best to participate [in] my joys, & then they would be complete. For though I possess a share of that monstrous, ugly thing called selfishness, in common with our fallen race, yet I can say my own pleasure is always enhanced by the pleasure of others, & always embit[t]ered by their sorrows. Thanks be to God, for it is by his grace that I am what I am. Oh, for that fulness of love which destroys self and fills the soul with heaven born generosity.[47]

Catherine was in Brighton again for her health. But she was not the only one there for that reason, for she reported,

> Brighton is very full of company. Many a poor invalid is here, strol[l]ing about in search of that pe[a]rl of great price–Health. Many, like the fortunate diver, espy the precious gem, & hug[g]ing it to their bosoms return rejoicing in the possession of real riches, but many, alas, find it not, and return only to bewail their misfortune. Which ever class I may be amongst, I hope I shall not have cause to regret my visit. But that if I find not health of body, I hope my soul will be strengthened with might, so that if the outward form should decay, the inward man may be rewarded day by day.[48]

Catherine seems to have returned to London in the first half of October.[49]

---

47 Ibid., Letter P2, probably 25 Sept. 1851, pp. 12–14.

48 Ibid., Letter P2, probably 25 Sept. 1851, p. 14. Note that Catherine did say, 'the inward *man*'.

49 Ibid., Letter P3, late September or early October 1851, p. 15.

CHAPTER 5

Catherine Mumford and the Methodist Reformers

'This was one of the first great troubles of my life
and cost me the keenest anguish',

Catherine Mumford.[1]

We come now to a major event in Catherine Mumford's life, though one that was largely out of her control. Wesleyan Methodism in Britain experienced a major crisis in the late 1840s and early 1850s, known as the Fly Sheet affair. It was an attempt to reform how Methodism was governed, and it led to many defections from Wesleyan Methodism in what is sometimes called 'The Agitation.'[2] Catherine Mumford became one of those defectors, though not by intention.

It will be helpful at this point to say a little about the structure of most forms of Methodism. A local Methodist group was known as a 'society' (which contained smaller groups known as classes), and a group of societies in one area was known as a 'circuit.' Several circuits in a larger area formed a 'district.' They were all answerable to the annual Conference, which was a meeting of the denomination's leaders, usually held in the middle of the year.

As has been seen, it was not long after the death of John Wesley in 1791 that British Methodism began to divide. Because of ministerial dominance, one group broke away as early as 1797 to form the Methodist New Connexion. Another split occurred when Primitive Methodism was founded in 1811, and the Mumfords seem to have been associated with that for a brief while. This later became a large body. Another group of defectors, mainly in the south-west of England, broke away in 1815 to form the Bible Christians. Further defections led to the formation of the Protestant Methodists in

---

1 Booth-Tucker, *Catherine*, vol. 1, p. 49.
2 Brooks, *West End Methodism: The Story of Hinde Street*, p. 61; Edwards, *Methodism and England: A Study of Methodism and its Social and Political Aspects during the period 1850–1932*, pp. 28–29.

1827–28 and the Wesleyan Association in 1835. These two last groups amalgamated in 1836.[3]

The Methodist (Wesleyan) Reformers

The breakaway movement referred to in this chapter is the Methodist or Wesleyan Reformers. This resulted from a series of incidents, culminating in 1849. As many as 100,000 people left the British Wesleyan Methodists by the mid-1850s, most of whom joined the Reformers. In fact, the Wesleyans experienced a decline of over 56,000 in the year 1850–51 alone.[4]

For much of the first half of the nineteenth century the Wesleyan Methodists strongly emphasised the supremacy of the Conference, which was run by the autocratic Jabez Bunting (1779–1858) and what was seen as a clique of likeminded ministers, based in London. This antagonised many, particularly as Methodism was stronger in the south-west and north of England and in the midlands than it was in London.

In 1846 the first of a series of anonymous Fly Sheets criticising the ruling party was published and circulated to Wesleyan ministers. A second appeared later that year, another in 1847 and a fourth in 1848. They labelled Bunting as the main villain, and whilst raising valid points of objection they also, as Maldwyn Edwards put it, engaged in 'exaggeration, misrepresentation and personal abuse'. At the beginning of 1849 some of Bunting's supporters issued 'Papers on Wesleyan Matters' attacking the anti-Bunting faction, which, like the papers they criticised, were 'venomous in tone and scurrilous in detail'. To further add to the dispute, later that year the Fly Sheets were bound together and made widely available.[5]

The 1849 Conference investigated the authorship of the Fly Sheets and only succeeded in making matters worse. That Conference expelled three ministers, James Everett (1784–1872), who was assumed to be the author, and William Griffith Jr (1806–83) and Samuel Dunn (1797–1882), who had

---

3 Vickers (ed.), *A Dictionary of Methodism in Britain and Ireland (DMBI)*, pp. 29, 233, 281, 283, 385.
4 Smith, *History of Wesleyan Methodism*, vol. 3, p. 476. The Wesleyan Conference announced decreases in five successive years (1851–55), before the membership began to increase again. See also *DMBI*, p. 386.
5 Edwards, *Methodism*, pp. 22–25; see also *DMBI*, p. 125 and Smith, *Wesleyan*, vol. 3, pp. 458–62. An example of the interest of the secular press in the affair can be found in the *Leeds Mercury*, 14 July 1849, p. 5, col. 3, though many newspapers commented on it and repeatedly.

published material in support of the Fly Sheets.[6] Indeed, Griffith and Dunn had refused 'to satisfy the Conference as to their innocence in the matter of the "Fly-Sheets"' themselves.[7] Samuel Dunn was William Booth's minister in Nottingham.

These expulsions, however, did not solve the problem. These three ministers were now free to do and say what they liked, so they toured the country, speaking at meetings, strongly defending their viewpoint. This included a 'densely crowded' gathering at London's Exeter Hall on 31 August that year. When Dunn rose to speak, he had to wait for 'some time' because of 'the intense and protracted cheering' that greeted him.[8]

The three dissidents initially urged their supporters in meetings and in a published letter 'to keep their present relations with Methodism.' However, their activities were widely reported, so the whole sad affair snow-balled and it became the trigger for many rank and file Wesleyans to defect over the next few years, and in some instances whole societies were expelled. Memorials with 50,000 signatures supporting the Reformers' case were presented to the 1850 Wesleyan Conference. The Conference responded by expelling another minister, the Rev. James Bromley.[9]

In March 1850, before that year's Wesleyan Conference, about 400 Reformers met in Albion Chapel in London to form a new body. This gathering they called a 'Delegate Meeting.'[10] The term 'Conference' presumably had too many bad connotations for them and seemed to represent a form of government that they no longer accepted. This meeting drew up a sixteen-point constitution and issued a 'Declaration of Principles.'[11] This declaration assured that this new branch of Methodism, later to be called the Wesleyan Reform Union (WRU), would be democratic and largely congregational in government. Its members did not intend becoming subject to a ruling elite. The Reformers at this time, it needs to be understood, still considered themselves to be Wesleyans, as their name indicates. They were Reformers, yes, but they were Wesleyan Reformers.

---

6 *The Argus,* 'The Wesleyan Conference: Recent Expulsion of Ministers, Official Statement', Wednesday, 19 Dec. 1849, p. 4

7 Smith, *Wesleyan*, vol. 3, p. 581.

8 *London Daily News,* 'The Expelled Wesleyan Ministers', 1 Sept. 1849, p. 5, col. 5.

9 Edwards, *Methodism*, pp. 25–29; Smith, *Wesleyan*, vol. 3, pp. 471–72, 476.

10 Smith, *Wesleyan*, vol. 3, p. 474. The Reformer Delegates were called together twice in 1850, in March and August, see Jones and G. A. M., *One is Your Master: The Story of One Hundred Years of the Wesleyan Reform Union*, pp. 7, 106.

11 Jones & G. A. M., *One Hundred*, pp. 7–9.

The Wesleyan Reform movement was never strong in London, for it was a protest from the provinces against the stranglehold that some ministers in London had upon Wesleyan Methodism. Indeed, the WRU had no churches at all in London after 1880.[12] However, the movement did have some in the early 1850s, when Catherine Mumford was there.

One of the main London circuits badly affected by this division was the 'sixth London', which was centred on the Hinde Street Church in London's West End. The leading lay Reformer at Hinde Street was Frederic Grosjean, 'a thriving West End tradesman', a local (that is, lay) preacher and a class leader. He had chaired two meetings in London at the end of 1849, which were held to discuss the recent expulsions, and at least one other meeting in Yorkshire. He also asked some awkward questions of members of the Methodist hierarchy at a meeting of the Wesleyan Methodist Missionary Society the following January, but, as a known Reformer, he was silenced. That March he was appointed secretary of the London Corresponding Committee, which had been established to promote the reform movement and to look after the welfare of its members.[13] He was still speaking at meetings for the Reformers in December 1852, when Catherine Mumford planned to hear him, but she was unwell and unable to do so.[14]

Joseph Beaumont, the superintendent of the Hinde Street Circuit, had tried to steer a middle course in the dispute, but as matters worsened this became impossible. He was instructed by the District Meeting to bring Grosjean to trial, which he failed to do, though he did suspend him from his role as a local preacher. Other lay preachers were also suspended. Beaumont, for his trouble, was hauled up before the Conference for failing to act on the instructions of the District Meeting.[15]

Catherine leaves the Wesleyans

Catherine Mumford followed these events with considerable unease. She attended a major Reformers' meeting at Exeter Hall, presumably the one in August 1849, and she was stirred by their cause.[16] Catherine strongly favoured the Reformers. In a letter to her parents from Brighton in 1851,

---

12 Ibid., *One Hundred*, p. 68.
13 Brooks, *West End*, pp. 63–64, 68.
14 Booth, *Letters*, Letter CM10, 19 Dec. 1852, p. 38, see also letter Booth, *Letters*, WB20, 21 Dec. 1852, p. 35; Booth, *Letters CD*, p. 42, see also p. 40.
15 Brooks, *West End*, pp. 64–66, 74.
16 Booth-Tucker, *Catherine*, vol. 1, p. 48.

she wrote, 'I feel indignant at the conference for their base treatment of Mr Burnett, but I quite expected it when he gave a conscientious af[f]adavit [sic] in Mr Hardy's case.[17] Well, it will all come down on their own pates. The Lord will reward them according to their doings. If they only persevere a little longer, *reform is certain.*[18] Mr Burnett seems to have been Rev. W. Burnett, who was censured by the Wesleyan Conference in 1851, for apparently supporting William Cozens-Hardy of Norfolk, who was expelled by the local Wesleyan Methodist District meeting in 1850 because he had supported the Reformers.[19]

Catherine appears to have supported the Reformers for two main reasons. First, because of their desire for a more democratic form of Methodism. Secondly, she also thought that the Reformers' brand of Methodism would be more evangelistic. She later seemed disappointed on both counts. When she had seen the Reformers in action, she thought that they tended to be chaotic rather than democratic, and they proved less evangelistic than she expected. The chaos in the movement seems to have been widespread, and largely attributable to the vast numbers leaving the Wesleyans in just a few years. That Catherine thought them less evangelistic than she expected was probably due to her limited, London-only, experience of the movement, for it was evangelistic in other areas.

At some stage, probably after her visit to Brighton in 1851, Catherine expressed her support for the Reformers to her female class leader, a Mrs Key, with whom Catherine had been very close. Mrs Key was not pleased and tried to persuade Catherine to change her view, but Catherine refused. The class leader then withheld Catherine's class ticket, no doubt after consultation with the minister (who seems to have been her husband).[20] This effectively expelled Catherine from the Wesleyan Methodist Church.

Catherine later remembered,

---

17 This is presumably a reference to the Wesleyan Methodist Conference held at the end of July 1851 in Newcastle-upon-Tyne, see https://archive.org/details/minutesseveralc18churgoog. Catherine's 1851 visit to Brighton was soon after that Conference.

18 'CBLP', Letter P2, probably 25 Sept. 1847, p. 14.

19 Information provided by Gordon Taylor. Mr Hardy was almost certainly William Cozens-Hardy of Letheringsett Hall, Norfolk, who was expelled by the local Wesleyan Methodist District meeting in 1850, Vickers, *DMBI*, p. 82.

20 Mrs Key was the wife of a minister, see the article on Catherine Booth in the *Wesleyan Methodist Magazine*, 1893, 6th series, vol. xvii, p. 134.

This was one of the first great troubles of my life and cost me the keenest anguish. I had been nursed and cradled in Methodism and loved it with a love that has gone altogether out of fashion amongst Protestants for their Church. At the same time, I was dissatisfied with the formality worldliness, and defection from what I conceived Methodism ought to be... I believed that through the agitation something would arise which would be better, holier, and more thorough... In this hope and in sympathy with the wrongs that I believed the Reformers had suffered, I drifted away from the Wesleyan Church, apparently at the sacrifice of all that was dearest to me, and of nearly every personal friend.[21]

Concerning the loss of friends, this was very evident in the case of Mrs Key. In numerous diary entries from May to July 1847, Catherine had referred favourably to her. She said, for example, 'there is non[e] I find so much communion of spirit with as dear Mrs Key', and Catherine called her 'a valuable friend'. She even considered Mrs Key her 'mother in Christ'.[22] In one entry late in June Catherine said, 'In the afternoon I went to dear Mrs Key's. I enjoyed the coming very much and was much blessed in prayer'. Ten days later she wrote, 'Dear Mrs Key called last night, bless her. She has a lively interest in my welfare. Lord, reward her and I will praise thee'.[23]

However, after Catherine's departure to the Reformers there was a sharp conflict between them, and Catherine felt that Mrs Key was snubbing her. According to a letter Catherine wrote to William Booth in February 1853, one day she found herself in the same chapel as Mrs Key. When Catherine passed the end of the pew where her old class leader sat, Mrs Key looked at Catherine but 'turned her head away'. Catherine continued, 'I could have shook hands with her with all my heart, and could have buried in oblivion her undeserved coldness & unprovoked unkindness', but Mrs Key

---

21 Booth-Tucker, *Catherine*, vol. 1, pp. 48–50.

22 Booth, *Diary*, 19 May and 15 July 1847, pp. 4 & 25; *Diary CD*, pp. 9 & 30; see also Booth, *Diary*, pp. 8, 10, 15, 24, 26, 31, 40; see also *Diary CD*, pp. 13, 15, 20, 28, 29, 35, 36, 44. The spelling of this name in the diary entries is uncertain, quite simply because Catherine's writing of it is hard to read and the various renderings of it never look precisely the same. For the diary entries Booth-Tucker, vol. 1, p. 35, gives 'Keay', while Bramwell-Booth, pp. 37, 41 and 48, has 'Leay'. However, it sometimes looks more like 'Key', and 'Mrs Key' also appears in some of Catherine's letters. In addition, the article on Catherine Booth in the *Wesleyan Methodist Magazine*, 1893, 6th series, vol. xvii, 134, specifically says that the name of her class leader was 'Key' not 'Keay', which was presumably intended as a correction of Booth-Tucker.

23 Booth, *Diary*, 28 June and 8 July 1847, p. 24; *Diary CD*, pp. 28–29.

withheld her greeting. In September that year Catherine was out walking when she came across Mr and Mrs Key. She told William, 'They passed me like strangers.'[24] Their friendship had been shattered. Yet Catherine clearly thought the fault was not hers, for the snub was 'undeserved' and 'unprovoked'.

Catherine's leaving the Wesleyans was not taken lightly. Her future was unclear, but Catherine Mumford was always a woman of principle. Fortunately for her the Reformers established a church at Binfield House, near where she lived. She was soon given a class of teenaged girls to look after, a task that she took very seriously. She used to get each member of her class to pray and sometimes these 'prayer-meetings' lasted an hour-and-a-half and left her with no voice. She also encouraged them to speak to her individually about what she had said in class and sometimes they would 'pour out their hearts' to her.[25] Catherine was now a Wesleyan Reformer.

It was presumably in 1850 that the Mumfords experienced a major disappointment. Their only living son, John, emigrated to America at, it is claimed, the age of 16.[26] The reasons for this are unknown, but it is likely that there was conflict between him and his father and possibly even with his mother. Little detail is known about his later life, but he remained in America, married a woman named Lizzy, does not appear to have been a Christian, and seems to have avoided fighting in the American Civil War (1861–65).[27]

Catherine in a letter to William Booth gives us another clue to the young John Mumford's life and character. In the context of contemporary evangelistic practices, she said,

> My own Brother was much injured thro' injudicious treatment in this respect. He went one Sunday evening to hear Mr Richardson at Vauxhall. He was quite unconcerned when he went but was much wrought upon under the sermon and induced to go to the communion rail, where he professed to find peace. There certainly was a change in him for a

---

24 This assumes that the name 'Key' is correct, see two footnotes back, and that the various references in the different documents are about the same person, which they almost certainly are. See Catherine's letters to William, Booth, *Letters*, CM21, 6 or 13 Feb. 1853, and CM57, possibly 19 Sept. 1853, pp. 69, 152; Booth, *Letters CD*, pp. 72, 154.

25 Booth-Tucker, *Catherine*, vol. 1, p. 50.

26 Bramwell-Booth says that he went to America when he was 16, see *Catherine*, p. 18.

27 John Mumford Jnr is mentioned fairly often in Catherine's letters to her parents. We will just give here the letter and page numbers of the most relevant letters: 'CBLP', Letters P5, P8, P32, P52, P190, P236, P272, P282, pp. 20, 24, 56, 87, 251, 322, 363–64 & 374.

short time, but, alas, there was no foundation & in a week or two the fair blossoms faded, and tho' he continued to meet in class, his conduct was far worse than it had ever been before. He was more impatient of restraint and reproof; in fact, his heart was closed against conviction by the vain idea that he was converted... Poor boy, he was young & ignorant in spiritual things & therefore easily deceived. I hope & pray that the spirit of God will become his instructor & reveal to him the true state of his heart & the broad & deep requirements of his law.[28]

John never returned to England. In this letter, Catherine said that he had gone to the communion rail, where, presumably he had been counselled and 'he professed to find peace.' Yet, she adds, later his conduct declined and 'his heart' proved to be 'closed against conviction by the vain idea that he was converted.' That with her phrase 'injudicious treatment' suggests she knew that some who used altar call methods did so in ways that were not helpful, and sometimes even counterproductive.

Years later, she said, 'We should be very careful, in all our dealings with anxious souls, first to find out their exact position with regard to sin.' She knew that some who present themselves at a communion rail or penitent form may be 'anxious', concerned about their soul's welfare, but, like King Agrippa, were not willing to give up their sins. She added that the counsellor needs to find out the 'true state' of the person they were counselling, 'and working together with the Holy Ghost to deepen conviction and drive them up to real submission to God.'[29]

---

28 Booth, *Letters*, Letter CM29, 20 Mar. 1853, p. 87; Booth, *Letters CD*, p. 90.
29 Booth, *Papers on Practical Religion*, pp. 103–104.

CHAPTER 6

Enter William Booth

'That little journey will never be forgotten by either of us',
Catherine Booth.[1]

William Booth's childhood

When Catherine Mumford was less than three months old, a boy was born in Nottingham, not much more than 40 kilometres from Ashbourne. His parents, Samuel and Mary Booth, named him William. He was born on 10 April 1829.

Samuel Booth, like several others in this story, was born in Derbyshire, though he later went to live in Nottingham. His first wife Sarah died in 1818 or 1819, and upon a later return to Derbyshire to visit the health-giving spas, Samuel met a tall young woman named Mary Moss. Samuel and Mary married on 2 November 1824 and settled first in Nottingham.

The Booths had four other children: Henry (b.1826), who died at the age of two, Ann (b.1827), who married and moved to London, Emma (b.1831), who did not marry, and Mary (b.1832), who also married. They were a lower middle class, nominally Anglican family.[2] William later portrayed his father as one 'who knew no greater gain or end than money.'[3]

William Booth received a longer and superior education to Catherine Mumford. As an adult his spelling, punctuation and handwriting were all better than Catherine's. For a few years the Booth family lived in the village of Bleasby, and William seems to have begun his schooling there in the vestry of St Mary's Church. When they returned to Nottingham in 1836 William was sent to Biddulph's Academy. Samuel Biddulph, the principal,

---

1 Begbie, *William*, vol. 1, p. 131.
2 Bennett, *The General: William Booth*, vol. 1, pp. 15–18.
3 Begbie, *William*, vol. 1, p. 25.

was a Methodist local preacher and class leader.[4] However, while Biddulph gave Booth a reasonable education, he seems to have made little impact upon him spiritually.[5]

The late 1830s and 1840s were a time of much poverty in England, and Nottingham was not exempt from it. William's schooling came to an abrupt end in about 1842, after his father had become bankrupt. Suddenly the family had become poor, and William was then apprenticed to a pawnbroker, a position and a trade that he came to hate.[6] But matters grew worse: late in September 1843, Samuel Booth died.

One bright spot at this time of gloom and difficulty was a Wesleyan couple named Dent, who took an interest in William Booth. And he took an interest in one of their daughters, though that came to nothing. The Dents encouraged him to attend the massive Broad Street Wesleyan Chapel. Whatever some reports say, it was a keenly evangelistic church. Samuel Dunn, who had been involved in a significant revival in the Shetland Islands, was the minister there for at least part of the time that Booth attended. In addition, travelling evangelists such as Isaac Marsden and James Caughey were invited to preach at Broad Street, and Booth heard them both. Marsden, with his vigorous, even 'violent', approach, impressed him and seems to have triggered the process that led to Booth's conversion. Caughey, with his quieter and 'heavenly' preaching, inspired Booth to mission, to evangelism. The teenaged William Booth then became a local preacher and a fervent outdoor evangelist.[7]

William Booth meets Catherine Mumford

When his apprenticeship ended, probably in 1849, he was unable to find work in Nottingham, so, like many before him, he went to London. The only job he could find was as a pawnbroker's assistant. He also attached himself to the local Wesleyan Church, and once more served as a local preacher and continued to preach in the open air. But the troubles in Methodism hit him as they had hit Catherine Mumford. Booth decided to concentrate more upon his open-air preaching, so he resigned his position as a local preacher.

---

4 Denise Amos, 'General William Booth.'

5 Begbie, *William*, vol. 1, pp. 40, 46; Bennett, *General*, vol. 1, p. 27.

6 Bennett, *General*, vol. 1, pp. 25–26.

7 Bennett, *General*, vol. 1, pp. 35–46; Booth, *Letters*, Letter CM29, 20 Mar. 1853, pp. 86–87; Booth, *Letters CD*, p. 90.

At a time when thousands were leaving the Wesleyan Church to join the Reformers, it was not a good time to resign from anything in Wesleyan Methodism. Such an act was bound to arouse suspicions about one's loyalty, and it did. William Booth, like Catherine Mumford, was dismissed from the Wesleyan Methodist Church, probably in the middle of 1851. So, he then joined the Reformers.

While, as has been seen, the Reformers were not strong in London, they were active in the area in which William Booth lived. He became a lay preacher for the Reformers and preached in what few chapels they had. When he preached at Binfield House in Clapham in March 1852, Catherine Mumford and her mother were present. Catherine was most impressed by this new preacher.[8] However, contact between William and Catherine in the period immediately after appears to have been limited to pulpit and pew. It was not love at first sight, as some have claimed.

William Booth's preaching also impressed Edward Harris Rabbits, a wealthy shoe-maker. Rabbits became Booth's long-term supporter, who impacted his life in two major ways. Rabbits formally introduced Booth to Catherine Mumford and he also paid him a salary for three months, so that he could leave his job and preach fulltime. So, early in April 1852, Booth left his hated job and the room that went with it; which made him, in the short term, homeless.

Soon after that, perhaps even that same weekend, an incident occurred that was crucial in the lives of William and Catherine. Some have cast doubts about whether it happened; however, Garth Hentzschel's research strongly suggests that the story is authentic and that the account may have come from William Booth via Booth-Tucker. It says that William Booth went to an informal Reformers' meeting organised by Edward Rabbits, where one of the other guests was Catherine Mumford. Rabbits must have had a mischievous streak, because he asked Booth to recite a lengthy temperance poem, knowing that it would create a debate, and perhaps a heated one, among his guests. The poem was called 'The Devil and the Grog-Seller: A Ditty for the Times' (also known as 'The Grog-Seller's Dream') and written by an American poet, W.H. Burleigh.[9]

---

8 Bennett, *General*, vol. 1, pp. 65, 68–75, 78.

9 Garth R. Hentzschel has carried out extensive research into and written two articles about the poem and this occasion: 'A recitation to romance: a study on the poem and event which led to the romance of William Booth and Catherine Mumford' and 'A new look at an old poem: The poem that changed William Booth's life', *AJSAH*, vol. 1, iss. 1, pp. 27–71. For

It has been stated that Booth was reluctant to do this recitation.[10] He does not seem to have been a drinker, but at this stage he may not have had strong feelings against alcohol. However, it is claimed that he was already familiar with the poem, and may have already known it by heart, as he certainly did later. But whatever his knowledge of the poem was at this time he agreed to recite it.[11]

The poem began

> The grog-seller sat by his bar-room fire,
> With his feet as high as his head and higher…

It then recounted the grog-seller's lack of sympathy for his drunken customers and their suffering families. The trade was legal and he was making plenty of money, so why should he be concerned? Then a terrifying figure appeared before him. It had an 'uncouth form with an aspect grim,' and

> From his grisly head, through his snaky hair,
> Sprouted of hard rough horns, a pair–
> And redly, his shaggy brows below,
> Like sulphurous flame did his small eyes glow–
> And his lips were curled with a sinister smile,
> And the smoke belched forth from his mouth awhile.

The grim figure vividly praises the bar man at length on his activities and closes with, 'You rival in mischief the Devil himself.' The grog-seller wakes from his dream

> And sad and silent, his bed he sought,
> And long of the wondrous vision thought.[12]

It is easy to imagine the tension in the room as the story unfolded, and it can be guaranteed that William Booth presented it in living colour. When Booth had completed his recitation there was silence for a moment or two and then the debate began. Who started it is unclear, but some defended their practice of 'drinking in moderation' and stated that the Bible allowed that.

The foremost speaker, at least for the abstinence side, was Catherine Mumford, who strongly put her case.[13] It is worth describing Catherine's

---

Hentzschel's discussion about the authenticity of the event see especially pp. 34–37.

10 Begbie, *William*, vol. 1, p. 129; Ervine, *Soldier*, vol. 1, p. 51. See Hentzschel's discussion on this, 'Recitation to Romance', *AJSAH*, vol. 1, iss. 1, pp. 37–39.

11 Hentzschel, 'Recitation to Romance', *AJSAH*, vol. 1, iss. 1, p. 44.

12 Hentzschel, 'A new look', *AJSAH*, vol. 1, iss. 1, pp. 54–62.

13 Hentzschel, "Recitation to Romance", *AJSAH*, vol. 1, iss. 1, pp. 40–41.

appearance in her young womanhood to grasp her full impact on this occasion. She has often been considered small in stature, but she only appeared that way when standing next to the gangling William Booth. Her eldest son said that she was 'some five feet six inches in height'[14], so a good height for a woman in the Victorian era. But she was not particularly attractive, and her bad back may have marred her posture. She would have been modestly dressed. She was shy in unknown company. If you passed her in the street, you would not necessarily pay much attention to her. So, as far as her appearance goes, she may have been easy to ignore.

But when Catherine spoke a change came over her, or, more accurately, a change came over people's perception of her. If she did not, perhaps, then have the power and command of her later years, there can be no doubt that even as a young woman she had the passion and knowledge to argue a case convincingly. Years later, her son, Bramwell, said that her 'countenance' had 'such strength and intensity' that it was 'almost mesmeric in its power to hold the attention even of the indifferent and casual.'[15] And it can be guaranteed that on this occasion Catherine Mumford held the attention of her listeners, as she argued forcibly for total abstinence, for she knew well the dangers of alcohol and feared anyone going down that path.

What exactly she said on this occasion is not known, but her general arguments can be safely guessed from what she wrote at other times. Eight months later, just after Christmas, she told William Booth,

> You ask my opinion about your taking port wine. I need not say how willing, nay, how anxious I am that you should have any thing & every thing which would tend to promote your *health* & happiness, but so thoroughly am I convinced that port wine would do neither, that I should hear of you taking it with unfeigned grief. You must not listen, my dear, to the advice of every one claiming to be experienced. Persons really experienced & judicious in many things not infrequently entertain notions the *most fallacious* on this subject. I have had it recommended to me scores of times by such individuals, but such reccommendations [sic] have always gone for nothing because I have felt that however much very superior such persons might be in other respects, *on that subject* I was the best informed. I have even argued that point with Mr. Stevens [her doctor], & I am sure set him completely fast[16] for arguments to

---

14 Booth, *Fifty*, p. 10.

15 Ibid., p. 10.

16 'Lost' may be intended, but 'fast' is definitely the word written in the original.

defend alcohol, even as a medicine… I abominate that hackneed [sic] but monstrously inconsistent tale, 'A teetotaller in principle, but obliged to take a little for my stomach's sake.' Such teetotallers aid the progress of intemperance more than all the drunkards in the Land… I dare take the responsibility (& I have more reason to feel its weight than any other being)[17] of advising you to abandon the idea of taking wine altogether. I have far more hope for your health *because* you abstain from stimulating drinks than I should have if you took them.[18]

It is easy to imagine that she argued along similar lines the previous April when her future husband had made the 'Grog-Seller' recitation.

It is also easy to believe Catherine argued that the Bible did not support the drinking of alcohol even in moderation. After she had given a temperance lecture early in 1861, she told her parents,

We had a very good meeting. Wm spoke *well* for about an hour. I followed him for 40 minutes, & according to the account of the folks got on well… I took up the most common objections to Teetotalism, which I had met with in private argument, etc. 1st, Why can we not take it in moderation? 2nd, What is it for? Is it not a good creature of God, etc? 3rd, The Bible does not prohibit it, etc. 4th, Don't like to sign the pledge; & 5th, Temperance advocates extravagant, & I forget the other. *I said some strong & pointed things on the Scripture argument, which told well* (emphasis added).[19]

Whether she was right or wrong is another issue, but that was Catherine Mumford Booth's belief, and it can be guaranteed that in the post-recitation debate she put her case forcibly, because she knew no other way. She was not the kind of woman who would try to crack a nut with a velvet glove.

After that debate it was William Booth's turn to be impressed. It was probably the first time he had heard Catherine Mumford in action, and there can be no doubt that he quickly realised that she was no ordinary woman.

Both Booth-Tucker and Begbie seem to indicate that William Booth took Catherine to her home in a carriage directly after this event.[20] Catherine's account of this ride is most illuminating and some of the wording (e.g. 'although such a stranger') confirms that it was very early in their relationship. Some of what Catherine says may also indicate that they

---

17 This is, no doubt, a reference to her father.
18 Booth, *Letters*, Letter CM11, 27 (& 29) Dec. 1852, p. 44, *Letters CD*, p. 48.
19 'CBLP', Letter P198, 22 Feb. 1861, p. 259.
20 Begbie, *William*, vol. 1, pp. 130–31; Booth-Tucker, *Catherine*, vol. 1, p. 63.

were not alone in the conveyance. She said,

> That little journey will never be forgotten by either of us. It is true that nothing particular occurred, except that as W.[21] afterwards expressed it, it seemed as if God flashed simultaneously into our hearts that affection which afterwards ripened into what has proved at least to be an exceptional union of heart and purpose and life, and which none of the changing vicissitudes with which our lives have been so crowded has been able to efface.

> He impressed me.

> I had been introduced to him as being in delicate health, and he took the situation in at a glance. His thought for me, although such a stranger, appeared most remarkable. The conveyance shook me; he regretted it. The talking exhausted me; he saw it and forbade it. And then we struck in at once in such wonderful harmony of view and aim and feeling on varied matters that passed rapidly before us. It seemed as though we had intimately known and loved each other for years, and suddenly after some temporary absence, had been brought together again, and before we reached my home we both suspected, nay, we felt as though we had been made for each other, and that henceforth the current of our lives must flow together.

> It was curious, too, that both of us had an idea of what we should require in the companion with whom we allied ourselves for life, if ever such an alliance should take place. Singular to say, W. had formed very similar notions, and here we were thrown together in this unexpected fashion, matching these pre-conceived characters, even as though we had been made to order.

When they arrived at Catherine's home in Russell Street, Brixton, Mrs Mumford invited William to spend the night, as he had nowhere definite to live at that time. Catherine was strongly drawn to this would-be preacher, and, she later reflected, the next day her mother 'was nearly as interested in him as I was.'

William, however, was confused. He was greatly attracted to Catherine, 'who filled up his life's ideal of what a wife should be', but he had just

---

21 This account is drawn from Begbie, but the fact that he has transcribed 'W' here (and later) and not 'William' suggests that he has made few if any alterations to the original, which does not now seem to exist. Research has been carried out into the origins of this story and Begbie's account is the earliest discovered.

escaped a job he hated and was starting on an uncertain course in Christian ministry. He had made vows to God about not being side-tracked by issues that might prove contrary to his new calling. It did not seem quite the right time to begin a relationship that would lead to marriage. It is said, that as he left the Mumfords' home the next day, he muttered, 'It cannot, must not, shall not be.' But as Catherine, almost triumphantly, later said, 'it was not many hours before he found himself at that door again.'[22]

Soon after that encounter Booth found temporary lodgings at Princes Row, Walworth. William and Catherine then began a series of letters to each other which commenced early in May and ended in the middle of August. Some of William's letters bear his Walworth address. That these letters came to a temporary end in mid-August and did not recommence until he moved to Lincolnshire at the end of November[23], suggests that he lived with the Mumfords during that period. Some comments in a few of Booth's early letters also hint at that. Indeed, his brief note dated 13 August sounds as though it was left somewhere at her home where she would find it rather than posted.[24]

From this time, it is impossible to understand Catherine Mumford Booth without some understanding of William Booth. It is also impossible to understand William without a reasonable understanding of Catherine. Long before they were married their lives were intertwined spiritually and emotionally, and to some degree mentally, though they had their disagreements. Physical union would have to wait.

---

22 Begbie, *William*, vol. 1, pp. 131–33.
23 See Booth, *Letters*, pp. 3–17; Booth, *Letters CD*, pp. 8–21.
24 Booth, *Letters*, Letter WB11, 13 Aug. 1852, p. 13; Booth, *Letters CD*, p. 18.

CHAPTER 7

The Engagement

'Most gladly does my soul respond to your invitation to give myself
afresh to Him, and to strive to link myself closer to you,
by rising more into the image of my Lord',

Catherine Mumford to William Booth.[1]

From early in May 1852 a host of letters passed between the two lovers,
and these were only halted when they were living under the same roof.
Catherine's letters were usually longer than William's. While she often
protested that she hated writing, her letters are numerous and frequently
long. While many of their personal letters have been lost, including the first
that Catherine wrote to William, about 350 still exist whole or in part.[2] In
the early 1850s, when this flood of correspondence began, Catherine had
more time to write than William. He was extremely busy with ministerial
matters, looking after several congregations, while Catherine, when well
enough, helped her mother with the household chores, read and taught a
Sunday School class.

The doubts

We will discover the story of their early romance and engagement mainly in
their letters and Catherine's diary, which she recommenced soon after they
were engaged. The first three letters we have are from William, all written
in the first half of May 1852, and they each start rather demurely, 'My dear
Friend', 'My dear Catherine' and 'My Dear Friend', and the first has at the
end 'Miss Mumford', which accurately expressed their relationship thus far.
It was hopeful and exciting but cautious. It was also rather confused, as

---

1 Booth, *Letters*, Letter (CM3), probably 15 May 1852, p. 8; Booth, *Letters CD*, p. 12.
2 Most of these letters are in the Booth Papers in the British Library but extracts of others are
found in the early biographies. All these existing letters and parts thereof have been brought
together in *The Letters of William and Catherine Booth*, edited by David Malcolm Bennett.

neither had been looking for a potential marriage partner in the period immediately before and thus they each had to readjust their thinking.

It was also made more hesitant because Catherine had strong views about the relationship between engagement and marriage. Years later she said, 'I regarded a betrothal as a most sacred act. That having once mutually decided on an engagement to be terminated with marriage, it was a very serious offence against God, and against the human heart, for any violation of such promises to take place.' William, it seems, regarded her views on this as 'very strict', but he accepted them.[3] Catherine had a friend who was engaged and then deserted and humiliated by her fiancé. She may also have known of other such cases that influenced her beliefs on this.

William's first letter, probably written less than three weeks after the carriage ride, clearly shows that they had already discussed the possibility of an engagement and thus marriage. But then panic set in.

> You may perhaps deem me to be taking another step in the wrong direction, but I must, after the very abrupt manner in which we parted last evening, say a word. I believe that you think me sincere, and I have only one fear, that is that you will make yourself ill. If you do, and I hear of it, it will drive me into delirium. My mind is made up. My hopes are set on things below of the same nature as things above. My heart prays that *His* will may be done on earth as it is done in Heaven.

He then referred to John and Mary Fletcher of Madeley, viewed as the ideal Methodist couple. 'With them' William wrote, 'it was not the impulse of passion, but the clear and unmistakable teaching of Providence. I would that it should be so in our experience.' But William was concerned that an engagement leading to marriage would 'injure' his 'usefulness' and draw off his 'heart from entire and complete devotion to God' with the possibility of 'setting up ... another god'; that is, Catherine Mumford. Also, in the foreseeable future he had no means of supporting a wife and family. For the first few weeks of their relationship there was a fierce 'Will we? Won't we?' struggle. They were both, it is no exaggeration to say, passionately drawn to each other, but they each feared that their developing relationship might hinder William's ministry as a Methodist preacher.

It also seems that Mrs Mumford had early on said something that had upset William. He did not state what it was, but her words were probably the result of her over-protective nature in relation to her daughter. But William

---

3 Begbie, *William*, vol. 1, p. 133.

was sufficiently hurt to consider those words 'unmerited and unjust'.[4] It appears that if William was to win the hand of Catherine Mumford, he would also have to win the heart and trust of her mother, which would not be easy.

After reading what was probably her first letter to him (now no longer available), he wrote to her in most uncertain terms.

> I have read and re-read yours of yesterday evening and in answer to it what can I say? My heart dictates what for the sake of your peace I dare not write, I mean, what I feel… I will love you as my sister, as I love my dearest friend. I cannot afford to lose your friendship. I *should* be lonely then. We can meet now and then and talk about books and Christ and Heaven, *nothing more, can we not?*

> … If I love you at all, if you wish to know *how much I love*, measure it by my calmness and my willingness in any way to do as you wish. I will. If you wish to see me, name the time and then nothing positively preventing I will come, though it be *every* night or only every year. I have nothing to say but I still write on. You will allow me to write to you now and then? I will not ask an answer … it seems to afford me unspeakable pleasure to be penning down words which I know will meet your eye…

> Whatever you do, whatever you think, do not imagine I question a word you have spoken. I declare before the throne of Eternal Truth that *I do not*. I love you as dearly as ever and that love is grounded on the highest esteem. But calmly, Catherine, let us do His will. I am perfectly the master of my feelings, at least to a great extent… May God comfort you now that I lack the power, and believe me to remain,

> Yours affectionately,

> Yours for ever in Jesus' love, William.[5]

According to Catherine Bramwell-Booth, Catherine's reply to that was 'Come and see me', though, if it was in a letter, it no longer exists. Bramwell-Booth's claim may refer to a similar comment in a later letter. However the invitation was expressed, William gladly accepted it. They talked, 'his hopes rose', but still there were doubts, and, as it appears, strong doubts.[6]

William then received two letters. The first was from his mother which

---

4 Booth, *Letters*, Letter (WB1), early May 1852, p. 3; Booth, *Letters CD*, p. 8.

5 Ibid., Letter (WB2), probably 7 or 8 May 1852, p. 4; ibid., p. 9.

6 Bramwell-Booth, *Catherine*, p. 68.

urged him 'to do nothing rashly.' As one might expect, Mary Booth knew her son well. According to William, she urged him 'that ere such an important step be taken I should *consider long* … but at the same time declaring that she will acquiesce in any decision at which I may arrive.'

The next letter was from Catherine (which again is unavailable). He answered it, saying,

> I know not that I have anything to write about in any way cheering to your feelings… I fear that I have blocked up for ever any possible way of my being made a blessing to you… Darkness gathers thicker than ever round the path I tread, and doubt, gloom, melancholy and despair would tread me down.

> I need not recapitulate my doubts, only that every day seems to blacken them and make them more worthy of consideration; I need not say here how highly I judge of you and how high in my estimation your virtuous soul I rank; I need not say that I have deemed and still do deem every, even the minutest, of your actions and words spotless and without blemish, that is, in my eyes.[7]

William clearly had a much higher estimation of Catherine than she had of herself. Indeed, in response to this she said, 'What you say of me in your letter gives me pain because I know it is not true, alas my soul bears a very faint impress of the Saviour's image, if it is visible at all.'[8]

Booth continued,

> my resolutions are unbroken to live and live only for the salvation of souls and the glory of God. I need not urge you to a more earnest searching out for the beauties and loveliness of the character of Jesus; I need not exhort you to entire consecration to His service and His constant hallowed communion; I would to God that my intercourse with *Him* was as *perfect* and my resemblance to *His* image was as divine as *your own*. I will to-day more earnestly than ever pray that you may find your all in all in *Him*. I say nothing decisive because I know nothing; I have neither advanced nor retrograded from the position I occupied when last we met.[9]

Catherine's first extant letter to William appears to have been written on the following evening. She told him,

---

7 Booth, *Letters*, Letter (WB3), probably 10 May 1852, pp. 4–5; Booth, *Letters CD*, p. 10.

8 Ibid., Letter CM1, 11 May 1852, p. 6; ibid., pp. 10–11.

9 Ibid., Letter (WB3), probably 10 May 1852, p. 5; ibid., p. 10.

I have been spreading your letter before the Lord & earnestly pleading for a manifestation of His will to your mind in some way or other, & now I would say a few words of comfort & encouragement. My heart feels for you far beyond what I can express. Oh, that I knew how to comfort you in an indirect way. The advice of your dear Mother is most judicious, the best she could possibly have given under the circumstances. May God answer her prayers and guide you *right*. You do grieve me by saying you fear you have blocked up every way of being a blessing to me. *I tell you it is not so*; your kindness & character will ever give weight to your advice & teaching & create a sympathy with your prayers which cannot fail to benefit me. If you wish to avoid giving me pain don't condemn yourself. I feel sure God does not condemn you & if you could look into my heart you would see how far I am from such a feeling. Don't pore over the past, let it all go. Your desire is to do the will of God & He will guide you. Never mind *who* frowns if God smiles. Though you are surrounded by a host of foes, He is *able* to deliver & He *will* deliver; only trust in Him & don't be afraid. The darkness & gloom that hangs about your path shall all flee away; when you are tried you shall come forth as gold. The words 'gloom, melancholy, & despair' lacerate my heart. Don't give way to such feelings for a moment. *God loves you*. He will sustain you. The thought that I should increase your perplexity & cause you any suffering is almost intolerable. Oh, that we had never seen each other. Do try to forget me as far as the remembrance would injure your usefulness or spoil your peace. If I have no alternative but to oppose the will of God or trample on the desolations of my own heart, my choice is made. Thy will be done is my constant cry. I care not for myself, but oh if I cause you to err, I shall never be happy again.

Their struggle was intense and ongoing.

Catherine went on to urge him not to 'take any step without some evidence *satisfactory* to your own mind of the will of God. Think nothing about me. I will resist to the uttermost. "I can do all things through Christ strengthening me."' Then she assured him, 'I do continually pray for you; surely God must answer our prayers when He sees it is our one desire to do His will. Let us *expect* an answer; perhaps our faith is deficient... May God bless and guide you into the path which will be most for His glory & your soul's interests is my constant prayer.'

Catherine ended this letter with 'My dear Mother's kind regards.' [10]

---

10 Ibid., Letter CM1, 11 May 1852, pp. 5–6; ibid., pp. 10–11.

Whatever William Booth had done earlier to upset Mrs. Mumford seems now to have been forgiven.

It was at about this time that William Booth wrote his fourth letter to Catherine. In it he says that he had 'offered ... to make the[11] engagement.' That is, presumably, he had tentatively proposed to Catherine Mumford. But she, it seems, 'declined', or at least deferred a positive answer, on what he believed to be 'good grounds'. Those 'grounds', as he understood her, were that she had been concerned about his 'circumstances', his prospects, in other words. It is also probable that his hesitant proposal had encouraged her uncertainty. He then continued in the letter, 'You know the inmost feelings of my heart', and there can be no doubt that she did. Yet, he said, 'I have not, as I could have wished, seen anything striking[12] to intimate the will of God.' William Booth, the decisive, was still incapable of making this most important of decisions.

The betrothal

He still, however, made one decision. 'After this is ended,' he said, 'this awful controversy, I shall call on you again. If you *accept* what I have stated, I will come Saturday. *If not*, I shall call as a friend in the course of a few days and show you how I bear the matter. If it be of man, if it be wrong, it will pass forgotten away. If it be of God, He will still bring it to pass.'[13]

Catherine quickly responded. No, 'It was *not circumstances*,' she said.

I thought I had fully satisfied you on that point. I thought you felt sure that a bright prospect could not allure me, nor a dark one affright me, if we are only *one* in *heart*. My difficulty, my only reason for wishing to defer the engagement was that *you* might feel satisfied in your own mind that the step is right. To cause you to err would cost me far more suffering than *any thing else*.

Then she added to confirm the point, 'You say if your circumstances were not so blighted, you could not desire so striking an indication of God's

---

11 The original of this letter has been lost. Of the existing records of it, Begbie, (*William*, vol. 1, p. 146) has 'the', Bramwell-Booth (*Catherine*, p. 68) has 'an'. Begbie usually transcribes accurately, and it seems more likely that 'the' would have been changed to 'an', than the other way around.

12 Begbie has 'striking'; Bramwell-Booth does not.

13 Booth, *Letters*, Letter (WB4) probably 12 May 1852, p. 6; Booth, *Letters CD*, p. 11.

will. I answer if you are satisfied of *His will* irrespective of circumstances, let circumstances *go* & let us be one come what will.'

Then significantly she said, 'come on Saturday evening and on our knees before God let us give ourselves afresh to Him & to each other; for His sake consecrate our whole selves to His service for *Him to live & die*.'[14] 'Come on Saturday', the crucial invitation.

So, William Booth arrived at 7 Russell Street, Brixton, on Saturday, 15 May, probably early in the evening. William and Catherine knelt side by side and committed themselves 'to each other and to God.' They were now engaged and, in their hearts, as good as married. If the road between their first formal meeting and this moment had been complex and confused, the time had been brief. It was a little more than a month since the 'Grog-Seller's Dream' event.

She wrote a letter to him probably later that evening[15], which is worth quoting in full. Her delight in her new situation blazes forth.

My Dearest William,

The evening is beautifully serene and tranquil, according sweetly with the feelings of my soul. The whirlwind is past and the succeeding calm is in proportion to its violence. Your letter – your visit have hushed its last murmurs and stilled every vibration of my throbbing heartstrings. All is well. I feel it is right, and I praise God for the satisfying conviction.

Most gladly does my soul respond to your invitation to give myself afresh to Him, and to strive to link myself closer to you, by rising more into the image of my Lord. The nearer our assimilation to Jesus, the more perfect and heavenly our union. Our hearts are indeed *one*, so one that division would be more bitter than death. But I am satisfied that our union may become, if not more complete, more divine, and, consequently, capable of yielding a larger amount of pure unmingled bliss.

The thought of walking through life *perfectly united*, together enjoying its sunshine and battling its storms, by softest sympathy sharing every

---

14 Ibid., Letter CM2, 13 May 1852, p. 7; ibid., p. 12.

15 Different dates have been given for this meeting, including 5 and 13 May. However, Catherine's letter CM2, written on Thursday 13 May, urged him to come that Saturday to make their commitment to each other. Letter CM3 was clearly written after the event and appears to have been written on Saturday 15 May, or, perhaps, Sunday 16 May. This letter is not in the Booth Papers and is drawn from the biographies, none of which give a precise date for it. Ervine suggests 'a day or two after', *Soldier*, vol. 1, p. 59, though it sounds as though it was written only an hour or two after it.

smile and every tear, and with thorough unanimity performing all its momentous duties, is to me exquisite happiness; the highest earthly bliss I desire. And who can estimate the glory to God, and the benefit to man, accruing from a life spent in such harmonious effort to do *His will*? Such unions, alas, are so rare that we seldom see an exemplification of the divine idea of marriage.

If, indeed, we are the disciples of Christ, 'in the world we shall have tribulation'; but in Him and in *each other* we may have peace. If God chastises us by affliction, in either mind, body, or circumstances, it will only be a mark of our discipleship; and if borne equally by us both, the blow shall not only be softened, but sanctified, and we shall be able to rejoice that we are permitted to drain the bitter cup *together*. Satisfied that in our souls there flows a deep undercurrent of pure affection, we will seek grace to bear with the bubbles which may rise on the surface, or wisdom so to burst them as to increase the depth, and accelerate the onward flow of the pure stream of love, till it reaches the river which proceeds out of the Throne of God and of the Lamb, and mingles in glorious harmony with the love of Heaven.

The more you lead me up to Christ in all things, the more highly shall I esteem you; and, if it be possible to love you more than I do now, the more shall I love you. You are always present in my thoughts.

Believe me, dear William, as ever,

Your own loving, Kate.[16]

Roy Hattersley said that their 'engagement went ahead as both William and Catherine, despite their protestations, always knew that it would.'[17] But Hattersley does not seem to understand the depth and strength of their commitment to Christ. No doubt, they always knew what they wanted the result to be, to have each other without disrupting their loyalty to Christ. Yet, at first, they seem to have had genuine doubts that they could have both.

A week after the engagement, Catherine was once more in reflective mood and full of worries about her betrothed. She told William,

I find that the pleasure connected with pure, holy, sanctified love forms no exception to the general rule. The very fact of loving invests the being beloved with a thousand causes of care and anxiety, which, if unloved,

---

16 Booth, *Letters*, Letter (CM3), probably 15 May 1852, pp. 7–8; Booth, *Letters CD*, pp. 12–13.
17 Hattersley, *Blood*, p. 46.

would never exist. At least, I find it so. You have cost me more real anxiety than any other earthly object ever did.

She worried that he went from place to place 'too thinly clad' and urged him to wear his 'greatcoat'. She also told him *'don't sit up singing till twelve o'clock after a hard day's work.'*[18] Her emphasis suggests that he often did so.

Inspired by her new situation, Catherine quickly adjusted her thinking. In one version of her reminiscences she said that after their engagement, life for her

> assumed altogether another aspect… The idea of the possibility of becoming a wife and a mother filled my life with new responsibilities, but the thought of becoming a Minister's wife made the whole appear increasingly serious. I assumed in imagination all these responsibilities right away, even as though they had already come, and at once set myself, with all my might, to prepare to meet them. I added to the number of my studies, enlarged the scope of my reading, wrote notes and made comments on all the sermons and lectures that appeared at all worthy of the trouble, started to learn shorthand in order that I might more readily and fully correspond with W., and in other ways stirred up the gift that was in me to serve God and my generation.[19]

It must be said that Catherine never took any responsibility lightly, and responsibilities such as these were doubly important to her. Concerning shorthand, both Catherine and William attempted to learn it and small portions of some of their letters were written in it, but it seems to have become more of a labour than a help, and the experiment ended.

Catherine's health

But Catherine also saw a major problem hovering over their future, her health. In those reminiscences she added, 'I was very delicate; in fact little better than a confirmed invalid, and [William] was afraid that my strength would never stand the strain and hardship involved in such a life as I imagined that of a Preacher's wife ought to be.'[20] But though Catherine may have been 'a frail thing', she was tougher than she or anyone else realised at that time, as subsequent events demonstrated.

---

18 Booth, *Letters*, Letter CM4, probably 21 or 22 May 1852, pp. 8–9; Booth, *Letters CD*, pp. 13–14.
19 From the reminiscences as in Begbie, *William*, vol. 1, p. 137.
20 Ibid., vol. 1, p. 138.

Roger Green said that Catherine 'had an almost unnatural preoccupation with health problems … throughout her entire life'[21], and that is a fair comment, especially concerning her early years. As W.T. Stead said, 'She was always ailing. If it was not one organ, it was another.'[22] The word 'poorly' (i.e. unwell) is one of the words she most commonly used in her letters. She most frequently said that she was poorly, but also at times William, or her children or her mother were poorly. That is not to say that these ailments were imagined, but rather that she focused on them so much that at times the stress seemed to make her worse. This may have been a trait she inherited from her mother, who, after all, had three of her children die in infancy.

One major concern was Catherine's back, which gave her much trouble. She frequently attended a galvanist named Franks to have this treated. Galvanism was electric shock treatment for bone and other disorders. Mr Franks seems to have exercised a general supervision of Catherine's health for a couple of years, and is one of the people most frequently mentioned in her letters to William. The fact that the Mumford family, for the most part, had to pay for this treatment shows that they were not poor, though at times they did have financial difficulties.

Soon after the engagement, Catherine also recommenced her diary, though most entries are more concerned about her relationship with God than her dealings with her fiancé. On the last Sunday in May she taught her Sunday School class in the morning, but at the service 'Received no good under the Sermon.' A different preacher in the evening gave a sermon she 'Enjoyed', but she found the congregation dead and 'almost at freezing point.'[23] Such criticisms were common in Catherine's letters and personal writings.

But her criticism was not only of others. The next day she wrote,

A day of pain & weakness of body & some depression of mind, arising from the consideration of my past unfaithfulness & present indifference. I have been calling to mind some by gone seasons of holy enjoyment & heart felt union with my Saviour, and as I have thought of those precious hours, my soul has filled with grief & my eyes with tears because I have not followed on to know the Lord more fully. Oh, if I had faithfully followed the light & improved the grace imparted, what heights &

---

21 Green, *Catherine*, p. 25.
22 Stead, *Catherine*, p. 43.
23 Booth, *Diary*, 30 May 1852, p. 40; *Diary CD*, p. 44.

depths of His love I might by this time have experienced. But regrets are useless, except as they produce Godly sorrow and stimulate me to greater diligence. My soul does hunger & thirst after righteousness. I feel the utter insignificance of every thing in comparison with a life of devotedness to God, & I will after all my unfaithfulness dare to expect grace & opportunity to glorify Him.[24]

A few days later she was reading Asa Mahan's *Scripture Doctrine of Christian Perfection*[25], which she thought 'the best work on the subject' that she had read, suggesting that she had read a few others. 'Oh, to enjoy this glorious salvation', she wrote. 'Satan would feign persuade me it were presumptuous in me to aspire after it, after so much unfaithfulness & so many backslidings. But I think I shall honour God more by hoping in His mercy & trusting in His faithfulness, than by despairing of it.'[26]

Two evenings later Catherine and William met and they 'Talked over some important matters' and 'parted in better spirits & with Sunnier feelings than on any previous occasion.' William's ministry for the Reformers was not going as well as hoped, and this must have caused some early concerns for them, particularly as Edward Rabbits had agreed to pay William's salary only for three months, which was now half through. They must have wondered what would happen after that. But 'Sunnier feelings' meant it was not all gloom. After William had left she 'enjoyed some liberty … in laying [their] case before the Lord & intreating Him to work the counsel of His own will.'[27]

With that entry on 5 June 1852, Catherine's diary came to a conclusion. But her letters, their letters, continued. However, none of Catherine's letters from late May until early December have survived, though we do have ten from William of that period, which tell us a little of their thoughts and activities.

Early in June an elderly lady gave William a note for Catherine. He sent it on with one of his own letters, with the message: 'Have just received the enclosed for you. The old lady has sent me word that I am to correct the spelling before I pass it you, but that I perceived to be a hopeless task and so pass it on & trust to your good nature and candour.'[28] No doubt Catherine

---

24 Ibid., 31 May 1852, pp. 40–41; ibid., p. 44.

25 Asa Mahan was an associate of Charles Finney.

26 Booth, *Diary*, 3 June 1852, p. 41; *Diary CD*, p. 45.

27 Ibid., 5 June 1852, p. 41; ibid., p. 45.

28 Booth, *Letters*, Letter WB6, 9 June 1852, p. 11; Booth, *Letters CD*, p. 16.

received and read it in that spirit.

It was probably at the end of July that William Booth encountered a young woman in great need. He and Catherine seem to have discussed a plan to help her, and it had been agreed that Catherine would visit her. William's next letter told Catherine where she lived. He said,

> It has just oc[c]urred to my mind that I did not leave you a correct address to that poor girl, and less you should be prevented from your benevolent undertaking, I post this to inform you. If you leave the omnibus at the Obelisk at the end of the London and at the foot of the Waterloo & Blackfriars Roads, you will be but a few yards from your destination which is No 3 or 4 Duke Street, next door to a Plumber & Glaziers shop. It is up two flights of stairs. Take with you a smelling bottle. A widow woman, who lives in the room as you enter from the street, if you ask her for the poor girl of the name of 'Leach', will show you her room, I doubt not. Speak pointedly to all you see of the family. Mention my name.[29]

Presumably Catherine made the visit, though we know no more. It is easy to imagine why William told his fiancée to take a smelling bottle with her, for Duke Street was in a slum area.[30] With this visit Catherine would have been doing Salvation Army work long before The Salvation Army existed.

William's employment ends

William's ministry with the London Reformers must have concluded at the end of July or early August. Exactly why that happened is unclear. Perhaps Rabbits was not prepared to put up any more money. Perhaps William Booth could stand the tension in his circuit no longer. Catherine later said that 'the connection was dissolved'[31], whatever that might mean. So, now he had no job, no income and thus no money for rent. It is almost certain that he went to live with the Mumfords early in August, which is when William's letters to Catherine cease until the end of November. The Mumfords commonly took in lodgers. The Census of March 1851 records that two young men were boarding with the Mumfords, an 'Architects Clerk', named Henry Hall, and an 'Architects Improver', called Frederick

---

29 Ibid., Letter WB9, late July or early August 1852, p. 12; ibid., p. 17.
30 'Slums in Southwark: Bradshaw's Handbook to London (No.85)', see Fig. 18, 'Duke-street, Southwark.'
31 Begbie, *William*, vol. 1, p. 138.

Pilkington.[32] They seem to have left later that year or early in 1852 and been replaced by a Mr Mackland, who is frequently mentioned in the letters that Catherine and William wrote to each other. In other words, in August 1852 the Mumfords had room for a second lodger. That respectable Victorians may not have approved of engaged couples living under the same roof, seems to have been overruled by necessity.

What may have been William's last letter to Catherine from Princes Row, Walworth, was written on 4 August. Presumably, by then his money had almost run out and he had to move. Life for them at that time does not seem to have been easy. Quite what was wrong is unclear. William's immediate future must have been one problem, but Catherine, too, had her own unstated difficulties. William, in that confused moment, wrote,

> My first thoughts are with you, and my first movement is to spell out your name and write. I scarce know why and so far I know not what.

> But if I spell out one word more and that word is *Love*, a multitude of thoughts come scrambling through my brain and a multitude of feelings come overshadowing my heart. The very affection we bare[33] each other seemeth to create darkness. What a dark day was your portion yesterday and if you had not loved me so well that would not have been endured. Our lot, our united lot, *so far* hath indeed been gloomy. But fear not; dark beginnings have often, if not always, bright endings. And we will hope that we have seen the ruggedest part of the journey we are to travel together.[34]

When one loves another person passionately and the object of one's affections suffers, then the lover shares the suffering. So, the 'very affection' that they bore each other sometimes created 'darkness' for each of them.

In the middle of August, William, in a more optimistic even playful mood, wrote her a brief note, which said,

> My own dear Catherine needeth not that I should assure her of the affection I bear her. 'Actions speak louder than words' is an aphorism often quoted by her, and one that William thinks is fully borne out in his brief acquaintance with her, whose eye this may meet. He the chosen of her heart wishes her all earth's pure and hallowed joys, promises to

---

32 '1851 England, Wales & Scotland Census, 7 Russell St.'

33 This word is unclear in the original, but looks like 'bare', and presumably is intended to be 'bear'.

34 Booth, *Letters*, Letter WB10, 4 Aug. 1852, p. 13; Booth, *Letters CD*, p. 17.

increase them so far as he hath power, and to aid in the formation and development of that character which is the Golden Key to unlock the Gates to another, brighter, happier sphere,

William.

There is a date but no address at the heading of this letter, and the phrase 'whose eye this may meet' suggests that it was left at a visible spot in the Mumford home, rather than posted.[35]

---

35 Ibid., Letter WB11, 13 Aug. 1852, p. 13; ibid., p. 18.

CHAPTER 8

The Dilemma

'I argued, that once settled in a Congregational pulpit, [William] could impart into his services and meetings all that was good and hearty and soul-saving in Methodism',

Catherine Booth.[1]

As their romance developed and their love deepened, they faced a major problem. What was William to do now his time with the London Reformers had concluded? Ervine said that his pawnbroker employer offered him his job back.[2] Whether that happened or not, it was not an option that Booth is likely to have taken, having once experienced fulltime Christian ministry. Yet there do not seem to have been any favourable Methodist options in the summer of 1852. Catherine, meanwhile, had fallen out of love with the Reformers, who were disorganised, even chaotic, and she also felt that they had treated her fiancé unfairly. Indeed, she later said that the Reformers, or at least the London group, tended to regard their minister 'as nothing, denying him every shadow of authority, and only allowing him to preside at their meetings when elected for this purpose, and speaking of him in public and private as their "hired" preacher.' Catherine says that they even denied her fiancé 'reasonable opportunities for preaching.'[3] She therefore began considering other options both for her own worship of God and her fiancé's ministry.

The Congregational ministry

Catherine began to attend a Congregational (Independent) church in 1852, though in which month is uncertain. There are references to Catherine hearing Rev. David Thomas, minister of Stockwell Congregational Chapel,

---

[1] Begbie, *William*, vol. 1, p. 139.
[2] Ervine, *Soldier*, vol. 1. p. 56.
[3] From the reminiscences as in Begbie, *William*, vol. 1, p. 138.

in the Booth correspondence early in December 1852, and those letters give the impression that she had also heard him earlier that year.[4] Catherine came to greatly admire Mr Thomas, and she loved his orderly, doctrinal preaching. In her letters, she at times gives the impression that his sermons were of a much higher standard than those she heard in various Methodist chapels. By this time, she seems to have become disillusioned with the Methodist Reformers.

It has been claimed that Catherine first heard David Thomas as far back as 1847, but this is clearly wrong. It is based partly on two misreadings Catherine Bramwell-Booth made of one of her grandmother's diary entries. In Catherine Mumford's diary entry of 25 July, 1847, Catherine had written that she had attended 'Southvill' chapel, which Bramwell-Booth reads as 'Stockwell' (the name of Mr Thomas's church) and the preacher was 'Mr Thompson', which she reads as 'Mr Thomas.'[5] It seems that Catherine Mumford first heard Rev. Thomas in 1852, perhaps in the middle of that year.

Catherine also greatly admired the American evangelist Charles Finney, who was a preacher for the Congregational Church in the USA. She may have thought then, and certainly did later, that if her fiancé entered the Congregational ministry, he could be the Charles Finney of England.

So, William's 'attention was turned to the Congregational Church.' Catherine said, 'I think this was my doing'[6], and there can be no doubt that William Booth approached the Congregationalists after a hefty nudge from his fiancée. As shall be seen, at least twice Catherine tried to persuade him to join the Congregationalists, yet, though he thoroughly investigated the prospect, he never joined them. William Booth was a General long before he became one, and did not readily take orders from anyone, not even Catherine. He listened to her advice, sometimes accepted it, but just as often argued against it or proceeded in another direction.

W.T. Stead said, 'although [Catherine] never commanded, she frequently led.'[7] However, Catherine did at times command, but she discovered that it was difficult to successfully command a would-be General, and she preferred to use oft-repeated suggestions to try to persuade her fiancé to adopt her viewpoint. But William was strong-willed and would usually

---

4 Booth, *Letters*, Letter WB16, 6 Dec. 1852, and CM6, 5 Dec. 1852, p. 23; Booth, *Letters CD*, p. 27.

5 Bramwell-Booth, *Catherine*, p. 45; Booth, *Diary*, 25 July 1847, p. 26; *Diary CD*, pp. 30–31.

6 From the reminiscences as in Begbie, *William*, vol. 1, p. 139.

7 Stead, *Catherine*, p. 50.

only give way if he thought her case was right.

With regard to entering the Congregational ministry, Booth carefully considered the possibility. But the first hurdle was William's love of Methodism, which Catherine described as 'almost … idolatry'. Catherine also had 'a fair share of love' for Methodism, but it did not run as deeply as William's, possibly, she thought, because she 'had not been actively engaged' in it as her fiancé had been. The second problem was the Congregational reputation for having and favouring an intellectual ministry. Was he, William wondered, clever enough?

William leaped over those two hurdles and went to meet Dr John Campbell, a leading Congregationalist and magazine editor. It needs to be borne in mind that at this time Congregationalism was entering a period of change, and there were conflicting camps within the denomination. Campbell received Booth in a kindly manner and arranged for him to meet the church's Committee for Home Mission work. That committee interviewed Booth, liked what they saw and heard, and suggested that Booth consider going to Cotton End, a Congregational ministerial training college. William seriously considered this, with Catherine's full support. It is known that Catherine was keen for William to study more and to go to a ministerial training college.

But William Booth was a man of action rather than a student. That does not mean that he was unintelligent or uneducated, for his writings demonstrate a lively intelligence and he read many books. But Booth was happiest dashing from chapel to chapel preaching the word of God, not studying. Yet this would not have deterred him from going to Cotton End. Then he came to the third hurdle, bigger and more imposing than the other two. The committee chairman asked Booth to read two Calvinistic books. Booth began to read one and he quickly rejected this area of Congregational theology.[8] He, therefore, decided against joining the Congregationalists and, thus, did not go to Cotton End.

Catherine, however, had not yet closed the door on the Congregationalists. She raised the issue again in a letter in February 1853. She protested that she was not trying to persuade him, just sharing her thoughts, but the tone of the letter does sound as though she was hoping he would change his mind.[9]

It was probably in the middle of July 1852, when William's time with

---

8 From the reminiscences as in Begbie, *William*, vol. 1, pp. 139–42.

9 Booth, *Letters*, Letter CM17, 1 Feb. 1853, p. 62; Booth, *Letters CD*, p. 66.

the London Reformers was reaching its end and negotiations with the Congregational leaders were continuing, that he received another offer. Rev. R. Ferguson of Ryde on the Isle of Wight approached Booth about becoming his assistant minister. Surprisingly, Ferguson and his church were also Congregational.[10] William seems to have replied to the offer, telling Ferguson that he was considering going to Cotton End College.

Ferguson then wrote a forceful and critical response from the island, which must have shocked Booth and may have helped move him towards his final decision concerning Congregationalism. 'Their college whitewash is only garnishing the sepulchre of dead souls,' complained Ferguson. He then added,

> We want a quickening, soul-saving ministry, affectionately brought to bear on the consciences and hearts of sinners... Here [in Ryde] is the place for your social, and I believe loving, heart to expand and quicken. Don't go to college. Your thoughts were directed here. The experience of thousands of students says, 'Don't go to college.' Their theology has become stereotyped, their social and moral nature has lost its vigour and power, while immured within the college walls.[11]

Strong words! And, no doubt, William Booth would have been in sympathy with them. Despite the pleading William turned down Ferguson's invitation; yet, as has been seen, neither did he go to college, at least not at that time. A little over 15 months later William again thought about going to Cotton End, but the idea flew quickly through his mind and vanished.[12]

So, it was 'No!' to Ryde and 'No!' to Cotton End. Where, then, could an earnest preacher of the gospel find satisfactory work in Victorian England without starving?

Lincolnshire

The answer came from near in a denominational sense, but rather far geographically. Booth heard that some Wesleyan Reformers in Lincolnshire were looking for a preacher. Lincolnshire was Catherine's county before her move to London, though the approach was from the Spalding and Holbeach area of that county, not Boston. However, the link may have come via

---

10 Booth-Tucker, *Catherine*, vol. 1, p. 74; 'Ryde Congregational Church.'
11 Booth, *Letters*, Letter (WB8), 28 July 1852, pp. 11–12; Booth, *Letters CD*, p. 16.
12 Ibid., Compare Letters (WB43), 3 Nov. 1853, and (WB45), probably mid-November 1853, pp. 169, 174; ibid., pp. 171, 175.

people who knew the Mumfords. And this group was not only Methodist, it was a collection of Methodist Reformer churches. William and Catherine must have viewed it as divine intervention, after the problems with the Congregationalists.

But immediate contact did not go smoothly. The British postal service was a fast-developing and generally efficient organisation in the middle of the nineteenth century. Yet in the autumn of 1852 it let William Booth down. It was probably in September that Booth heard of the opening in Lincolnshire and applied for it. It appears that he sent his initial letter to 'Mr Ward, Builder, Spalding, Lincolnshire.' Mr Ward was one of the leading Reformer laymen in the Spalding circuit. Unfortunately, he was a farmer, not a builder, so the letter went astray. However, months later when Booth tried to find out why his original letter had not arrived, he thought that it still 'ought to have been forwarded' and it probably would have been, but, it seems, the local 'postman [did] not like reformers.'[13] Feelings were still running high in the Methodist disputes of the time.

Eventually contact was made and it was arranged for Booth to be the sole paid preacher for several Reformer churches in the Spalding area. There was one major problem. Spalding was about 200 kilometres from London and, as they were not married, Catherine would not be able to go with him. This meant an unwanted, probably long-term, separation, as their chances of soon getting married were poor. This separation was to be hard for William, but much harder for Catherine. He had plenty of work, too much Catherine thought, so, while he missed her a great deal, he was able to lose himself in preaching, visiting and leading meetings. Catherine had less to occupy her at this stage in her life, which meant she had more time to fret and worry, and Catherine was always a worrier.

---

13 Ibid., Letter WB15, 6 & 7 Dec. 1852, p. 21; ibid., p. 25.

CHAPTER 9

A time apart

'Here I sit all alone in our comfortable little parlour. My dear Mother & Mackland have gon[e] to hear Mr Thomas, while I, wearied with the previous exertions of the day, have been endeavouring to get good at home, and now feel a strong inclination to talk with you a bit',

Catherine Mumford to William Booth.[1]

On 30 November 1852, William left 7 Russell Street, Brixton, and his loving fiancée, boarded a train and travelled to Spalding, in Lincolnshire, just north of The Wash. His new job was as the sole paid preacher to several Wesleyan Reformer churches in that area, and it was a Reformers' stronghold. But the situation in Methodism in that area was also chaotic. It was common to have a man worshipping with the Wesleyans, while his wife worshipped with the Reformers, and vice versa. In one village the Wesleyans had the chapel, with ten or even less in attendance, while the Reformers packed dozens into a home for worship, and inevitably there was tension between the rival groups.

However, the Lincolnshire Reformers, unlike those in London, received William Booth warmly. They loved him and he came to love them and his ministry among them. He preached in Spalding, Holbeach, Gosberton, Weston Hills, Fleet Fen, Donnington, Risegate, Quadring Endike, Pinchbeck Bars and even occasionally, by invitation, in Boston, though that was not in his circuit. Sometimes he was given a ride in a carriage to his preaching appointments, occasionally he was able to travel by train, but usually he walked, and he walked many, many miles. He was busy, too busy. The situation may have been chaotic, but he loved it.[2]

---

1 Ibid., Letter CM6, 5 Dec. 1852, p. 23; ibid., p. 27.
2 For a detailed account of William Booth's ministry for the Reformers in Lincolnshire see the latter part of chapter 7, in Bennett, *General*, vol. 1, pp. 114–40.

Catherine alone

But our focus is on Catherine Mumford, though the 14 months of William's absence was not generally a dramatic time for her. Catherine continued to teach a Sunday School class for the Reformers, but she was much happier worshipping with the Congregationalists. Her admiration for David Thomas continued to increase. He was one of the people that she mentioned most often in her letters to William.

During their time apart (except for two, possibly three, brief visits to London by William) their only means of communication was by letter, and an illuminating array of letters passed between them. A contrasting feature in these letters is that though they clearly loved each other deeply, it did not stop them arguing and that frequently. They argued about a variety of subjects and, at times, quite vigorously. This does not mean that they spent their later lives arguing; rather, it was the inadequacies of communication by letter when they were apart that caused many a misunderstanding.

Catherine wanted him to study. 'Everything depends on it' she said, and repeatedly she urged him to study.[3] But, as has already been suggested, Booth was not a student, but a man of action, and there was plenty of opportunity for preaching action in Lincolnshire. Study would have to wait. But wait till when?

Catherine, as we have seen, was also a worrier. One issue that especially concerned her was that she knew that her fiancé, left to himself, was a workaholic, and she worried that he would kill himself or, at least, make himself seriously ill. William Booth was not especially strong, but he had a remarkable capacity for hard work. While on several occasions, well into the future, he became ill, he rebounded back to his calling with energy and enthusiasm. If William Booth was not strong, he was tough and resilient. But Catherine did not know the future, she knew William was working too hard and it naturally worried her.

When William told Catherine how often he preached, she was most upset. She told him that she was considering writing to one of the leaders in the circuit, to complain about it, and, she added,

> I certainly shall if you continue to do it. Nine sermons in one week! Monstrous! I am sure you will not be able to do it, neither ought you.

---

[3] Booth, *Letters*, see especially letter CM7, 12 Dec. 1852, p. 29, Booth, *Letters CD*, p. 33, but there are many other examples.

They told you they did not wish more than 5. How very wrong of you to go beyond your strength, & wrong yourself of time to study when they do not wish it. Is this scolding? If it is, I really cannot help it, so forgive me.

But there was the softer side. Immediately after that outburst she added 'And if you were here, I would *make* you forgive me. I *know how* I could do it. So do you, don't you, dearest?'[4]

Catherine was also learning to play the piano, a common accomplishment for young women in the Victorian era, and William was very keen that she did so. Here it must be said that William Booth loved music. Catherine, it seems, could take or leave it. But practice she did. The first possible instance of her playing the piano was in May 1847, so well before William Booth had entered her life. It was on her first visit to Brighton. She recorded in her diary, 'Spent the afternoon at Mr Wel[l]ses [sic] in reading and playing peices [sic].' However, the meaning of that passage is a little uncertain. The first part of the word transcribed 'playing' is partially obscured by a blot. It could be 'playing' or 'praying', though the former fits better with the following word, but what does 'playing peices' mean? (She usually spells 'pieces' as 'peices.') Was she already playing the piano, or did she not start that until William Booth appeared on the scene? Or on this occasion was someone else playing and not her?[5]

When we come to the flood of letters between William and Catherine in 1853, references to her playing the piano are frequent. William seems to have been the driving force behind it, and Catherine perhaps a little reluctant, though later as a young married woman she did seem to treasure her piano.

Another dispute erupted while Booth was in Lincolnshire, over the purchase of a piano. Just after one of William's brief return visits to London, Catherine acquired a piano, having already discussed it with him. She reported the purchase, and he wrote back to say that she had bought the wrong piano and he seems to have become upset about it. Catherine's response to the two letters he wrote concerning this is most unlike her normal writings.

I have a great deal to say. Oh, that I could *speak* it. But the Piano is up[p]ermost. I feel *very, very* sorry I did not write before I let it come, but *I did not think* I was acting on my own responsibility. What you said

4 Ibid., Letter CM30, 30 Mar. 1853, p. 90; ibid., p. 93.
5 Booth, *Diary*, 20 May 1847, p. 5; *Diary CD*, p. 10.

in both your letters made me think that you in your heart prefer[r]ed Bartlet's, & felt doubtful about the other, & you remember, dear, after you had seen it you did not want to go to the other again, & in both letters you say how *mortified* you should be that we did not have this if the other did not suit. I thought you would be better satisfied with this. I *am sure* I was not influenced by any thing but a desire to do for the best, & I feared the other had been much *more worn*. But *I shall not think of keeping* it if *you prefer the other*. It is all nonsense about 'Must keep it now it is here.' Not all the people in Brixton could persuade me, if I thought you were not in your heart pleased. It came yesterday & I thought it looked magnificent & Sounded *splendid*. But this morn'g all its charms are gon[e], & I have wished it out of the house over & over again. I do not care who is offended, I *shall not keep it*, if you would rather have the other. I did not think I was acting without you. I talked about you at the time & said I would write & ask you what I must do about mine, & when I went to take Miss T[abart] to look at it. I did *not intend* to let it come till I had received an answer. But he asked me if he should send it, & I said I would wait for a letter, but when he came next morn'g, as I was only to have it a fortnight, I thought it might as well come. But I did wrong, and I am real grieved & I hate to see it, and I shall return it early next week, unless you wish me not. *Forgive me*. I did not think I was acting without you. Nay, I wished in my heart you had bought the other, even tho' I did not think it so good, rather than I should have had to choose between them, which I *thought* you *wished me to do*.[6]

It was most unusual for Catherine to take a backward step as she did on this occasion However, the two letters from William, mentioned above, are both missing.[7] It was not unknown for Catherine to destroy some of his letters[8], if she thought them unkind, and she may have done so on this occasion.

Another matter that Catherine seems to have worried about was that her dynamic fiancé was more than 200 kilometres away, and surrounded, she imagined, by adoring young women. In one letter in March 1853, William told her that at one meeting that he 'was very *popular* among the young folks. There was some fine crushing to get along side of *me* at Tea.' While

---

6 Booth, *Letters*, Letter CM36, possibly 26 May 1853, pp. 103–104, Booth, *Letters CD*, p. 106.

7 See Booth, *Letters*, p. 103, fn. 305, Booth, *Letters CD*, p. 105, fn. 344.

8 For example, Booth, *Letters*, Letter CM53, 22 or 29 Aug. 1853, p. 142, Booth, *Letters CD*, p. 144.

only boys are mentioned in this letter, it is far from clear that only boys were present, which⁹ means that probably Catherine would have been unclear.⁹ Catherine must have wondered who was doing the crushing? Booth was at that time nearly 24, a young man. It is easy to imagine that some of the young ladies found him attractive, even exciting, and there can be little doubt that Catherine did imagine that. But William Booth was a faithful man. He knew that he could have no better woman to share his life than Catherine, so he was happy to wait. But Catherine still worried.

In July Catherine excelled herself. She wrote her fiancé a letter of 18 pages. It was reflective and, in part, an emotional examination of her own spiritual condition. It began with a common complaint. 'This has not been a happy day with me,' she said. 'My mind has been much agitated through not receiving a letter yesterday. I expected one with *unusual anxiety* in answer to my two written this week, and cannot imagine the reason it has not come to hand. A thousand conjectures harrass [sic] me, so that I have been in a tremour [sic] most of the day.'

Changing direction a little, she continued,

I went to chapel this morn'g but felt ill and so have spent the evening at home alone. It is very good to be alone sometimes. I often think that you are not alone enough. You are very fond of company & your manner of life favours it, but, my Love, you should often *try to be alone*. All that Poets have said in praise of solitude falls short of its actual deservings. The wise man communes with his own soul in solitude. It brings the christian, as it were, into the immediate presence of God. It removes all outside[r]s & shows the soul to itself. It quickens conscience by giving it breathing time & exercise. For it is when we are *alone* that conscience speaks most effectually and shows us our past conduct and presents motives in their true colours. Solitude antidotes the dread hour when the soul must bare itself before God, and *alone* unaided by any external being or circumstance answer his requirements and receive his sentence, either 'Well done!' or 'Depart from me.' Solitude is all this to me, & I believe would be to every soul of man if he would let it. It is one of man's best friends, but like *himself*, true to his own infatuated heart, he shuns it like his greatest enemy. The wicked hate solitude. It is to them a prelude of hell, the time when conscience stings like a scorpion. You might sometime bring this subject into a sermon. It would *do good*

---

⁹ Ibid., see Letter WB28, 14 or 15 Mar. 1853, pp. 81–82, ibid., p. 85.

perhaps. You might press it home to the heart of the sinner. The time will come when he *must* endure solitude.

… to day my soul has been in some measure going out after God. Oh, I do long to be restored to all his salvation, to experience his fulness of love, but there is such a shrinking from the *only* condition of this restoration, viz., taking up the cross & *following* Christ. It is *here* I have stumbled & fallen a thousand times. The Spirit of God seems to lead me to such a *peculiar* work, to such a strange path, to such a *hard task*, I cannot do it! My soul swells as I write it, my eyes fill & my whole frame *trembles*. Oh, that he would give *me power*, & work in me to *do* as well as to *will* of his 'good pleasure.' Scores of times I have determinedly opposed what I cannot doubt were the direct leadings of the Spirit to some particular work, & thereby brought condemnation & barrenness & hardness into my soul. I am the subject of such *strange feelings*. Many a time when passing a person in the street whom I had never seen before, I have felt as if I must speak to them or be guilty of their soul's blood. I have felt as if my heart would burst with feeling, as tho' I could kneel down in the street & pray for them, & yet I have times without number resisted & gon[e] on, feeling a burden almost intolerable to be borne. In 3 or 4 cases where persons have been on my mind weeks & months death has cut them off in their sins before I ever opened my lips to them. This has been my case ever since I knew the love of God. If ever I omit[t]ed to *reprove sin* or to follow the light of the spirit, I have invariably sunk further from God. What am I to do? Do you think this *has* been the Spirit of God? I have tried to believe it was temptation, fanaticism, any thing but the voice of God, but always when my soul has prospered & revived, this extraordinary experience has revived also, & whenever I have been careless & cold this has subsided. I have thought, if I could only get on as other christians seem to do, I could do it. But why should *I* have such a *singular* & & [sic] difficult work assigned me, & one for which nature has so unfit[t]ed me?

Narrowing her call to specific persons, she continued,

I have obeyed in one case lately in writing to that poor woman a long, plain, full, simple account of the plan of salvation, with abundant scripture references. May God own it. There is another case pressing on my mind continually, & I *must*, I *will* obey in this also. It is a poor, degraded, sinking drunkard, living in Russell Gardens. What I feel every time I see him I cannot discribe [sic], but I am *decided* I will go & invite him here, not letting him know what I want him for till he comes, & then I will just tell him what is in my heart to say to him, not forgetting to look up to God for guidance nor [sic] to leave the result in his hands. I feel convinced, if I must prosper in my soul, this is the way for *me* & I *must* walk in it. *Do* pray that I may be *strengthened* to do so. Oh, if you knew what I feel, if you knew what I have lost, you would pity me. Tell me what you think. *Advise me.*[10]

John Gough the temperance speaker

In the end, Catherine seems to have advised herself. One of her great heroes was John Gough, a vibrant American temperance speaker, and a month after she had written that letter Gough was in London on a speaking tour. Early in August she sent William a letter and enclosed a pamphlet, which told Gough's story and advertised his meetings. The leaflet described how Gough the drunkard had become, in Christ, Gough the temperance speaker. She urged William, 'Be sure to read' the leaflet 'at once, & then *lend it*, & when you have your book parcel, *order some to sell*.' Her letter continued,

I never read any thing with such intense interest in my life. *It* is *true*. Its subject is a *living man* & a *christian*, & I have heard him for myself. I was at the Hall[11] last night, & tho' it was the third oration the body of the Hall was *very full* & the Platform above half full at 2/6 a ticket. I did not intend going again, but I really cannot stay away, so I am going, all well, to night to the Whittington Club. Talk of eloquence & oratory! I never heard any before in comparison with this. I thought I must have come out; it almost overpowered me. I have witnessed much enthusiasm in that Hall, but nothing to equal it last night; kept up through the whole address. Oh, in some parts it was *awful*.

Her father was with her, and Gough's message seemed to have had a profound impact upon him, as she explained,

My father sat next to me. He kept turning as pale & his hands & the mussels [sic] of his face were in most sensible motion. [Gough's] discription [sic] of the *gradual* process of intemperance could only have been given by one who had experienced it. It was truly awful, but oh, *splendid* in the extreme, & *true* as God is true. His eloquence is

10 Ibid., Letter CM45, 3 July 1853, pp. 125–26; ibid., pp. 128–29.
11 This is almost certainly Exeter Hall, which commonly hosted such meetings as this. It is known that Catherine was at a meeting later that year at Exeter Hall, at which Gough spoke.

irresistible... After speaking of his *'blessed'* Mother (& oh, what he said of her was sublime) the people stood up & shouted till the place echoed. He spoke most powerfully on the mighty influence of Woman & told some telling anecdotes on the subject. He appealed to the young ladies present with earnestness, which I trust sunk into many hearts, & what he said to young men is beyond *eulogium*... But it is useless me writing. I am so excited.

In fact, she was so excited she could not keep it all to herself and her fiancé. She explained,

I have been to 3 or 4 *places* this morning to get persons to go to night, who I know are going down to destruction through drink. Praise the Lord, all have received me kindly & 3 are going, one of them is the poor man I told you about. He has just been here for a ticket I bought him last night, & is going. Praise the Lord with me.[12] He tells me that he has not tasted a *drop* since I first spoke to him & that he begins to feel better, & indeed his parched lips & palsied limbs begin to assume a more healthful appearance, but oh, the struggle is fearful... But the Lord is able to keep him from falling... I intend to work *more* in this good cause... Oh, I praised God for giving me to see the importance of abstaining from the ac[c]ursed stuff, & I praised him *too* for enabling me to keep my *early ressolution* [sic] to give my affections to *no man* who was not of the same mind. Bless the Lord that we both see alike *here* & shall be able to train up our children perfect *Samsons*. Oh, *do all you can* in this cause...[13]

What happened to that 'poor man' is unknown. At least two of her following letters are missing, which might have given us a clue. However, it needs to be noted that on the two occasions she refers to him, she shows pity rather than condemnation. Judging by the many things she said on the subject, she seems to have blamed the drink and those who sold it, more than the drinker.

The Reformers or the New Connexion

William Booth found the Wesleyan Reformers chaotic but seemed, for the most part, to rejoice midst the muddle. Catherine Mumford also found the Wesleyan Reformers chaotic and was repelled by the confusion. William's dashing about from chapel to chapel preaching sermon after sermon also

---

12 This could be as written, or '& is going, praise the Lord, with me.'
13 Booth, *Letters*, Letter CM 51, 5 Aug. 1853, pp. 138–39; Booth, *Letters CD*, p. 141.

greatly worried her. She thought it would kill him or at least make him permanently ill. Surely, she thought, there has to be a better way, a better Christian group, in which her fiancé could use his talents.

She began to direct his thoughts to the Methodist New Connexion. The New Connexion was another breakaway Methodist group. It was begun in 1797 and established as a more democratic form of Methodism. It was a protest against the rule of the dominant group of clergy in Wesleyan Methodism.

There was hope for a while in 1853 that the New Connexion might unite with the Wesleyan Reformers, and the former bring some order into the latter's disconnected administration and conduct. The two groups had left the Wesleyans for similar reasons (ministerial dominance), though about 50 years apart, so there was some basis for hope.

William Booth was involved in discussions on this matter in Lincolnshire. As early as February 1853, William told Catherine, 'How I wish the Reformers would amalgamate with the New Connexion or with the [Wesleyan] Association and that all this agitation were ended.'[14] In the middle of April the Reformers in the Lincolnshire District called a meeting to discuss the issue of amalgamation. William was present. He told Catherine,

> The District Meeting yesterday was a poor affair. Got myself a little *insulted*; a large Meeting yesterday, it is true, at *night*. Spoke with some considerable liberty and was well received. Came home more than ever out of love with the Movement generally [i.e. the Reformers], and more in love than ever with my own Circuit, and half resolved to write off directly and offer myself to the New Connexion. But I must learn to wait. Mr Shadford, Mr Hardy, Mr Brown, and others from our Circuit strongly pressed a motion in favour of amalgamation with the New Connexion, but it was lost. I supported it of course very warmly.[15]

So, as early as April 1853 William Booth had thought of joining the Methodist New Connexion, but he decided that then was not the time.

Catherine responded,

> I was sorry to hear that the District meeting turned out so poorly & that the motion for amalgamation was lost. What a pitty [sic] it is they cannot, or will not, see what would be to the best interests of the church

---

14 Booth, *Letters*, Letter (WB27), 21 or 28 Feb. 1853, p. 76; Booth, *Letters CD*, p. 80.
15 Ibid., Letter (WB30), 12 Apr. 1853, 96; ibid., p. 99.

generally. I have not the least confidence in the stability or durability of the movement. I fear its best days are over. It is most important for you to look around and step cautiously. You 'came home *half* resolved to offer to the New Connexion.' It appears then your mind is unsettled on the subject. I do think it would be your highest wisdom, if you are determined to remain in the ministry, unless your circuit amalgamates and takes you with it... If the [circuit leaders] can once be brought to look at their interests ... apart from the movement generally, they will doubtless amalgamate. But while they cling to the worn out ressolutions [sic] of the Delegates and view the movement in a false light they will cling to it. But you know all this far better than I do.[16]

Catherine and William began to read about the origins and constitution of the New Connexion. It was not long before she became convinced that it was an attractive option for her future husband. William, still 'in love' with his Reformers' circuit, was more hesitant. However, it was probably early in June that he contacted Rev. William Cooke of the New Connexion, expressing interest in attending a small college that he ran from his home in London.[17]

Yet Booth remained hesitant for much of the remainder of the year. His ministry with the Reformers in Lincolnshire was successful, and he was fond of them, and they of him. It continued a major topic of discussion in these letters. Then in the middle of September Catherine became so frustrated with William's indecision that she decided to push the matter. She told him,

I received your very kind letter this morning. I had been anxiously expecting the report of the quarterly meeting & your thoughts about the New Connexion. I hope you did not *forget* that my remarks on the subject were in *answer* to what you have said in two or three letters. It is certainly time to settle the matter some way, as it paralizes [sic] you & agitates me. I have thought a great deal about it, & reasoned it over all ways, & prayed earnestly for light & direction for us both, & I now want to give you my thoughts & conclusions. Listen to me & then act as your *judgment* dictates...

First then, you '*love the* polity of the Connexion very much.' You consider it to possess Methodism as it should be. You regard its organisation as peculiarly adapted to spread the gospel & subserve the interests of

---

16 Ibid., Letter CM33, possibly 14 & 15 Apr. 1853, p. 97; ibid., p. 101.
17 Ibid., Letter CM39, possibly 8 June 1853, p. 113; ibid., p. 116.

christian freedom, & the position and claims of its ministers you hold to be exactly scriptural. In union with *it* you would have a *certain* sphere of usefulness, in which you could labour in sure & certain hope that your successor would build up & not *pull down* the work of your hands. In it you would have freedom from pecuniary anxiety, which in *your case* would be absolutely *necessary* to usefulness, etc., etc.

On the other hand, the movement [i.e. the Methodist Reformers] you *never have* been in thorough harmony with. You consider its leaders are likely to lead it to destruction. You consider its aims wild & extravagant, & the position of its ministers, at least theoretically, degrading & *unscriptural*, & it promises no *certain* sphere beyond 2 or 3 years, & not even for that time, & your views & feelings are not in harmony with it as a whole, nor ever have been. You consider *amalgamation* would be a blessing & ultimately save it from ruin, & *have done what you could* to promote it but in vain, & all such efforts *will* be in vain, I feel persuaded. Then the question seems to me to be *only* this: shall you amalgamate *yourself* & join a constitution in thorough harmony with both *your* views & feelings & *mine*, & consequently enjoy all its privileges? Or shall you, for fear of the censure of some & for fear of loseing [sic] the respect of others, continue to labour in your present sphere independent of all consequences? I consider it would be perfectly *honourable* to join them. *You have tried your best to take the movement with you*, & it *will not go*. Then surely it cannot be dishonourable to leave it *quietly* & go yourself. Remember it involves no sacrifice of *principle*. I believe your conscientious views are on *the side* of the *Connexion*. As to your circuit, they have done no more for you than you have *deserved*. You have been worthy of your hire, & also of their kindness. I consider there is no *obligation* whatever, & they may easily get another whose views are more in keeping with their position & will be equally useful, & as to leaving such a loving people I fully sympathise with you, but it is only like leaving one Circuit to go to another, a thing essential to Methodistic rule & which must come sooner or later.

As to providence putting you there, I believe it *did*, but I see no reason why the same providence may not have opened your way into a more sure, & certain & happy sphere. I think it has done so in making it possible for you to marry & yet join them, & you know our *judgment* was given us to *exercise* and act upon in humble dependence on God's guidance.[18]

18 Ibid., Letter CM57, possibly 19 Sept. 1853, pp. 151–52; ibid., pp. 153–54.

The drama continued. Booth applied to join the New Connexion ministry, but then what seems to have been a Reformers' circuit in London made him a tempting offer, which further confused him.[19] This he eventually declined, and so he went to London early in February 1854 to join the Methodist New Connexion as a ministerial student. It can be safely said that Catherine was greatly relieved. Indeed, with respect to their relationship and hoped-for marriage they were both delighted. They had been a long time apart, a little over 14 months, and had written dozens of letters to each other. Their relationship had been tested and found to be loving and strong. As Catherine said in a letter at that time, 'This long correspondence should have developed our characters to each other. For my part I am sure I have written the very workings of my soul & I am sure you know me *far better* than you would have alone by personal intercourse of twice or thrice the length of time (except, alas, the faults of my daily life which I pray God to reduce both in number & magnitude).'[20]

One major problem still confronted them. As William Booth was a ministerial student, the leaders of the New Connexion would not allow them to marry yet.

William Booth's successful 14 months in Lincolnshire was the confirmation of his calling as a preacher. The people of Spalding, Holbeach and the surrounding area heard him gladly and many were converted. If he had any doubts about what his ministry should be in November 1852, he had none by the beginning of 1854. William Booth was called to preach the gospel of Jesus Christ and he knew it.

---

19 Ibid., Letter WB51, possibly 10 Jan. 1854, and WB52, possibly 11 Jan. 1854, pp. 206, 208; ibid., pp. 207, 209.
20 Ibid., Letter CM85, possibly 6 Feb. 1854, p. 215; ibid., p. 215.

CHAPTER 10

The Methodist New Connexion

'I just write you a note to cheer your soul and comfort your heart, but just as I begin I hear Mr Cooke calling out breakfast. I have been up some time and have been reading English History',

William Booth to Catherine Mumford.[1]

Catherine Mumford and William Booth were once more living in the same city. William was staying at Albany Crescent near the Old Kent Road at the home of William Cooke, who conducted his ministerial training school on the premises. This was situated near the pawnshop where William had worked when he first moved to London, and about three kilometres from where Catherine lived. Close contact between the two lovers was now much more frequent. As Catherine later put it, 'We were once more within reach of each other', and after a year of frustrating communication by letter she was delighted that they were now able to discuss issues face to face and 'compare notes.' However, William was under the discipline of Dr Cooke, so he could not go to meet her whenever he chose. But Catherine was pleased that at last her fiancé was undergoing a course of study.[2]

Catherine's sermon sketches

One way in which Catherine helped William at this time was taking notes of addresses she heard by David Thomas and other preachers, to give him ideas for his sermons. She also drafted sermon sketches and gave them to him. She was still not preaching and despite her developing feminist thinking she seemed to have no desire to do so at this time.

Her sermon sketches were not brief. In fact, they were long enough to need little editing to make them complete and useful orations. Indeed, one could develop each 'etc' a little and have a long sermon. One sketch runs to

---

1 Ibid., Letter WB53, late February or March 1854, 216; ibid., 216.
2 Presumably from her reminiscences in Begbie, *William*, vol. 1, pp. 223–24.

well over 2000 words. It is based on Revelation 2:10, 'Be thou faithful unto death, and I will give thee a crown of life.' It will be useful to quote part of it, as it demonstrates some of her thinking at this stage. She said,

Faithfulness or fidelity in any position or relationship of life is one of the highest virtues a creature can possess. Whatever may be the powers or qualities of a being, if that being be unfaithful to his trust, or inconstant in his relations, he is a moral bankrupt, a wandering star in God's universe, & most, if not *all*, the misery of our world is traceable to unfaithfulness in one form or another. All the woes of our race consequent on original depravity spring from man's infidelity to his trust when he had but one to keep. He betrayed it & fell from his high & holy estate, etc., etc.

From matrimonial, parental & filial unfaithfulness spring the multiplied *domestic* broils & sorrows which poison society at its heart & send through its endless ramifications one pestilential stream of evil, etc., etc.

From unfaithfulness amongst Friends & acquaintances in the betrayal of secrets & the exposure of faults, & amongst tradesmen & professional men in their different commercial transactions with each other spring nearly all what may be termed *social* evils, & we learn from history that the infidelity of statesmen, governments & sovereigns has given rise to most of the political evils which from age to age have devastated our world with fire & sword, & sent thousands reeking in the blood of their fellow men to the awful tribunal of a just & holy God, etc. Would to God that the direful effects of unfaithfulness were discernable [sic] *alone* in the domestic, Social & Political worlds, but, alas, there is yet *another* in which unfaithfulness has been more prolific of evil & suffering than in all the others put together, viz. the religious. Under the old dispensation, the infidelity of the Jews to their covenant relation with God brought upon them a succession of persecutions & sufferings unpresidented [sic] in the history of any other nation, & then final banishment from their land & dispersion amongst all the nations of the earth, etc., etc.

And after the establishment of christianity, when the pure & glorious light of the gospel shone on the primitive churches, *unfaithfulness* to the *spiritual simplicity* of Christ's doctrines caused the gathering of that cloud of error & superstition, which tho' at first not larger than a man's hand, gradually spread till it overwhelmed christendom with its horrors, & entombed the human mind in worse than Egyptian darkness. The church, having left her first love & departed from the simple teaching of Christ & his Apostles, receiving for doctrines the traditions & commandments of men, & refusing to repent & do her first works, the candlestick was removed & the awful consequences of her unfaithfulness soon began to manifest themselves...

Unfaithfulness in the exposition & application of the pure & peaceful doctrines of the cross has riven more hearts, caused more cruelties, & damned more souls than all other causes united. Christ foresaw the consequences if his church proved unfaithful to her sacred trust, and to warn & save her from such a catastrophy [sic] he dictated these heart searching appeals to the 7 churches, coupling with his solemn injunctions to fidelity promises & threatenings as they improved or neglected his words. Would to God they had taken warning & been faithful to their trust, but alas, etc. (You will doubtless find something highly instructive & interesting relative to the history of the 7 churches in [Adam] Clark[e]'s commentary. There is something very striking & peculiar in the history of the church at Philadelphia, which Jesus promised to 'keep from the hour of temptation', etc. because it kept the word of his patience, etc. This might be made very telling here.)

There was a fearful *necessity* to sound in the ears of the members of those primitive churches, 'Be thou faithful', & there is an equal necessity to reiterate the solemn injunction in the ears of every christian *now*. Who can tell *how much* may depend on the fidelity of the churches of this age, on their adherance [sic] to the *simplicity* of gospel institutions & to the pure & unadulterated word of God, on their rejection of mere cerimonial [sic] forms of worship, & their maintaining the inner life of religion in the soul? And yet what formality, indifference & externalism everywhere abound.

Surely, the ter[r]ible voice of the past borne to us on the blood & groans & tears of suffering humanity, the ominous voice of the present & the aspect of the future, *as well* as the faithful & loving accents of the Son of God cry in our ears, 'Be thou faithful', *thou* christian, whatever be thy position in the church or the world, whether thou be entrusted with one tallent [sic] or ten. '*Be faithful!*' *To thee* Christ has made himself known & commit[t]ed to thy trust the riches of his salvation. 'Be thou faithful' in exhibiting his character & dispensing his treasure as far as he gives the opportunity. *To thee* he has given a full & clear revelation of his will, & revealed many of his purposes. *Be faithful* in carrying out the one

& seeking to hasten the accomplishment of the other. 'Be thou faithful unto death & I will give thee a crown of life'…

Catherine then followed with a sequence of numbered points, though not all her numbers tallied. She closed considering

a few of the most powerful incentives to faithfulness. The first & most precious is the attainment of personal *peace*, a peace passing understanding, etc., etc. 'My peace I leave with you,' etc., *etc., etc.* 2nd, positive safety in all circumstances of trial or danger. The consciousness of fidelity leaves us no room to doubt of Christ's presence & support in seasons of trial. With Stephen the *faithful* christian can look 'steadfastly into heaven,' etc., etc. Having kept the 'Word of Christ's patience,' he looks to Christ to keep *him* in 'the hour of temptation' & suffering, & rests on his promises in perfect peace. It is the *unfaithful* who are racked with doubts, etc., etc. [3rd] Final & eternal salvation. 'I will give thee a crown of life.' Enlarge on the felicities of implied in the phrase, 'crown of life,' etc., etc., etc.

Then she told her fiancé, 'It is strictly & purely my own, so if it is useful, it is *yours*.'[3] In June 1854 she sent him another on 'Be not deceived.' William thought that one was 'admirable.'[4]

On 11 April the local Quarterly Meeting unanimously recommended Booth as a suitable person for the New Connexion ministry. The Conference in 1854 was held at Halifax in Yorkshire and began on 5 June. One question asked at that Conference was, 'What Preachers are now received on trial?' Seven names were then read out, including William Booth's. He was also listed as a preacher in the London Circuit.[5] Perhaps oddly, when he heard that news, he told Catherine, 'This is very good, but for some unaccountable reason I do not feel at all grateful, neither does it at all elate me.'[6]

Meanwhile Dr Cooke and his associates quickly realised that William Booth was not the keenest student, but he was a powerful evangelist. This was good, but it had its down side, as it meant that William would travel for the Connexion preaching the gospel. Quite how far he would travel and how often no one knew at first, but Catherine would on occasions be left behind again and they would have to communicate by letter once more. At

---

3 Booth, *Letters*, CM86, undated sermon sketch, pp. 216–19; Booth, *Letters CD*, pp. 216–19.

4 Ibid., Letter (WB58), 12, 19 or 26 June 1854, p. 223; Booth, *Letters CD*, p. 223.

5 *MNCM*, 'Extracts from the Minutes,' 1854, pp. 664–65, 668.

6 Booth, *Letters*, Letter (WB56), 8, 9 or 10 June 1854, p. 221; Booth, *Letters CD*, p. 221.

first Booth ministered in London, but there were only four New Connexion churches there, with collectively 228 members.[7] He travelled to Nottingham to visit his mother early in June and then moved on to Caistor, where he had conducted a successful mission at the end of his time in Lincolnshire. Once more 'he preached to crowded congregations.'[8] Then he appears to have returned to Nottingham unwell with a fever.

Cholera

There was a fearful outbreak of cholera that year, which hit London especially badly. That August Catherine decided to visit her friend Emma Smith in Burnham-on-Sea, in the south-eastern county of Essex. The visit seems to have had two purposes, first to visit an old friend, and secondly to escape the ravages of cholera in London. Burnham had been a cholera-free village in earlier outbreaks in 1832 and 1849.

It seems to have been her first visit to Burnham. She told William,

Instead of the wide extensive coast I expected, I find an arm of the sea about 20 miles in length, with beautiful green banks. A very strong sea breeze is blowing & the roar of old Ocean in the distance creeps soothingly over me. I think I shall enjoy it. Burnham seems a nice, prosperous village & does a good trade in Oysters. Miss Smith is *very much better*, poor girl. She is delighted to see me. I am agre[e]ably surprised to find her so much better, but yet there seems a deep, settled cloud on her spirit. I like her Mother & Father. They are real old fashioned, Country folks, & I shall have the advantage of a real Country life while here… At present I find it impossible to divest my mind of all anxiety about home & the health of those I have left. I feel twice as apprehensive about the sickness of London now that I am away.[9]

Once more Catherine felt the separation keenly. William was in the north, she was in the south-east and his letters took two days to reach her. Though this separation was likely to be of a much shorter duration than during his time in Lincolnshire, it still troubled her greatly, for she feared that if his health grew worse the news would be slow in reaching her. She wished he had 'come to Burnham.'

Catherine had fallen in love with Burnham. She had a keen eye for the

7 *MNCM*, 'Extracts from the Minutes,' 1854, p. 670.
8 Booth, *Letters*, Letter (WB58), 12, 19 or 26 June 1854, p. 223; Booth, *Letters CD*, p. 223.
9 Ibid., Letter CM89, late August 1854, p. 224; ibid., p. 224.

beauty in nature and could see the spiritual lessons in it, and Burnham displayed plenty of such treats. Later in her stay she told William,

> It is one of the loveliest days the earth ever rejoiced in. The water is running up in dimpling ripulets [sic] just before me, & all nature seems to be luxuriating in the perfection of happiness. It is a joyous thought that altho' the world *is* so marred & blighted by sin, there is still so much of beauty & enjoyment in it left, as it were, as a type & earnest of its coming emancipation. Oh, how glorious it will be when we walk together the streets of the new earth, 'wherein dwelleth righteousness.' Oh, how strange it is that *we* can deign to grovel among the husks as we do. Let us try to rise into the life of God. Let us make even this affliction work out for us a brighter & holier experience. I pine, I long, to be a temple of indwelling God. Alas, that my faith & obedience bears [sic] so little proportion to my desires. 'Lord, quicken *thou* me according to thy word.'[10]

Catherine had long suffered from diarrhoea. It was an oft repeated and troubling condition for her throughout her life, and it was also the major symptom of cholera. While the people of Burnham had escaped cholera in earlier outbreaks, it was not to do so this time. A man in the house next door to the Smiths caught it and died 'in 24 hours', she told William. Not surprisingly, it made Catherine 'feel rather nervouse [sic] when [she] was suddenly seized with violent pain & dieareah [sic].' But she went straight to bed and 'took a very strong dose of brandy & ginger, which,' she said, 'made me completely tipsy. Sent me in a nice perspiration & the next morn'g I felt better.'

Catherine did not have cholera, just one of her annoying bouts of diarrhoea. But there is another issue here that needs to be considered. Catherine Mumford Booth was a life-long opponent of alcohol and even rejected its use as a medicine. This letter has certainly caused concern for some researchers. In the original letter several words in this sentence have been crossed out by another hand, including the word 'brandy'. In the amended form it reads, 'took a very strong dose of ~~brandy &~~ ginger, which ~~made me completely tipsy~~ sent me in a nice perspiration...' This amendment was not done by Catherine.[11] She also confirmed that she

---

10 Ibid., Letter CM90, 3 Sept. 1854, pp. 225–26; ibid., pp. 225–26.
11 Ibid., Letter CM93, 13 Sept. 1854, p. 231; ibid., p. 231.

drank brandy at about this time in a letter to her parents.[12] The word 'tipsy' is not completely clear in the original but is a probable reading. Bearing in mind Catherine's strong opposition to alcohol, even as a medicine, it is strange to hear her admit this, and that without any word of regret. No other evidence of Catherine drinking alcohol has been discovered. The fear of cholera must have been, shall we say, a powerful stimulant.

William Booth, a travelling evangelist

The yearly Conference, usually held mid-year, was the governing body of most forms of Methodism, including the New Connexion. However, some decisions needed to be made between Conferences, and such decisions were made by a group called the Annual Committee, which consisted of leading men in the denomination. Their decisions would then be ratified or not by the next Conference. It appears to have been towards the end of 1854 that the Annual Committee appointed William Booth as the denomination's evangelist. This was confirmed and made ongoing by the Conference at Sheffield held in late May and early June 1855. The Conference report stated that Booth would be 'stationed' in the Manchester Circuit, 'for special Connexional Services', i.e. evangelistic meetings, 'under the direction of the annual Committee.'[13] It was a strange appointment in one sense, in that Booth did not go on to spend much time in Manchester. The special services were held in many places. It is also crucial to note that this was an official appointment, because later many in the New Connexion believed that the position of denominational evangelist should never have been created, and the battle over it became fierce.

For about six months from the end of 1854, William Booth, though still a minister on trial, acted as a travelling evangelist for the New Connexion. First, he went to Guernsey in the Channel Islands, between England and France. Next, as shall be seen, he preached in the Staffordshire towns, Longton, Shelton and Burslem. It was then on to other towns in the north of England and the midlands.

There seems to have been some tension between William and Catherine as the year 1855 began. The details are unknown as they were both living in

---

12 'CBLP', Letter P4, probably 4 Sept. 1854, p. 16.
13 For a list of where preachers were to be stationed for the following twelve months see *MNCM*, 1855, p. 651.

London at that time, so there are no letters to guide us, and some of the letters written soon after are available only in part. In a letter now only available in edited versions, William told her '... I am yours, wilful, impulsive and fitful as I am. I am yours in affection, *enduring* and tender and *faithful*.'[14] That first quoted sentence may mean anything and the unavailable part at the beginning was probably the key to it. These comments, as they stand, do not indicate a great problem between them. However, on 6 January, clearly in response to this letter, Catherine said, 'Praise the Lord the horrid controversy is ended and I am once more happy. My fears are hushed, my doubts dissipated, & my mind at rest, precious, most precious *rest*.'[15] William and Catherine do not fit the picture of lovers who never argued, but they do demonstrate to us that those in love can disagree but still love passionately.

---

14 Booth, *Letters*, Letter (WB68), 5 Jan. 1855, p. 242, Booth, *Letters CD*, p. 241.
15 Ibid., Letter CM98, 6 Jan. 1855, p. 242, ibid., p. 242.

CHAPTER 11

'The daughters of my people'

'My heart often aches & weeps over the hurts of the daughters of
my people & I often make their cause a matter of supplication to
the God of Heaven',

Catherine Mumford, February 1854.[1]

Catherine Mumford was born into Methodism, and it has been said that 'the greatest breakthrough in opportunities for women to proclaim the gospel came with the Wesleyan revival'[2] that saw the birth of Methodism. However, while Methodism allowed women to speak and pray at class meetings, it had a varied history on allowing women to preach.

John Wesley had some reservations about women preaching, at least in the late 1760s. In 1769 he issued the following instructions to at least two women, Sally Crosby and Grace Walton. He said, '1) Pray in private or public, as much as you can. 2) Even in public, you may properly enough intermix short exhortations with prayer; but keep as far away from what is called preaching as you can. Therefore never take a text; never speak in a continued discourse, without some break, above four or five minutes.'[3] It could be said that at that time Wesley had adopted a moderate position on women's ministry.

In his Journal in December 1786 Wesley recorded that he met Sarah Mallett, who was aged in her early twenties. Upon talking with her he learned that she often had 'fits' (or trances) in which she imagined that she was preaching the gospel, which she took as a call to do so. However, at first, she resisted the call, and the fits persisted. Finally, she began to preach and

---

[1] Booth, *Letters*, Letter CM85, probably 6 or 13 Feb. 1854, p. 215; Booth, *Letters CD*, p. 215. This letter is often thought to have been written in 1852. However, a February 1854 date is almost certain.

[2] Kari Torjensen Malcolm, *Women at the Crossroads*, quoted by JoAnn Shade, 'Let the women speak,' *The Officer*, May/June 2010, p. 10.

[3] Wesley, *Works*, letter to Mrs Crosby, 18 Mar. 1769, vol. 12, p. 355.

then the fits ceased.[4] Catherine Booth mentioned Sarah Mallett in one of her books. She said, 'From the Methodist Conference held at Manchester, 1787, Mr Wesley wrote to Miss Sarah Mallett, whose labours … had been opposed by some of the preachers, "We give the right hand of fellowship to Sarah Mallett and have no objection to her being *a preacher in our connection*, so long as she preaches Methodist doctrine, and attends to our discipline."'[5] Dorothy Graham, a leading authority on women's ministry in Methodism, confirms that the 1787 Conference did authorise Mallett to preach.[6]

But, whatever Wesley thought, more than 20 female preachers emerged in British Methodism towards the end of the eighteenth century, including Mary Bosanquet (1739–1815), who married John Fletcher, a leading Methodist preacher, and Mary Barritt Taft (1772–1851). In 1771 Bosanquet wrote a letter to John Wesley defending the right of Methodist women to preach.[7] Not surprisingly, Catherine Booth had a high opinion of Mary Bosanquet Fletcher and her husband.

The Wesleyan Conference of 1803, so twelve years after Wesley's death, placed a ban on women preaching, except to their own sex. But like most bans, it was only partially effective. On the other hand, the Primitive Methodists and Bible Christians did allow female preachers, some of whom travelled extensively.[8] One early Primitive preacher was Sarah Kirkland (later Harrison), who came from Derbyshire but exercised a powerful ministry in Nottingham and its surrounds in 1816. Later she ministered in Yorkshire. Others followed her.[9] In other words, there were female Methodist preachers at the end of the eighteenth century and into the next, but not many.

Catherine's letter to William

Catherine had always been a thinker, and now her thought was expanding and maturing. One of the main issues she considered was women's equality

---

4 Wesley, *Journal*, 4 Dec. 1786 in *Works*, vol. 4, p. 356.

5 Booth, *Papers on Practical Religion*, pp. 164–65. The emphasis is in Catherine Booth's book.

6 *DMBI*, 'Sarah Mallett', p. 221.

7 Ibid., 'Mary Barritt,' 'Mary Bosanquet,' and 'Women,' pp. 21, 37, 399; Chilcote, *The Methodist Defense of Women in Ministry: A Documentary History*, pp. 17–19.

8 *DMBI*, 'Women,' p. 399; Chilcote, *Defense*, p. 6.

9 Werner, *Primitive*, pp. 88–89, 106–107.

with men, a topic that became dear to her heart. Consequently, on this subject her words often burst forth into fire. Her first significant written venture into this was in a letter to William early in April 1855. So hot is this letter that the pages must have burnt Booth's hands as he took them from the envelope and the words must have exploded in his mind as he read them. The letter is long, stretching to 16 pages; most of it deals with this issue, powerfully and passionately.

She began with a paragraph on the 'curse' of drink, then launched into 'that *other* subject.'

> You know I feel no less deeply on this subject & perhaps you think I take rather a prejudiced view of it; but I have searched the word of God through & through, I have tried to deal honestly with every passage on the subject, not forgetting to pray for light to *perceive* & grace to submit to the truth, however humiliating to my nature. But I solemn[l]y assert that the more I think & read on the subject, the more satisfied I become of the true & *scriptural* character of my own views.
>
> I am ready to admit that in the majority of cases the training of woman has made her man's inferior, as under the degrading slavery of heathen lands she is inferior to her own sex in christian countries. But that *naturally* she is [in] any respect, except in physical strength & courage, inferior to man I cannot see *cause* to believe, & I am sure no one can prove it from the word of God, & it is on *this* foundation that professors of religion always try to establish it. Oh prejudice, what will it not do? I would not alter woman's domestic position (when indeed it is scriptural), because God has plainly fixed it. *He* has told her to obey her husband, & therefore she ought so to do, if she profess to serve God; her husband's rule over her was part of the sentence for her disobedience, which would, by the bye, have been no curse at all if he had ruled over her *before*, by dint of superiority. But God *ordained* her subjection as a punishment *for sin*, & *therefore* I submit. But I cannot believe that *inferiority* was the ground of it. If it had, it *must* have existed prior to the curse & thus have nullified it.
>
> Oh, I believe that volumes of light will yet be shed on the world on this subject. It will *bear examination* & abundantly repay it. We want a few mighty & generous spirits to go thoroughly into it, pen in hand, & I believe the time is nor far distant when God will raise up such. But I believe woman is destined to assume her true position & exert her proper influence by the special exertions & attainments of her *own sex*.

She has to struggle through *mighty* difficulties to[o] obvious to need mentioning, but they will eventually dwindle before the spell of her developed & cultivated *mind*. The heaving of society in America (that birthplace of so much that is great & *noble*), tho' throwing up, as all such movements do, much that is absurd & extravagant & which I no more approve than you; yet it shows that p[r]inciples are working, & enquiry awakening.

May the *Lord*, even the just & impartial one, overrule all for the true emancipation of woman from the swad[d]ling bands of prejudice, ignorance & custom, which almost the world over have so long debased & wronged her. In appealing thus to the Lord I am deeply sincere, for I believe that one of the greatest boons to the race would be woman's exaltation to her proper position mentally & spiritually. Who can tell its consequences to posterity? If what writers on physiology say be *true*, and experience seems to render it unquestionable, what must be the effects of neglect of mental culture, and the inculcation of frivilous [sic], servile, & self-degrading notions into the minds of the *mothers* of humanity? Oh, that which *next* to the plan of salvation endears the christian religion to my heart is what it *has* done & *is destined* to do for my own sex; and that which excites my indignation, beyond anything else is to hear its sacred precepts dredged forward to favour degrading arguments. Oh, for a few more Adam Clark[e]s[10] to dispel the ignorance of the church, then should we not hear very *pigmies* in christianity reasoning against holy & intelligent women opening their mouths for the Lord in the presence of the church.

Whenever you have to argue with such, just direct them to read the three following passages & Clark[e]'s comment on the 2 first: Exodus 15 c. 20-22 verse[s]; Judges 1 c. from the 4 v. and 2nd Chronicles 34 c. from the 21st v.[11] On the first he says the same word in the orriginal [sic] is used in reference to *Moses* & the other prophets, and therefore Mirriam [sic] was as truly inspired, and that she was chosen & constituted joint *leader* of the people. We have the express word of God for it, viz., Micah 4 c. 4

---

10 Adam Clarke was an early Methodist Bible commentator.

11 The first of these passages speaks about 'Miriam the prophetess' encouraging 'all the women' to praise God, and the last speaks of 'Huldah the prophetess' giving words of divine wisdom to some of Judah's leading men. The second reference, however, is incorrect. Though Catherine has clearly written 'Judges 1 c.... 4 v.,' she means chapter four, verse four, which commences the story of 'Deborah, a prophetess.'

v.[12] 'For I brought thee up out of the land of Egypt, & *I sent* before thee Moses, Aaron & *Mirriam*' [sic]. On the latter, Clark[e] says that Deborah seems to have been supreme as well in civil matters & in spiritual. 'She judged Israel;' the same term as is used to denote the functions of the regular judges. *She appointed* Barak as general of the armies, as well as declared God's will to him, & Barak most unhesitatingly recognised her authority. But read *carefully* the whole account, as also that in the 34th c. of 2nd *Chron[icles]* and say whether in *any* respect you can discover any difference between the exercise of the prophetic power or the recognition of its reality & force in these cases & those of Is[a]iah or Jeremiah.

It is worthy of remark that there are no less than *six* Prophetesses mentioned in the old Testament, one of whom was was [sic] unquestionably *Judge* as well as prophet. And these are not mentioned in a way which would lead me to suppose that the inspired writer regarded them as any thing very *extraordinary*. They are simply introduced to our notice like the other prophets. Now, God having *once* spoken *directly by woman*, and man having once recognised her divine commission & obeyed it, on what ground is omnipotence to be restricted or woman's spiritual labours ignored? Who shall dare say unto the Lord 'What doest thou?' when he 'pours out his spirit upon his *handmaidens*,' or when it is poured out shall render it null with impunity? If *indeed* there is in 'Christ Jesus neither male nor female,' but in all touching *his kingdom* 'they are *one*,' who shall dare thrust woman out of the church's opperations [sic] or presume to put *any* candle which God has lighted under a bushel? Why should the swad[d]ling bands of blind custom, which in Wesley's days were so triumphantly broken, & with such glorious *results* thrown to the moals [sic] & bats[13], be again wrapped round the female disciples of the Lord, as if the natural & in some cases distressing timidity of woman's nature were not sufficient barrier to her obeying the dictates of the spirit, whenever that spirit calls her to any public testimony for her Lord.

Oh, it is cruel for the *church* to foster prejudice so unscriptural, & thus make the path of *usefulness* the path of untold suffering.

However, as has been seen, Wesley did not break with 'blind custom' quite as completely as Catherine seems to have thought.

---

12 Catherine has once more given a wrong reference. It should be Mic 6:4.

13 This probably should be 'moles & bats' and is presumably a reference to the assumed blindness of those creatures.

She then threw out a challenge directly to her fiancé.

Let me advise *you*, my Love, to get settled views on this subject & be able to render a *reason* to every caviller, & *then* fearlessly incite *all* whom you believe the Lord has fitted to help you in your master's work, male or female. Christ has given them no *single tallent* [sic] to be hid in a napkin, & yet, oh, what thousands are wrap[p]ed up & buried, which used & improved would yield 'some thirty, some sixty, yea, and some an *hundred* fold'. If God has given her *the ability*, why should not woman persuade the vascilating [sic], instruct & console the penitent, & pour out her soul in prayer for sinners? Will the plea of bashfulness or *custom* excuse her to *him* who has put such honour upon *her*, as to deign to become her *Son* in order to redeem her race? Will these pleas excuse her to *him*, who last at the cross & first at the sepulchre was attended by women, who so far forget bashfulness as to testify their love for him before a taunting rabble, & who so far overcame *custom* that when *all* (even fellow disciples) forsook him & fled, they remained faithful to the last, & even then lingered 'afar off', loath to loose [sic] sight of an object so precious?

Oh, blessed Jesus! He is indeed 'the *woman's* conquering seed.' He has taken the bitterest part of her curse 'out of the way, nailing it to his cross.' In *him* she rises to the dignity of her nature. In *him* her *equality* with her *earthly Lord* is realized, for 'in *him* there is neither male nor female,' & while the outward semblance of her curse remains, in him it is nul[l] ified by *love* being made the law of marriage—'husbands *love* your wives *as* Christ loved the church & gave *himself for it*'. Who shall call subjection to such a husband a curse? Truly, *he* who 'was made a curse for us' hath beautifully extracted the venom, for what wife who *loves the Lord* can feel it a burden to '*reverence*' a husband thus *like him*, and glory to his name while his death did *this*, & his precepts are so *tender* & so *easy*.

His *example* is no less endearing. In her society he *loved* to spend his hours of repose & holy retirement in the *lovely little home* at Bethany. To her at the road side well he made his only *positive* avowal of his Messiahship & set aside the trammels of national custom to talk with her. For *her* he made a way of escape from her merciless tho' no less guilty accusers, & while sending *them* away, conscience smitten, to *her* he extended his tender mercy, 'Neither do *I* condemn thee. Go in peace.'[14]

---

14 Here Catherine misquotes Jn 8:11, which concludes 'go, and sin no more,' not 'Go in peace.' Catherine may have done this deliberately to relate it to Christ's encounters with

He never slighted her, overlooked her, or cast a more *severe construction* on sin in *her* than in *man*; no, he treated her in *all respects* the same. His last affectionate solicitude, in the midst of expiring agonies, was exercised for *her*, & oh, best of all, his rising sallutation [sic], the first view of his *glorified* body, that pledge of his victory over her ancient enemy, was given to *her* with a commission to go & *publish* to his disciples the facts of his resurrection. Methinks if some of our modern quib[b]lers had been amongst them, they would have hesitated to receive such tidings from *her*, but not so Peter & John, they *ran* as swiftly at *her* word as if it had been a man's, & 'stooping down & looking in' realized the glorious truth. Oh, that many Marys may yet *tell* of his wonderful salvation.

Catherine then said, 'I have long wanted to put my thoughts on this subject on paper.'[15] This suggests that she had never done so before, at least not in any detail.

William's answer

One suspects that if William Booth was standing when he first opened the envelope, he had to sit down long before he had read the whole letter. The power of it must have swept over him and left him stunned. W.T. Stead no doubt exaggerated when he said that 'Sometimes William Booth must have felt as if he had caught a Tartar,'[16] but on this occasion he must have wondered who was this sweet, innocent, young lady that he had promised to marry. Booth must have asked himself, 'How am I going to respond to that?'

But he did respond, though hesitantly, almost nervously. We do not have the complete letter in this case and must rely on edited versions in the biographies, but there is no reason to suppose that they omitted anything related to the subject of women. If this is correct, his response was brief, cautious, and, it must be said, confused. It was also, as usual with William Booth, pragmatic. He said,

The remarks on *Woman's* position I will read again before I answer. From the first reading I cannot see anything in them to lead me for one *moment* to think of altering my opinion. You *combat* a great deal that I hold as firmly as *you* do, viz. her *equality*, her *perfect equality*, as a whole, as a *being*. But as to concede that she is man's *equal*, or *capable* of becoming

---

two other New Testament women, see Lk 7:50 and 8:48.
15 Booth, *Letters*, Letter CM122, 9 Apr. 1855, pp 283–86; Booth, *Letters CD*, pp. 282–85.
16 Stead, *Catherine*, p. 68.

man's equal, in intellectual attainments or prowess–I must say *that* is contradicted by experience in the world and my honest conviction. You know, my dear, I acknowledge the superiority of your sex in very many things; in others I believe her inferior. *Vice versa* with man.

I would not stop a woman preaching on any account. I would not encourage one to begin. You should preach if you felt moved thereto; felt equal to the task. I would not stay *you* if I had power to do so. Altho' *I should not like it*. It is easy for you to say my views are the result of prejudice; perhaps they are. I am for the world's *salvation*; I will quarrel with no means that promises help.[17]

No doubt William did read her letter again, but if he did give a fuller answer, it no longer exists. Perhaps he was too busy to consider the matter in detail and it was never written. He was, after all, the New Connexion's travelling evangelist at this time, serving in Bradford, so he was busy. Perhaps he did respond again, but Catherine was not happy with what he said, so she destroyed it. We will never know. However, while the extent of Catherine Booth's influence over William Booth's opinions is often exaggerated, there is no doubt that this is one area where she got him to change his mind.

Catherine's letter to the New Connexion Magazine

Catherine's letter to William on women was written on 9 April 1855. Four days later she wrote a letter to the *Methodist New Connexion Magazine* on 'How to Train New Converts.' It contained some excellent advice on the subject and was in four sections. The last was on 'freedom from undue restraint in the use of the faculties.' One concern she expressed under that heading was that Methodism had slipped from its leading role in allowing women to minister publicly. 'There seems,' she said, 'in many [Methodist] societies a growing disinclination in the female members to engage in prayer, speak in love-feasts and meetings, or in any public manner bear testimony for their Lord … and this false, God-dishonouring timidity is but too fatally pandered to by the church, as if God had given any talent to be hidden in a napkin.' Once more she complained about women being bound by 'the swaddling bands of blind custom.' She then asked, 'Where are the Mrs Fletchers and the Mrs Rogers of our churches now, with their numerous and healthy spiritual progeny?' Then surprisingly, in her closing

---

17 Booth, *Letters*, Letter (WB95), 12 Apr. 1855, p. 287; Booth, *Letters CD*, p. 286.

paragraph, she said, 'Mistake me not, *I am not advocating female preaching*, but female efforts in other ways, especially for the benefit of their own sex' (emphasis added).[18]

Catherine's letter to Rev. David Thomas

Later that April she sent a letter to Rev. David Thomas about women's equality with men, which echoed many of the thoughts she had expressed to her fiancé and in the magazine article. We have noted that she had great admiration for Mr Thomas and loved his preaching, but that does not mean that she blindly accepted his views. One Sunday she heard him and was not happy. Thomas had said something she considered derogatory to her sex and she penned a letter in response.

The date that this occurred has long been debated and needs a brief comment here. The suggested dates are 1850[19], 1853[20], and, for the sermon, 22 April 1855.[21] The 1850 date is clearly wrong, as it is based on Catherine Bramwell-Booth's misreading of the two names in her grandmother's diary, which were mentioned before. There is no evidence that Catherine Mumford heard David Thomas preach before 1852.

An 1855 date for the letter seems certain, not least because the manuscript of this letter in the British Library has the date of the sermon as 'Sunday morning, April 22nd '55' in the body of the letter. (However, it appears that the handwritten letter in the British Library is not in Catherine's own handwriting, but even if this is so, there is no evidence to suggest that the date has been incorrectly copied.) That 22 April that year was a Sunday gives the ring of truth to this date. In addition, as has been seen, on Monday 9 April, just thirteen days before, Catherine wrote that lengthy letter to William mainly on this same subject, and in that she said, 'I have long wanted to put my thoughts on this subject on paper,'[22] thus implying that she had not written on women's issues in depth before.

18 C[atherine] M[umford], *MNCM*, 'How to Train New Converts', 1855, pp. 319–21.
19 Bramwell-Booth, *Catherine*, p. 50; Major Douglas Clarke, 'Female Ministry in the Salvation Army', pp. 232–33; Murdoch, 'Female Ministry in the Thought and Work of Catherine Booth', p. 349, and Murdoch, *The Origins of The Salvation Army*, p. 32.
20 Booth-Tucker, *Catherine*, vol. 1, pp. 83–86; Green, *Catherine*, p. 307, fn. 2; and Hattersley, *Blood*, p. 61, fn.
21 Walker, *Devil's Kingdom*, pp. 251–52, fn. 50.
22 Booth, *Letters*, Letter CM122, 9 Apr. 1855, p. 285, Booth, *Letters CD*, p. 285.

Pamela Walker is justified in saying, 'There is absolutely nothing to support any other date than the one clearly given in the text of the letter.'[23] Therefore we conclude that 22 April 1855 is the correct date for the sermon, and the letter was probably written later that same week.[24] But what did she say to David Thomas? Like her letter to her fiancé it is very long, so only the main points will be given.

She began respectfully and apologetically, acknowledging the quality of David Thomas's abilities and teaching. She continued,

> I had the privilege of hearing you preach on sunday morning April 22[nd], '55, and it is for a few remarks in that discourse that I would ask your second consideration. When descanting on the policy of Satan in first attacking the most assailable of our race, your remarks appeared to imply the docterine [sic] of woman's intel[l]ectual and even moral inferiority to man. I cannot beleive [sic] that you intended to be so understood, at least with reference to her moral nature, but I fear the tenour [sic] of your remarks would but too surely leave such an impression on the minds of many of your congregation, and *I* for one cannot but deeply regret that a man for whom I entertain such high veneration should appear to hold views so derogatory to my sex, and which I beleive [sic] to [be] so unscriptural & dishonouring to God.

She then, a little cheekily, asked him whether he had 'ever made the subject of woman's equality as a being [a] matter of calm investigation and thought?' She added, 'If not, I would with all deference suggest it as a subject well worth the exercise of your brain and calculated amply to repay any research you may bestow upon it.' She next affirmed her belief that the Scriptures taught woman's 'perfect equality.'

Catherine admitted that women are generally 'inferior to man intel[l]ectually,' but this was because she had received an 'inferior education.' It was not something that was innate. She then asked, 'has not her education been more calculated to render her a serf, a toy, a plaything, than a self-dependent, reflecting, intel[l]ectual being?' She continued,

> As you, my Dear Sir, often say in reference to other subjects a 'brighter Day is dawning', and ere long woman will assume her true position and rise to the full h[e]ight of her intel[l]ectual stature. Then shall the

---

23 Walker, *Devil's Kingdom*, p. 252, fn. 50.
24 For a detailed argument for the April 1855 date, see Bennett, *Catherine Booth on Women's Place and Ministry*, pp. 4–6.

cherished, tho' but human dogma, of her having 'a cell less in her brain', with all kindred assumptions, explode and perish before the spell of her developed and cultivated mind...

I must hasten to say a word or two on the moral side of the question. And here I am quite sure your remarks implied more than you intended, for I cannot believe that you consider woman morally more remote from God than man, or less capable of loving him ardently and serving him faithfully. If such were the case, would not the great and just one have made some difference in his mode of dealing with her? But has he not placed her on precisely the same moral footting [sic] and under the same moral government with her companion? Does she not sustain the same relation to himself and the moral law, and is she not exposed to the same penalties, and an heir of the same immortality? This being the case, I argue that she possesses equal moral capacity...

Oh, the thing which next to the revelation of the plan of salvation endears Christianity to my heart is what it has done and is destined to do for my own sex, and any attempt to deduce from its historical records or practical precepts views and doctrines derogatory ther[e]to, I cannot but regard with heart felt regret.

Catherine then used some of the same Scriptures that she used in her letter to William to argue her case. She also once more admitted that 'God, who had a right to determine the penalty for sin, has clearly defined and fixed woman's domestic and social position.' But this did not mean that she was inferior to man either intellectually or morally.

She then became more passionate, saying,

Oh, that Christians at heart would throw off the tram[m]els of Prejudice and try to arrive at the truth on this subject. Oh, that men of noble souls and able intellects would investigate it and then ask themselves and their compeers, *why* the influence of woman should be so underestimated that a book, a sermon, or a Lecture addressed to her is a rarity, while books, sermons and Lectures to young men are multiplied indeffinitely [sic].

If it be only partially true that 'they who rock the cradle rule the world,' how much greater is the influence weilded [sic] over the mind of future ages by the *mothers* of the next generation than by all the young men living. Vain, in my opinion, will be all efforts to impregnate mind gennerally [sic] with noble sentiments and lofty aspirations, while the *mothers* of humanity are comparitivly [sic] neglected, and their minds indoctrinated from the school room, the press, the platform, and even the *Pulpit*, with self-degrading feelings and servile notions of their own inferiority. Never till woman is estimated and Educated as man's equal, the literal '*she man*' of the Hebrew, will the fountain of human influence become pure, or the bias of mind noble and lofty.

Oh, that the ministers of religion would search the original records of God's word in order to discover w[h]ether the general notions of society are not wrong on this subject, and w[h]ether God really intended woman to bury her gifts and talants [sic] as she now does, with reference to the interests of his Church. Oh, that the church gennerally [sic] would enquire w[h]ether narrow prejudice and lordly userpation [sic] has not something to do with the circumscribed and limited sphere of woman's religious labours…

Would to God that the truth on this subject, so important to the interests of future generations, were better understood and more practically recognised, and it is because I feel that it is only the truth that needs to be understood, that I make this appeal to one who I believe loves truth for its own sake, and who I know possesses the ability to aid in its manifestation. Forgive me, my Dear Sir, if I have spoken too boldly. I feel deeply on this subject. Tho' God knows it is not on personal grounds. I love my sex and desire above all earthly things their moral and intel[l]ectual Elivation [sic]. I believe it would be the greatest boon to our race, and tho' I deeply feel my own inability to help it onward, I could not satisfy my *conscience* without making this humble attempt to enlist one whose noble sentiments on other subjects have so long been precious to my soul… I have no sympathy with those who would alter woman's domestic & social position, providing it be scriptural. I believe God has clearly defined and as clearly given the reason of his conduct, and therefore I submit, feeling that in wisdom and Love as well as in judgment, 'He has done it.' But on the subject of equality of nature I believe my convictions are true…[25]

That is passionate and powerful. It is the kind of writing (and that kind of preaching) that helped make Catherine Booth famous.

It has been suggested that Catherine did not send this letter to Rev.

---

[25] This letter is on one side of three large sheets of paper in the Booth Papers in the British Library, MS64806, *ff.199–201*.

Thomas, but kept it. It would, then, have ended only as a means of her letting off steam. This is possible. While there is no evidence to support that, nor is there any evidence of a response from David Thomas. If Mr Thomas did receive it, it must have come as a shock to him. It is unlikely that he received many complaints about his teaching, and certainly not from young women. If Catherine did send it, she did so anonymously (according to the closing part of the letter), though it is likely that David Thomas would have known who the writer was.

One distinctive, non-feminist point needs to be noted in these two magnificent letters. W.T. Stead captured it well when he said, 'Mrs. Booth, loyally bowing to the letter of the scripture, never cavilled about or disputed the headship of the husband, nor questioned the obedience which was due from the wife.'[26] This point is in danger of being missed.

In his book on the Victorians, A.N. Wilson says that Britain's 'male-dominated' society 'seriously began to change' to one more favourable to women in the 1860s.[27] Thus it can be argued that Catherine Mumford's thinking in the mid-1850s has the spirit of a pioneer and can even be expected to have had some originality. Catherine Mumford was, in part, paving the way for an unforeseen Christian Army, which would employ many women preachers, and preachers who did not just minister to their own sex but to both. As her eldest son later said, 'No work on the emancipation of women would be complete without a record of her service.'[28]

---

26 Stead, *Catherine*, p. 50.
27 Wilson, *Victorians*, p. 308.
28 Booth, *Fifty*, p. 25.

CHAPTER 12

The Wedding

'I don't care much for [having] a family. I would rather be with *you* always than have *ten* sons.'[1]

Catherine Mumford to William Booth, Jan 1855

Success in Staffordshire

At the beginning of 1855 William Booth continued his travelling ministry for the New Connexion. It was first to the pottery towns in Staffordshire. He arrived in Longton in the first week of January, after a long and arduous journey, which concluded with 'a 3-miles walk' in a strong wind. Fortunately, he did not have to carry his luggage, which was delivered to his host's home later.[2]

Catherine was greatly relieved when she received William's first letter from Longton. She had just heard about 'a very serious accident on the same line' that Booth had travelled, in which 'two persons were killed and many wounded', plus two accidents on other lines.[3] In mid-Victorian England, railway travel was an exciting and convenient innovation, but it was not always safe. Catherine had been understandably even more worried than usual.

Booth's campaign in Longton did not begin well. The congregations were 'very good', but Booth at first found the work 'heavy, very heavy', and fewer people came out to the communion rail than he expected. He also knew that with frequent preaching he continually needed fresh ideas, so he asked Catherine to jot down anything that struck her during her 'own reading or meditation' that was 'likely to be useful' to him.[4] Then, a week

---

1 Booth, *Letters*, Letter CM100, 13 Jan. 1855, p. 247, Booth, *Letters CD*, p. 247.

2 Ibid., Letter (WB67), probably 3 Jan. 1855, p. 240, ibid., p. 240.

3 Ibid., Letter CM97, 5 Jan. 1855, p. 241, ibid., p. 241.

4 Ibid., Letter (WB68), 5 Jan. 1855, p. 242, ibid., p. 242.

later, he said, 'I want to make a sermon on the Flood; if anything strikes you on the subject note it down.'[5]

After another five days of the Longton mission, results and Booth's mood had both improved remarkably. 'The revival is progressing with mighty power and influence', he told her. They had had 'Several very interesting cases … and some important persons have been converted.' (The Booths commonly used the word 'cases' for those who had come forward to the front of the chapel or hall for counselling, so they were not necessarily all converts.) They had taken 'about 140 names' of those who had come forward, all recorded in a notebook, and, 'a great number of persons [were] under deep conviction.'[6] When Catherine heard that news she was delighted, but ever the realist she said, 'If only *half* the converts stand, there will be a goodly harvest from a week's labours.'[7] On the final night in Longton, William preached to the largest congregation he had ever faced and another 50 'cases' were written into the notebook. It must have been a relief to Catherine when he told her that though he had worked 'very hard' his health was better than when the campaign began.[8]

It was then on to Hanley. If the congregations in Longton had been good, they were even better in Hanley. John Ridgway, a local Methodist layman, said that there was 'upwards of 3,400' at the first evening service.[9] It is tempting to believe that that figure is an exaggeration, and it probably is, yet it comes from a local man, whom one would have expected to know the chapel's capacity. Booth's letter referring to the attendances on that Sunday has been lost, and the versions of it in the biographies give contradictory figures.[10]

Booth went next Burslem at the end of January and to Newcastle-under-Lyme in February, then back to Longton, and visited Oldham and Mossley in Lancashire. The New Connexion authorities allowed him a rest period in London for about two weeks, though he may not have allowed himself that much rest, as he seems to have still been officially attached to the London circuit.

5 Ibid., Letter (WB71), 12 Jan. 1855, p. 246, ibid., p. 245.

6 Ibid., Letter (WB70), 10 Jan. 1855, p. 244, ibid., p. 244.

7 Ibid., Letter CM99, 12 Jan. 1855, p. 245, ibid., p. 244.

8 Ibid., Letter (WB71), 12 Jan. 1855, p. 245, ibid., p. 245.

9 Ridgway, 'Revival at Hanley', *MNCM*, 1855, p. 96. (The page is given in the magazine as 66, but this is incorrect.)

10 Booth, *Letters*, See Letter (WB72), 13 & 15 Jan. 1855, p. 246; Booth, *Letters CD*, p. 246.

Once more he stayed with the Mumfords for at least part of that time, and, presumably, occupied the room he had used before. While there he seems to have injured his finger. In Catherine's first letter to him after his return to the Midlands, she said, 'The first thing which met my eye on returning to the room you had just left was a bit of rag, [covered] all over [in] blood from your poor finger. I cannot tell you with what feelings I seized it. It seemed so really a part of yourself that I could not but press it to my sorrowful bosome [sic] in – –.' The two concluding dashes were inserted by Catherine. Then she lamented 'Oh, these *partings!*' William seems to have left her a '*special* letter' to comfort her during his absence. She kept it under her pillow and read it when she needed that comfort.[11]

Next it was back to Longton for William for another campaign, and on to Oldbury and Smethwick. Then he went further north to Bradford, Newcastle-upon-Tyne, Gateshead, Manchester and Sheffield. Most of these visits resulted from invitations from the churches concerned.[12] In little more than a year, William Booth had become a much sought-after evangelist, at least in his own denomination. Yet, while at this time he only preached in New Connexion chapels, many from other denominations went to hear him.

William Booth was busy and loving it. Catherine Mumford, while rejoicing in her fiancé's successful missions, was once more concerned about the strain upon his health.[13] She knew that he was not one to take it easy in ministry of that kind and she feared that his body would not stand the strain.

Plans for marriage

But there was good news, great news. They had been given permission to marry, and they had begun to plan for that day. However, Booth still had much work to do in the north of England.

Yet not all were convinced that it was wise for Booth to marry. Early in June he told Catherine, 'Some friends seem to fear my marrying standing in the way of my extensive usefulness, and I *should much love to disappoint*

---

11 Ibid., Letter CM117, 26 Mar. 1855, pp. 275–76; ibid., p. 275.

12 Bennett, *General*, vol. 1, pp. 189–90. See accounts of some of Booth's missions in *MNCM*, 1855, pp. 146–53, 219–22, 540–43, 613–17.

13 See, for example, Booth, *Letters*, Letters CM108, 5 Feb. 1855, and CM128, 19 May 1855, pp. 260–61, 296; Booth, *Letters CD*, pp. 260, 295.

them, in fact I trust it will *rather* increase, nay, considerably increase it.'[14] Clearly, some of Booth's friends did not know Catherine, and they certainly could not have known what she would become. William Booth was right. Being married to Catherine would 'considerably increase' his usefulness.

However, Catherine was already making arrangements for the wedding. In the middle of May William was then campaigning in Manchester and was being 'pulled to pieces' by the New Connexion Methodists from other towns, fighting over his labours. While he was there, Catherine sent him a letter (now missing) that seems to have suggested they get married during the week ending 16 June. William, with too much on his mind, appears to have been glad that Catherine was making the decisions, and tentatively agreed.[15]

William Booth was not always tactful, a trait he shared with his wife-to-be. About three weeks before the wedding he sent her a letter about her health, which is no longer available. Most likely, Catherine was so upset by it that she burnt it. We can glean what it said from Catherine's irate response. She began 'My dearest William,' which did nothing to hide the storm that followed. 'This [is] the *fourth* sheet of paper I have thus commenced since yesterday morn'g in attempts to answer your Monday's letter.' Clearly, she was having difficulty controlling her thoughts and pen. She continued,

> However, I will leave what I have to say on the subject of my health untill [sic] you come, *then* I will tell you *all* I *know, think*, hope, or fear, & give you *perfect liberty* to act as your *judgment* dictates. You shall *never* lead me to the alter [sic] in the spirit of a martyr going to the stake, depend upon it. No! You shall act *freely* and *willingly* in *that* act, if you never do again. I will not *consent* to be married as a matter of *necessity*. Your 'fate' is not yet irrevocably fixed. It is in your own power. It is of no use torturing me about it any more. I have done *all* I can, & the very anxiety you *continually* excite on the subject frustrates your own wishes. Of course, I cannot *guarentee* [sic] health in the future. Can you? And is it not a fact that often the strongest women become delicate after marriage, while delicate ones become strong? But I have no more to say, only that at present I am very much better. I am taking no medicine & feel pretty well. My constitution is *dellicate* [sic], tho' Mr F[ranks] says I have about me no *disease*, but I will have the thing *clearly settled* when you come.

---

14 Ibid., Letter WB108, 5 June 1855, p. 302; ibid., p. 301.
15 Ibid., Letter (WB104), 15 May 1855, p. 296; ibid., p. 295.

Perhaps we can blame William's lack of tact in this instance on the pressures he was under. Catherine's response, if his letter was as unfeeling as it seems to have been, is understandable, though it does not read like a missive from a lover to the one she loved. But disagreements between them never seem to have lasted for long. Their love was too strong and deep and their sense of shared purpose under the direction of God was too clear and uniting to wreck their relationship. Indeed, while writing that letter she received another letter from him, which, she said, 'was a great comfort to me. It breathed a more *loving* spirit.' Suddenly, all, or nearly all, was forgiven and she moved on to discuss the plans for the wedding.[16]

A crucial question for any bride was what should she wear for the wedding? That was a topic that William entered into with enthusiasm. On 22 May he urged, 'Write me per return how much black silk you will want for a flounced dress and whether you would prefer that to a satinet or satinture – I intend having a first rate one. If I buy it without your letter, I shall get black silk and *16 yards*.'[17]

Catherine responded,

As to the dress, *thy* choice is absolutely *mine*; just which *you* prefer, only I do think flounces will neither become our position nor profession. My dear, you must act on *principle* in this matter; the people will look at us for an *embodiment* of the truth you preach. Let not our appearance contradict it. Besides, if you wish people to form a *true* estimate of *my* character, you will let me dress plain, as *good*, & as full as you like, but *don't* insist on the flounces. 14 yards will make a handsome, full dress, plain skirt, 12 yards wide width [sic], which it *should be*. I *will* 'look up & be happy.'[18]

William wanted her to look lovely; Catherine wanted to look 'Christian.'

William had a rethink. In his next letter he said, 'I am not sure whether I shall get the black silk. Without flounces I don't like them, and I don't want to cross your wish.'[19] So the questions remain: did Catherine wear black silk for her wedding? And if so, was it with or without flounces? We do not know the answer to those questions. No photographs were taken and there is no detailed account of the ceremony. If black seems a strange choice for

16 Ibid., Letter CM129, 23 May 1855, p. 298; ibid., pp. 297–98.
17 Ibid., Letter (WB105), 22 May 1855, p. 298; ibid., p. 297.
18 Ibid., Letter CM129, 23 May 1855, 299; ibid., p. 298.
19 Ibid., Letter (WB106), 24 May 1855, p. 300; ibid., p. 299.

a wedding, white was not as common a choice for brides as it later became, and, as is clear, William Booth liked it.

There was also a difficulty over where to hold the wedding, which Catherine and her father had to sort out. First, there was a problem with William's residency. He did not really live anywhere, as he moved from place to place. They considered Dover Street [aka Brunswick] New Connexion Chapel, where William Cooke was the minister, but there seems to have been doubts about even Catherine's residential qualifications for that. In the end they settled on Stockwell Congregational Chapel, with David Thomas to officiate.[20] The thought of a trainee minister of one denomination being married by a minister from another denomination did not seem to be a problem.

By this time, Saturday, 16 June had been confirmed as the date for the wedding. On 6 June Booth was in Nottingham, no doubt advising his family about the wedding preparations. Two days later he wrote Catherine a letter from Spalding in Lincolnshire, where he had served as a preacher for the Reformers. This appears to have been his last letter to her before their marriage. In it he told her, 'how soon once more shall we meet again.'[21] He returned to London the following week, probably a day or two before the wedding, apparently taking his sister Emma with him.

The ceremony was conducted, as planned, by Rev. David Thomas at Stockwell Congregational Chapel. The generally accepted list of those present at this wedding is strange, though more for its absentees than for those who attended. It seems to have been a small gathering, with John Mumford and Emma Booth acting as witnesses, and the only others present seem to have been John Barnett (the Registrar), and, according to Catherine Bramwell-Booth, the church caretaker. Noticeable absentees were the two mothers, Mary Booth and, it seems, Sarah Mumford.[22] It is easy to explain the absence of Mrs Booth. She lived over 200 kilometres to the north and travelling such distances in those days was still not common.

---

20 Ibid., Letters CM128, 19 & 21 May 1855; (WB105), 22 May 1855; CM129, 23 May 1855; and CM130, 25 May 1855, pp. 297–99 and 301; ibid., pp. 296–98 and 300.

21 Ibid., Letter WB110, 8 June 1855, p. 303; ibid., p. 302.

22 Details from a copy of the marriage certificate, courtesy of the International Heritage Centre of The Salvation Army. See also Booth-Tucker, *Catherine*, vol. 1, p. 134; Begbie, *William*, vol. 1, p. 275; Ervine, *Soldier*, vol. 1, p. 130; Bramwell-Booth, *Catherine*, p. 145; Green, *Catherine*, pp. 66–67; Hattersley, *Blood*, p. 73 (Hattersley gives an incorrect date for the wedding); and Bennett, *General*, vol. 1, pp. 214–15.

But why did Sarah Mumford miss her only daughter's wedding? After all, she lived walking distance from Stockwell Chapel. While she may not have been well, it is hard to imagine that ill health alone would have kept her away. It is much more likely to have been that she could not bear the thought of losing her daughter. As has been seen, the bond between mother and daughter was extremely close. Sarah now had only her husband for company and comfort, and he does not seem to have been the man she had once admired and loved.

It is possible that a few others were present at the wedding, or, at least, attended the following reception at the Mumfords' home. There had been talk earlier about hiring two carriages for the wedding party, instead of one, which suggests a group of more than four, though whether this was done is unknown. In addition, in one letter before the wedding Catherine told William that her mother was 'sadly put about at the idea of having Mr C[ooke] and Mr R[abbits]' and presumably their wives, at the Mumfords' home, for, apparently, a reception.[23] If Messrs Cooke and Rabbits and their wives did attend the reception, it is also possible that they were at the wedding, though there is no known evidence to support that.

But one thing is unquestioned, that day in June 1855 William Booth married Catherine Mumford, and then began a relationship that would impact not only late-Victorian Britain, but also the world.

The newly-married Booths went for a week's honeymoon to Ryde on the Isle of Wight. The decision to go there may have been because of William's contact with Rev. Ferguson, who three years earlier had invited him to go to Ryde as his assistant minister.

---

23 Booth, *Letters*, Letter CM130, 25 May 1855, p. 301; Booth, *Letters CD*, p. 300.

CHAPTER 13

Travellers for God

'Well, I got through the journey far better than I expected. I was
only sick *once*, & then not very bad',

Catherine Booth to her parents.[1]

Together in the Channel Islands

In typical Booth fashion, after the honeymoon, it was back to work, for
William at least. He had accepted an invitation to preach for a second time
for the New Connexion Methodists in Guernsey in the Channel Islands.
So they both made the sea crossing. Catherine feared sea voyages and her
fragile health seems to have taken a pounding on this one.

They were, however, well received, and Booth conducted what seems to
have been a frenetic evangelistic campaign on both Guernsey and Jersey.
The Methodist New Connexion was not strong in these islands. It had only
one minister, two societies (presumably one in Guernsey and the other in
Jersey), one chapel, and 148 members.[2] However, vibrant guest preachers
tend to attract crowds, particularly if they have made a successful earlier
visit, and that is what happened.

Catherine probably wrote more than once to her parents from the
islands, though only one letter from their visit remains. It comes from the
end of her husband's Guernsey campaign. It gives insights into William
Booth's character, methods and popularity, and her pride in him.

> Wm is preaching his farewell sermon to night. I feel so sorry I cannot
> hear him. The doors were to be open at half past 5 to admit the seat
> holders *before* the *crush*. The interest has kept up all through the services,
> so as I never saw it before. It would do you good to see some of the
> prayer-meetings, chapel crowded, upstairs and down. There have been
> some precious cases of conversion, but not so many as Wm expected.[3]

---

1 'CBLP', Letter P6, 26 Aug. 1855, p. 21.
2 *MNCM*, 'State of the Connexion, 1855,' 1855, p. 653.
3 'CBLP', Letter P5, 7 or 9 July 1855, p. 20.

That account was a sign of things to come. Crowds crushing in to hear the new evangelist, exciting 'prayer-meetings' (that is, counselling sessions), 'precious conversions', and, despite it all, William Booth was still not satisfied.

Separated again

When they returned to England, Catherine was unwell. This was probably partly because of her usual health problems, partly because she was still recovering from a rough sea voyage, and partly because she was already pregnant. William journeyed to the north of England to conduct evangelistic services for the New Connexion, mainly in Yorkshire, and Catherine stayed with her parents.

So, it was back to letters for them. Her pregnancy seems to have followed a rather typical course. In one letter to William she told him, 'The sickness continues very distressing at times. Sometimes all my meals come up again almost directly, but not often... everybody tells me it is only the common lot of woman, so I must be patient & wait, but it is wearisome work.' She had been eating onions for 'supper,' but the craving for onions was replaced by the desire for raisins, which, she then said, she 'cannot do without.' In fact, she was eating raisins while she was writing one letter to William, which made her hands 'sticky.'[4]

She was missing him desperately, and she knew that he was missing her. She wrote,

> I have been thinking about thee in thy lonely chamber, picturing thee going comfortably off to sleep without being disturbed by a little wife pottering about the room half an hour before she gets in. I can see thee sleeping nice & cool without anybody slipping into the middle of the bed and taking up all the room, and I can hear thee say when thou wakes up in the morning, 'My poor little wife, I wish she was here.'[5]

Catherine joins William

But Catherine did not get married to live apart from her husband. She naturally wanted to be with him, so, despite her sickness, towards the end of

---

4 Booth, *Letters*, Letters CB135, possibly 14 Aug. 1855; CB137, possibly 16 Aug. 1855, pp. 310, 312; Booth, *Letters CD*, pp. 308, 310.
5 Ibid., Letter CB133, 8 Aug. 1855, p. 309; ibid., p. 307.

August she travelled north to Hull in Yorkshire to join him. In a letter to her parents, probably written the day after her arrival in Hull, she told them,

> Well, I got through the journey far better than I expected. I was only sick *once*, & then not very bad. The guard was exceedingly kind & attentive. If I had been rich, I would have given him *half a sovereign*. I eat [sic] half of the pie & enjoyed *it much*. The last bit I had this morn'g for lunch. I got a cup of Tea at Peterborough all right. Had the carriage to myself all the way. My precious Husband met me at Milford & was delighted to see me.

Their hosts, Catherine told her parents, were 'a homely family, but one in which [she] felt at home directly. The Lady is a Mother of 9 grown up children, & she is truly *motherly*.'[6] Thus began a lengthy period of their lives in which they travelled much and had no home of their own. This was particularly hard for Catherine. She was pregnant and often sick, which she knew did not make her the ideal guest. However, while their hosts were very welcoming, Catherine did not like Hull. She described it as 'a horridly *close*, flat, unsightly place, & scarce one house in a *hundred* has even a decent yard, much less garden.'[7]

But William eased her difficulties by his kindness and attention. In that same letter she said, 'My precious Wm is kinder & more tender than ever. He is *very, very* glad I came. Bless him! He is worth a *bushel* of some soarts [sic].' He also gave her some welcome news, which she passed on to the Mumfords, 'The *work* wears the most encouraging aspect of any place he has visited (at the beginning), & he is, therefore, in excellent spirits.'[8]

William and Catherine had a relationship that was serious and earnest, but they could be playful at times. William annotated one of her early letters to her parents, thus: 'I am happy to tell you I am much better, tho' *comparatively* [completely *W.B.*] *useless*. I do *little* [nothing, *W.B.*] else but eat & drink & sleep.' To which she responded, 'My pest of a husband has been interlining the above, & making me out to be worse than I am.'[9]

That December, in a different vein, Catherine told her parents,

> I don't know what I should do in strange places with no mother to warm me up after I am in bed, if I had not such a loving, kind husband. But I soon get warm now of a night, & when I get comfortably e[n]sconsed

---

6 'CBLP', Letter P6, 26 Aug. 1855, p. 21.

7 Ibid., Letter P9, 11 Sept. 1855, p. 25.

8 Ibid., Letter P6, 26 Aug. 1855, p. 22.

9 Ibid., Letter P7, 3 Sept. 1855, p. 22.

in my beloved's arms with my cold feet on his legs, I often say, 'Two are better far than one.' If you know any poor wretch who dithers & shakes an hour every night, as I used to do, advise them to get married. There is nothing like animal heat, depend upon it.[10]

The work continued in Hull with 'mighty power.' God was doing 'great & marvellous things.' The only negative aspect was that William had been working so hard that he was 'sadly knocked up.' At the end of the first week of September he was given a brief break and the Booths went to Caistor in Lincolnshire again, though this time for a rest. This corresponded with a period when Catherine was feeling better.[11]

After two days William returned to Hull for one week's further ministry, while Catherine remained in Caistor. She fell in love with the place. 'It is such splendid country,' she said soon after William had gone.

> As I rambled out in the green lanes this morn'g, hemmed in on every side by fields of golden corn, in which the reapers are busy in all directions, and surrounded by the most lovely scenery of hill & dale, woods and gardens, I did wish my dear Mother could come and spend a fortnight…
> It is like being in fairy land *here*, after being [in Hull].[12]

God, however, continued to do great and marvellous things in less beautiful Hull. On the Sunday after Booth's return there were 'upwards of 40 cases' at the evening service, 'some of them very remarkable ones.'[13]

Sheffield

William Booth was in much demand, so towards the end of September they moved on to Sheffield, which Catherine found no better than Hull. Catherine thought that 'for smoke' Sheffield 'must rival the infernal region itself.' However, fortunately for her they were housed in 'a beautiful home, in the outskirts of the town, within ten minutes' walk of the cemetery, and overlooking some splendid scenery.'[14] Any negative thoughts that the cemetery might convey were clearly offset by the beauty of the area.

Sheffield was a rapidly growing town, famed for its steel. Triggered by the industrial revolution, the population had grown from 45,758 in 1801

---

10 Ibid., Letter P31, possibly 10 Dec. 1855, p. 55.
11 Ibid., Letter P8, 7 Sept. 1855, pp. 23–24.
12 Ibid., Letter P9, 11 Sept. 1855, p. 25.
13 Ibid., Letter P9, 11 Sept. 1855, p. 25.
14 Ibid., Letter P12, 24 Sept. 1855, p. 27.

to 135,310 in 1851.[15] Sheffield Methodism had also grown quickly in those years.

Catherine was well enough to attend two evening services during the first full week of her husband's Sheffield campaign. After witnessing events first hand, she thought that 'The work is rising in power, influence, and importance, and bids fair to become very mighty.' As predicted, it continued to progress with power into October.

Leading figures in Methodism, not just the New Connexion, were beginning to take notice of this new preacher. Catherine also heard at this time that her article on training new converts, which had been published in the *New Connexion Magazine*, had now also been published in the *Canadian Christian Witness*, widening her influence in an unexpected direction.[16]

Rest

Late in October they were able to have a time of rest in 'comfortable apartments' in Chatsworth Park, on the Duke of Devonshire's estate, 'just inside the Park gates.' This was in her native county, Derbyshire. On Sunday morning they worshipped at the local Church of England, and Catherine called the service 'a dry affair.' That afternoon they 'walked through the Park right up to the Duke of Devonshire's residence.' Catherine described the park as 'one of the most splendid spots I ever was in. It is all hill & dale, beautifully wooded and bestudded with Deer in *all directions*. The residence itself is superior to many of the Royal residences & the scenery around most picturesque & sublime.' And best of all, she added, 'This splendid spot is *ours* for a week in every sense necessary to its full enjoyment, without any of the anxiety belonging to its real owner.' In the evening William went to the 'reform chapel,' while Catherine stayed home, rested and wrote to her parents.[17]

The first day of November was 'frosty,' but fine, and they set off to explore, going 'for a walk … to see the rocks of Middleton Dale… The scenery all the way was enchanting' she told her parents.

> I could scarce get along for stop[p]ing to admire & exclaim; the dark frowning cliffs on one hand, the splendid autumnal tints of rich foliage on the other, and the ever varying views of hill and dale before us, all, as

---

15 Wickham, *Church and People in an Industrial City*, p. 20; Best, *Mid-Victorian Britain 1851–75*, p. 11.

16 'CBLP', Letter P13, 27 Sept. 1855, and P14, 5 Oct. 1855, pp. 28, 29.

17 Ibid., Letter P21, 28 Oct. 1855, p. 38.

it were, tinged with glory from a radiant sky, filled us with unutterable emotions of admiration, ex[h]ilaration and joy.

She continued,

Well, we reached the Dale, and were not at all disappointed with the scenery. It is a long, narrow road with cliffs from a hundred to two hundred feet high on either side, jutting out here & there like old towers of a bye gon[e] age, and frowning darkly on all below…

We walked about half a mile up the dale, & then I rested & got a little refreshment at a very *ancient* and comical kind of Inn, while Wm walked half a mile further. During which time I had a very cozy & to *me* amusing chat in *rich* Derbyshire brogue, with an old chap over his pipe and mug of ale.

After resting about half an hour, we bent our steps homeward where we arrived about half past two in prime time for Dinner. I felt tired but considering I had walked at least 9 miles during the day I considered myself worth many dead ones.[18]

A walk of 'at least' nine miles (14 kilometres) in one day suggests that Catherine may have been a little stronger than she usually thought.

Being married had modified Catherine's thinking in some respects. In her diary entries, written in her teens, she was happy to speculate that death for her might be a comfortable and welcome release from her ailing body. But now after a little more than four months of marriage those thoughts had changed, even though she was often still unwell. She wrote,

I could not tell you *how* happy we both are, notwithstanding my delicate health & our constant migrations. We do indeed find our earthly heaven in each other. Praise the Lord with me, & Oh pray that I may so *use* and improve this sunshine that if the clouds should gather & the storm arise, I may be prepared to meet it with calmness & resignation. Oh, I cannot tell you how I sometimes feel when I contemplate the bare possibility of death robbing me of all this bliss. It seems as tho' I could not bear it, but I know it is best to *trust* & not be afraid.[19]

A strong awareness of death, though, remained.

What were Catherine's concerns and hopes in early married life? As Catherine Mumford in April that year, she had written to her then fiancé and to Rev. David Thomas about her conviction concerning women's

---

18 Ibid., Letter P22, 2 Nov. 1855, p. 39.
19 Ibid., Letter P21, 28 Oct. 1855, p. 38.

equality with men. With that came the suggestion that women could and should be allowed to do more in Christian ministry. Yet in the early letters to her parents after her marriage, Catherine is not yearning after more opportunities for ministry, and certainly not expressing any hope to be a preacher. She appears content to be the wife of a Methodist minister, in whose success she takes great pride, and the bearer of his children. Indeed, she said, 'My precious William is all I desire.'[20] This may seem odd, and perhaps it is, but the letters up to and soon after the birth of their first child give that very strong impression.

Halifax

After their rest at Chatsworth Park, it was back to travelling and back to work for William. They returned to Yorkshire, this time Dewsbury, where the work progressed 'gloriously,' even though the people were initially '*frozen* and formal.'[21] It was then on to Leeds and Hunslet, where they still were early in 1856.

Booth's next mission was again in Yorkshire, this time Halifax, where for the first time they had a home of their own. It appears that one of the local Methodist families had recently purchased a house that they did not need immediately, so they let it to the Booths. It was well-furnished and '*very nicely* fitted up with gass [sic] & every convenience, in a beautiful & healthy locality.' This was a relief to Catherine as she was eight months pregnant. She said, 'I should not mind if [the birth] happened *here*. I feel so comfortable in a house to myself.' Another great relief was that they were able to acquire the services of an elderly nurse, who was prepared to act as a servant until her nursing experience was required at the birth.[22]

Their first-born

They were still in Halifax when on Saturday evening 8 March, Catherine Booth gave birth to their first child. They named him William Bramwell Booth. William and Catherine had great admiration for William Bramwell, a major north-country, Methodist evangelist and holiness teacher at the end of the eighteenth century and the beginning of the next, and they were

---

20 Ibid., Letter P11, 19 Sept. 1855, p. 26.
21 Ibid., Letter P25, 12 Nov. 1855, p. 44.
22 Ibid., Letter P43, 9 Feb. 1856, pp. 74–75.

pleased to name their firstborn after him. However, no one could have envisaged at the time that in his adult life this baby would become known as Bramwell Booth, and many male children born to Salvationists, would, in turn, be named after him.

The next day William Booth wrote to his parents-in-law to tell them the good news. The original of this letter has been lost and the transcripts of it vary in the biographies. Below is the Booth-Tucker version, with an added sentence in square brackets from Catherine Bramwell Booth's biography of her father.

> My Dear Mother and Father,
>
> It is with feelings of unutterable gratitude and joy that I have to inform you that at half-past eight last night my dearest Kate presented us with a healthy and beautiful son. The baby is a plump, round-faced, dark-complexioned, black-pated little fellow. A real beauty. The Lord has indeed been very good to us. [We wanted a *son*, and I wanted him to be like his mother.] Poor Kate has had a dreadful time, but the Lord in mercy has brought her safely through. Believe me as ever,
>
> Your very affectionate son,
>
> William Booth.[23]

About a week later, Catherine managed, 'By a little subtlety' to get 'hold of a bit of paper and a pencil' and wrote to her 'precious mother,' telling her

> I now know what it is to be a mother, and I feel as though I had never loved you half as well as I ought to have done. Forgive all my shortcomings and be assured I appreciate all your self-sacrifice on my behalf. My soul is full of gratitude to God for having brought me through! I am doing better than I could have expected considering how very ill I have been. My precious babe is a beauty and very good. Farewell until I can get hold of a pencil again.[24]

'Doctor' Catherine

Concerning general health matters, as was seen earlier, Catherine generally rejected orthodox medicine, and usually opted for alternative forms. She had already experienced galvanism, now she was favouring homoeopathy,

---

23 Booth-Tucker, *Catherine*, vol. 1, p. 171; Booth, *Bramwell Booth*, p. 7; 'CBLP', Letter WBM2, 9 Mar. 1856, p. 81.
24 'CBLP', Letter P49, mid-March 1856, p. 82.

famous for its 'infinitesimal doses,' and later it would be hydropathy. In September 1855 she told her parents, 'I have been reading a very good work on Homoeopathy which has removed my last difficulty on the subject, and If I should be ill, I should like a homoeopathic doctor.' Quite what Catherine's last difficulty was is unknown, but it appears that on an earlier encounter with a homoeopathic doctor, he asked some questions that she did not like, which may have been this problem. Now, she had come to believe that those questions were necessary, so she was ready to accept that form of treatment.[25]

Homoeopathy, then and now, tends to be controversial, but Catherine became a keen advocate of the discipline. She used homoeopathic medicines for herself and William, and later for their children. She recommended them to her parents, but they were sceptical about their benefits. At times she prescribed these remedies for some of her friends, and even on one remarkable occasion for a dog. Catherine claimed that the dog was 'cured … in about 24 hours.'[26]

William tended to rely on his wife's judgment in medical matters but took homoeopathy a little less seriously and a little less confidently than her. In one letter to Catherine in 1857 he said,

> If it does not get better, I shall go to the Homeopathic doctor. Chester is either blessed or cursed with three of them. But as you deem it a blessing, I am fain in this, as in many other respects, to pin my faith to your sleeve, and with me there the controversy ends! So I throw up my cap and shout, 'Hurrah for Homeopathy,' with its infinite quantity of infinitesimal doses, in whatever society I may be where the question is mooted. All because I have such a blessed little wife, in whose judgment I can confide on matters physical.[27]

After the birth of William Bramwell Booth, Catherine was unwell, and Sarah Mumford agreed to visit the Booths and help care for her daughter and the baby. Sarah probably arrived when they were still in Halifax and moved with them when they went to Macclesfield for another campaign, which the *MNCM* described as 'a series of special services unprecedented in the town'.[28] There was one interruption in the Macclesfield evangelistic

---

25 Ibid., Letter P13, 27 Sept. 1855, and P15, 9 Oct. 1855, pp. 28, 29.
26 Ibid., Letter P150, 28 Jan. 1859, p. 205.
27 Booth, *Letters*, Letter (WB123), late Jan. or Feb. 1857, p. 321; Booth, *Letters CD*, p. 319.
28 *MNCM*, 'Revival services, Macclesfield Circuit', 1856, p. 395.

services. William Booth held a special service to baptise about 30 children, including his son.[29]

The wider family

Catherine must have found having her 'dear mother' on hand a great blessing. But she continued 'very poorly,' and baby was at times 'very fretful.' At first Catherine breast-fed the baby, but she had some problems with that, so they acquired a wet nurse named Sarah.

Catherine did not write many letters to her father alone. She wrote many to both her parents and some to her mother, but, with her mother now on hand, she seems to have written several to him, though only one remains from this period. Catherine even wrote parts of these letters on behalf of her mother, reasoning that she could 'write much *quicker*' than the aging lady.

In the still existing letter, Catherine expressed great concern about her father's work situation and the Booths and Sarah Mumford held 'a very grave consultation' about his future, which was almost certainly initiated by Catherine. Indeed, it seems, they held more than one. It appears that they all inclined to him becoming an auctioneer. The Booths did not know whether William would continue the travelling ministry after the July 1856 Conference or be appointed to a circuit. Their idea was that if the Booths were sent into circuit work, the Mumfords could come and join them and live in the same house. Then John Mumford could become an auctioneer in that town. However, this scheme always seemed doomed by too many uncertainties. It was wrecked when the Conference agreed that Booth continue his travelling evangelism for the year 1856-57.

Catherine and William were also concerned about her father's spiritual condition. She told him,

> I do not know of anything in this world that would give [William] more pleasure than to see you brought to God and raised temporally. He gets increasingly anxious about you & so do I, and I do hope the time of your redemption draweth nigh. But why, my dearest Father, wait for a change in circumstances before giving yourself afresh to the Lord? True you have many difficulties, but non[e] that are insurmountable... Oh, take *this* step and the Lord will take care of the rest.[30]

29 Booth-Tucker, *Catherine*, vol. 1, p. 174.
30 'CBLP', Letter P50, 29 Apr. 1856, p. 84.

Great Yarmouth, then Sheffield again

William Booth, meanwhile, continued with his itinerant evangelistic work for the Methodist New Connexion, first to Great Yarmouth, a seaside resort on the eastern coast of England, just south of The Wash. They arrived on Saturday 19 June and had difficulty finding suitable accommodation. But, with the help of the local minister, they found 'comfortably furnished' apartments, looked after by a widow, 'within one minute's walk of the beach.' Catherine thought that Yarmouth exceeded 'Brighton in many respects, especially in the character of its beach', that is, sand versus pebbles, '& the *warmth* of its climate. I like it very much and hope it will do us all good.'[31] Yet, after a short while in residence, Catherine thought it a '*fashionable, wicked, godless* Town.'[32]

An unexpected difficulty arose on the day after their arrival. Sarah the wet nurse became ill. She was 'so bad in the ev'ng that Wm had to go & fetch a Doctor at 10 o'clock.' She had 'broke[n] out all over in great weals,' Catherine said.

> I never saw such a sight in my life, and towards night she began to complain of her throat & tongue swelling, which frightened us… However, the doctor soon allayed our fears by assuring us it was only a fit of indigestion & derangement of the stomach. He gave her a pill, etc., etc., and she is nearly well to day [Monday], for which we are truly thankful, I assure you.
>
> Wm & I had baby last night, as the Dr advised not to let him suck for 12 hours. Bless him! He was very good and took his bottle first rate. He gets fatter every day & more beautiful.

Despite that domestic difficulty, William began his campaign that Sunday, but 'to the poorest congregation he ever begun with,' the cause being '*dreadfully* low, almost dead.'[33] According to the denomination's magazine, the congregation had had financial problems for some years, which had damaged its progress. However, Booth's visit had been advertised well, and on that first Sunday night 'the congregation was treble its usual number.' In the five-week long campaign, 'upwards of one hundred had their names recorded as brought to God.' This was modest by the standards of some of

---

31 Ibid., Letter P51, 21 July 1856, p. 85.
32 Ibid., Letter P53, probably August 1856, p. 85.
33 Ibid., Letter P51, 21 July 1856, p. 85.

Booth's other campaigns, but, the writer thought, was satisfactory under the circumstances, though probably Booth did not think so. People from other Methodist denominations had joined them in the weeknight services and probably more than half the number of 'penitents' were associated with other churches.[34]

Late in August they moved on to the northern circuit of Sheffield. (Booth had earlier ministered in the southern circuit.) This proved much more fruitful than Yarmouth. A little more than a week into the campaign Catherine said, 'The work is rising gloriously, chapel full every night and packed on Sunday nights.' Yet William was 'tugging at it, full of anxiety and despondency. I never knew him more cast down than he has been of late.'[35] The *MNCM* confirmed that on some nights the chapel was so crowded that latecomers had to be turned away. In the first 17 days '225 persons ha[d] given in their names in token of decision for God,'[36] including, according to Catherine, 49 on one Sunday evening and 63 on the next.[37]

Their baby, meanwhile, was proving most playful, as was his father, despondent or not. Catherine told her parents, 'When his father first comes in sight he is fit to fly; they play all sorts of games, such as tossing, rolling, jumping, walking, etc., keeping me in a ferment all the time for fear of an accident.'[38] About a week later the little boy had teething trouble and was 'very cross.'[39]

Yet if William was despondent, he had his highs, and Catherine had her difficulties. For some reason Sheffield did not agree with her[40], perhaps because it was an industrial town, and she was not in the best of health, even by her standards. And in one letter she reflected,

> It is worth making sacrifices for to minister Bliss and salvation in Jesus's name. We are trying to lose sight of man & second causes and to do what we do more exclusively unto the Lord. I feel this is the only way to find satisfaction & peace in the prosecution of our mission. But I am not near such an apt scholar at it as my beloved. He can bear non-appreciation, etc., etc. much easier than I can. The simple reason is, he

---

34 *MNCM*, 'Revival at Yarmouth,' 1856, pp. 549–50.

35 'CBLP', Letter P57, possibly 7 Sept. 1856, p. 91.

36 *MNCM*, 'Sheffield North Circuit,' 1856, p. 549.

37 'CBLP', Letters P57, possibly 7 Sept. 1856, and P58, possibly 15 Sept. 1856, pp. 92–93.

38 Ibid., Letter P56, late August 1856, p. 91.

39 Ibid., Letter P57, possibly 7 Sept. 1856, p. 91.

40 Ibid., Letter P67, about 23–25 Oct. 1856, p. 101.

is in a much better state of soul, but I am trying to rise. May the Lord help me.[41]

It is worth noting the phrase 'the prosecution of *our* mission.' Though Catherine was not yet preaching she was still sharing in the efforts, troubles and trials of Christian mission, so it was their work, not just his, to win men and women into the Kingdom of God.

Another difficulty for Catherine was her on-going concern about William's health. His work was high-powered and exhausting. As she said in a letter describing one Sunday's activities,

> He preached hard this morn'g, and for an hour this afternoon never ceased talking, and I don't expect him home before ten or half-past. It astonishes every body how he holds out, and no one more than *me*. I live in perpetual fear of his breaking down. Sometimes I get quite distressed about it. But the Lord does strengthen him wonderfully. I must try & *trust* and not be afraid. *It is* a glorious work, without controversy. Let this comfort us in the sacrifices we are called to make for it.

But the results were worth it. That morning there had been

> a *splendid* congregation, a melting sermon, and a glorious *influence*. The people wept all over the place. We stayed near the chapel for dinner & went to the sacrament in the afternoon; one of the most precious services I ever attended, the bottom of the chapel quite full, and shouts of glory & Allalular, [sic] amidst tears & sobs from all parts of the chapel.[42]

The Sheffield mission closed with a Tea Meeting, as these campaigns usually did, at which 1200 sat for tea, and 2000 were present for the following meeting. Catherine described the gathering as 'a dense mass of heads and happy faces.' Catherine excitedly told her parents that after tea William 'spoke for near two hours, never for one moment loosing [sic] the most perfect control over the minds & hearts of the audience. I never saw a mass of people so swayed & carried out at the will of the speaker but once or twice in my life. The cheers were deafening & prolonged for several minutes.'[43] William Booth was clearly a gifted evangelist and Catherine Booth a proud wife.

Towards the end of October, after a week's rest, they moved to Birmingham in the Midlands. Her health improved there but, she told

---

41 Ibid., Letter P57, possibly 7 Sept. 1856, p. 92.
42 Ibid., Letter P60, possibly 28 Sept. 1856, p. 95.
43 Ibid., Letter P64, 11 Oct. 1856, p. 99.

her parents, William's mission 'drags on heavily.'[44] It was more like Great Yarmouth than Sheffield. Yet towards the end of the Birmingham campaign, Rev. B. Turnock said, 'about three hundred have found peace with God.'[45]

The Booths were invited back to Sheffield at the end of November, so that the grateful people could make a presentation of a portrait to William. Catherine reported to her parents, 'We arrived safe here at about half past three yesterday afternoon. I was not at all fit for the journey, having been ill from a severe cold & cough for several days. However, I managed it' travelling 'first class & laying down occasionally & being *sick* through the window.' Catherine was pregnant again. She continued,

> I did not attempt to go to the meeting for Tea but laid down & went in a cab just to hear the speaking. I sat on the Platform & I may say it was [the] proudest moment of my life. The meeting was a perfect triumph (as many as on the last occasion). The speaking very good, and the portrait the *best of all*. I like it much, altho' I do not think it flatters my beloved in the least. Indeed, it would not, be possible to transfer to paper that which constitutes his peculiar charm when speaking.[46]

This second pregnancy had her concerned. A month later she told her mother, 'I don't know what we are to do with another baby unless you can have it.' Did she mean that? Did she really expect her mother, whom she was always telling not to work too hard, to look after a baby for her? But she was 'cast down at the prospect' of another child so soon. 'One seems as much as ever we can do with, while I am so poorly.' Willie, now nine months old, 'gets such a rip[47], I cannot nurse him an hour without [k]nocking myself up.'[48]

---

44 Ibid., Letter P67, 23–25 Oct. 1856, p. 101.

45 *MNCM*, 'Revival at Birmingham,' 1856, p. 673.

46 'CBLP', Letter P72, 27 Nov. 1856, pp. 106–107. Catherine dated this letter 'Octb'r 27th', but this meeting took place at the end of November. The denomination's magazine confirms that the date of the presentation was 26 November, see 'Presentation to the Rev. W. Booth,' *MNCM*, 1857, pp. 102–103.

47 Catherine uses 'rip' on several occasions and in this context seems to mean 'a lively child.'

48 'CBLP', Letter P75, probably late December 1856, p. 110.

CHAPTER 14

North, South, East and West

Jesus said, 'A prophet is not without honour,
save in his own country'

(Mt 13:57, KJV).

Nottingham and London

Many people were likening William Booth to the prophets of old. In December he returned to Nottingham, 'his own country.' How would he be received?

Catherine excitedly reported to her parents that the people received him very well.

The work here exceeds any I have ever seen for the time. Yesterday the chapel, which is a very large one, was very full in the morn'g and at night hundreds went away unable to get in. I suppose it was so packed that all the windows & doors had to be set wide open. They took 67 names in the Prayer-meeting, amongst them some very important cases.

I went in the morn'g and to the sacrament in the afternoon. Two precious seasons they were. The movement is taking hold of the Town. The Preacher & his plans are the topicks [sic] of conversation in all directions. Numbers of Wm's old Wesleyan friends come, and the Infidels are mustering their forces. The Mayor & Mayoress, with a family of fine young men, are regular attendants and stayed the Prayer-meeting the other night a considerable time. The folks seem as if one of the old prophets had risen, or John the baptist come again, it is so different to their ordinary ro[u]tine. I never saw so respectable an audiance [sic] so rivited [sic] in their attention as on Sunday morn'g. The place seemed full of divine influence. How ready the Lord is to work when man will work too.[1]

---

1 Ibid., Letter P73, 15 Dec. 1856 p. 108.

The Mayor and Mayoress of Nottingham, mentioned in this letter, were John and Mary Bradley. They appear to have been related to some of the Booths' Sheffield friends. Sadly, one of the Bradleys' 'fine young men' was missing. He had died just over two weeks earlier.[2]

On family matters Catherine told the Mumfords that her husband was 'more [k]nocked up than usual.' However, Willie

is first rate. He gets a charming fellow. I often fear that we are getting too fond of him, but he is so intelligent & interesting that every body loves him at once. He will want firm dealing & then I hope he will make something, but he manifests a good deal of spirit even now. The other night I had a struggle with him, which lasted some half hour, but I conquered, and you would be surprised at the difference in him when I lay him down in his cot & when Sarah [the nurse] does. When she does, he jumps up again & sits straight up & screams if he does not want to lay down. When I lay him down and wrap him, he looks at me as knowingly, and turns his cheek to the pillow and begins singing. Bless him! I fear we shall have some little trouble with him… I intend him to *obey* from the heart. The Lord teach me the most excellent way.[3]

Then later she said, 'But he is a *good* child, and only wants good nursing– bless him! He gets so old-fashioned. I often wish you could hear him sing himself to sleep in his way; we put him to bed awake and then Sarah rocks him & sings to him & he often sings as loud as her.'[4]

That Christmas they played host to William's mother and two unmarried sisters, Emma and Mary.[5] Emma had recently been seriously ill, and at one stage was not expected to survive.[6]

Early in 1857 William, Catherine and Willie went to London to visit her parents. It was a rest for William and, no doubt, for Catherine too. On Sunday 11 January, William, though probably not Catherine, went to hear Charles Haddon Spurgeon, the great Baptist preacher. Spurgeon had begun his ministry at New Park Street Chapel three years earlier at the age of 19 and had quickly become a sensation, and at this time was preaching on Sunday mornings at the Surrey Gardens Musical Hall to thousands. Booth wrote in his diary that day, 'Heard Mr Spurgeon, and was much pleased

---

2 Crisp, *Visitation of England and Wales*, vol. 10, pp. 81–83.

3 'CBLP', Letter P73, 15 Dec. 1856, p. 108.

4 Ibid., Letter P75, probably late December 1856, pp. 110–11.

5 Ibid., Letters P74, mid-December 1856, and P76, 29 Dec. 1856, pp. 109, 112.

6 Ibid., Letter P62, 1 Oct. 1856, p. 98.

and profited—a truly simple, earnest, and faithful sermon. I doubt not he is doing a very great work.'[7] Two months later Catherine said, 'Spurgeon's popularity is astonishing. I *cannot* see much in his *sermons* to account for it.'[8] This suggests that she had read him but not heard him.

An important contact

Late in January, William went to Chester to conduct another campaign, and Catherine and Willie stayed with the Mumfords. The ministry in Chester progressed reasonably well, but trouble was stirred up by a newspaper, which accused Booth of bad behaviour and it attracted trouble-makers to the chapel, who disrupted some of the services.[9]

However, while there, William made a very significant contact, Reginald Radcliffe, a wealthy solicitor from Liverpool who was also a highly successful independent evangelist. He had heard about Booth and sought him out. Radcliffe offered to hire a theatre or other large hall in which Booth could minister, 'allowing the New Connexion to take the converts.' In other words, he does not seem to have suggested that Booth leave the New Connexion. But for such a venture to take place it would have needed the support of the New Connexion's Annual Committee, and Booth knew he was unlikely to get that. William told Catherine, 'I cannot at present entertain anything of this character.' As William and Catherine had both earlier been greatly influenced by the American independent evangelist James Caughey, they were sympathetic to that kind of ministry. In addition, Booth liked Radcliffe and was impressed by him[10], and any thoughts he may have had of becoming an independent evangelist must have now become stronger.

Radcliffe and Caughey were representatives of a growing host of independent evangelists, not all of whom aroused the sympathy of the Booths. William later said that he disliked some evangelists he met, for they seemed 'bragging and mechanical' in their 'revivalism.'[11] Yet William Booth and Catherine Mumford both greatly admired James Caughey, who seemed to be their ideal of what an evangelist should be. But they were

---

7 Booth-Tucker, *Catherine*, vol. 1, p. 188, quoting from Booth's Diary.

8 'CBLP', Letter P80, 17 Mar. 1857, p. 116.

9 Booth-Tucker, *Catherine*, vol. 1, pp. 188–89; 'Pepper Street Chapel,' *Chester Chronicle*, 14 Feb. 1857, p. 8, col. 3.

10 Booth, *Letters*, Letter (WB117), 13 Feb. 1857, p. 319; Booth, *Letters CD*, p. 317.

11 Ibid., Letter (WB150), possibly December 1864, p. 353; ibid., p. 349.

divided over another travelling preacher, Isaac Marsden. Marsden had had a major impact on the teenaged William Booth, and Booth remembered him fondly. But Catherine did not like Marsden. She regarded his preaching as 'exceeding injudicious and violent' and she did not 'believe that the gospel needs such roaring and foaming to be effective.'[12] A little later she gave a similar, but more general, criticism of preachers who seemed to think 'the salvation of the world depended on the amount of noise they make.'[13] She, at this stage, much preferred the measured tones and moderate methods of David Thomas. Later, in Christian Mission and Salvation Army days, she would have to adapt her thinking to be more in line with her husband's views, as some of the early preachers in those movements were rough and ready, more like Marsden than Thomas.

Bristol and Cornwall

After William's visit to Chester, the Booths were then reunited, and in March they went to Bristol in the south-west, where William conducted a brief and not too successful campaign. At the end of the first week, Catherine said, 'The work at the chapel goes on heavily, congregations but poor. Still, gradually increasing!' This campaign was causing William much anxiety[14], and it did not improve. Catherine later called it 'the worst we have had anywhere.' She described the New Connexion chapel as 'large & draughty, & *cold* enough to frighten the folks away.' In addition, while in most places other Methodist denominations supported the work, in Bristol the Wesleyan Reformers, at least, seem to have opposed it.[15]

By this time Sarah the nurse had left them, and they had employed a young lass named Eliza as a servant. Eliza seems to have been willing and caring, but inefficient. Catherine later described her as 'such a *muddler*, always doing & never done.'[16] The Booths by this time were able to afford one servant, often two, but these domestics were usually young and inexperienced girls, and, while cheaper than the more able servants, they at times caused Catherine much stress. She later called one 'a vile deceitful hussy', and complained that some of the servants they employed did not

---

12 Ibid., Letter CM 29, 20 Mar. 1853, p. 87; ibid., p. 90.
13 Ibid., Letter CM 68, possibly November 1853, p. 175; ibid., p. 176.
14 'CBLP', Letter P79, 13 Mar. 1857, p. 116.
15 Ibid., Letter P80, 17 Mar. 1857, p. 116.
16 Ibid., Letters P88, 31 May 1857, and P103, 28 Oct. or 4 Nov. 1857, pp. 124–25, 142.

'seem to have any moral sense developed, but just [said] what serve[d] their purpose at the moment without any regard to truth.'[17] Economies were also always necessary, particularly as Catherine found Bristol 'a very dear place, worse than London in most respects.'[18]

They did a little sightseeing while in Bristol. One Monday, early in their stay, they 'went up to Clifton downs … as far as the projected suspension bridge.' This famous bridge was designed by Isambard Kingdom Brunel. Work began on it in 1831, but its construction was hindered by various difficulties and it was not completed until 1864.[19] Catherine enthused about the scenery, which she found 'truly enchanting.' She thought Clifton was 'one of the most fashionable and aristocratic places' she had visited, and the buildings were 'very beautiful.' Indeed, she had never seen 'such terraces of fine houses any where, except round the London Parks.' She told the Mumfords that she intended 'to get on to the downs as often as possible, tho' it is too far & too steep a hill for me to climb on foot. I rode up in an omnibus and walked home, which I found quite enough at once.'[20] She was at this stage five-months pregnant.

They next moved further west to Cornwall, where the response was significantly different. Cornwall had a long history of vital Christian movements. John and Charles Wesley had both exercised highly successful ministries in that county in the eighteenth century, and at the end of that century there were more Methodists in Cornwall than there were in London, despite the former's much smaller population.[21] John Wesley frequently preached at Gwennap Pit in Cornwall in the 1770s and attracted enormous crowds. The Methodist movement in Cornwall had continued to grow in the nineteenth century, though it had also divided into numerous factions. Cornwall was a Methodist stronghold.

The Booths' first stop in that western county was Truro, where they arrived early in April. According to the Connexion's magazine, the congregations were good on the first few days, 'but little fruit was gathered.'[22]

---

17 Ibid., Letter P115, 8 Feb. 1858, pp. 157–58.

18 Ibid., Letter P79, 13 Mar. 1857, p. 115.

19 See 'Clifton Suspension Bridge,' https://visitbristol.co.uk/things-to-do/Clifton-suspension-bridge-p24661.

20 'CBLP', Letter P78, 9 Mar. 1857, p. 114.

21 *Minutes of the Methodist Conferences, 1765–98*, vol. 1, pp. 282, 303–304, 325, 354, 389, 424. (Add together the figures given for St Austle, Redruth and Penzance, and, later, Launceston for Cornwall.)

22 *MNCM*, 'Truro Circuit Revival Services,' 1857, p. 400.

But at the end of the first week there was a major breakthrough. William told the Mumfords,

> We had a very glorious stir last night–such a meeting for excitement and thrilling interest as I never before witnessed. The people had been restraining their feelings all the week. Many of them had been stifling their convictions. But it burst out last night, and they shouted and danced and wept and screamed and knocked themselves about, until I was fairly alarmed less serious consequences might ensue. However, through mercy all went off gloriously, twenty-seven persons professing to find salvation. Praise the Lord for ever! I am happy, but weary. I have had nine public services this week, have to attend a meeting to-night, and three more to-morrow.[23]

The mission in Truro also finished 'triumphantly,' nearly a month after it began, with the chapel so packed 'Crowds [were] unable to get in,' and they had 'above 30 cases' that night.[24]

It was then on to St Agnes, where they had a shorter, but still successful stay.

The 1857 Conference

There was one more port of call before the all-important Conference that was due to begin on 1 June. The Booths were aware that some leading figures were against Booth continuing his current travelling ministry and that they hoped to place him in a circuit. Catherine thought these men were motivated by jealousy, and perhaps some were, but others may have sincerely believed that Booth, who was still only 28, needed some circuit experience so that he could see the other side of Christian work. Roger Green is also probably right when he says that some of the ministerial opposition to Booth's evangelism was because of 'the whole revivalistic enterprise.'[25] Some probably viewed it as a bit of a circus.

The Booths had mixed feelings about circuit work. It was clear to anybody who had been taking any notice of William Booth's activities over the previous two years that he was a gifted evangelist, and the Booths strongly believed that that was what his ministry should be. But the continual travelling and packing and unpacking was tiring and disruptive,

23 'CBLP', Letter WBM3, 11 Apr. 1857, pp. 119–20.
24 Ibid., Letter P83, 8 May 1857, p. 120.
25 Green, *Catherine*, p. 82.

especially for Catherine.

Booth's last campaign before the Conference was in Stafford in the West Midlands. The Booths travelled to Stafford separately. William arrived first and was met by Rev. William Dunkerley, the local New Connexion minister, and together they began the search for apartments. Catherine later told her parents, they 'tra[i]psed miles ... before they could meet with any thing at all suitable. However, in their extremity the Lord guided them' to a lovely place, with 'large & lofty' rooms, including a 'sitting room [with] a large bow window,' which looked 'out on a garden & meddow [sic].'

Catherine, meanwhile, had difficulties with the journey. She told her parents,

We arrived safe here at about half past twelve last night, after one of the most harrassing [sic] & fatiguing journeys I ever experienced. In consequence of its being W[h]it Saturday there were great numbers travelling, and great confusion amongst the Trains. We had once to change Stations, & three or four times carriages, and having all the luggage to see to, you may imagine what it was. I felt ready to lay down on the road by [the time] we got to Wolverhampton, within 20 miles of the end of our journey. In this state of feeling, you can perhaps imagine how I felt when informed that we were to[o] late for the train to Stafford and must wait three hours & a half for the next.

I did not know what to do. However, I resolved to bear it as patiently as I could, so, first of all, dispatching a telegraphic message to Wm informing him of the cause of our non-appearance & telling him to meet us at the next train, we got a cup of Tea & some refreshment. I packed myself up with the rugs & lay down in one corner of the waiting room. Willie ran about the room like a little kitten untill [sic] 10 o'clock, then went to sleep, Eliza nursing him with great tenderness & self-forgetfulness, altho' very much [k]nocked up. And at a ¼ past 11 o'clock we set off for Stafford. We had not got two miles before we had to change carriages again, heaving all the luggage out in the dark.[26]

The Booths spent about two weeks in Stafford. According to Mr Dunkerley, Booth's labours there were 'crowned with abundant success ... believers were quickened, wanderers reclaimed, and sinners brought to God.' Then, mid-June, to Dunkerley's great disappointment, the mission was 'suddenly

---

26 'CBLP', Letter P88, 31 May 1857, pp. 124–25.

and unexpectedly terminated.'[27] The Conference had decided to remove Booth from the evangelistic work and send him to serve in a circuit, and there was nothing Dunkerley or Booth could do about it. Dunkerley, a 'much-loved and respected pastor,'[28] appears to have been more in sympathy with Booth's aims than most other New Connexion clergy.

27 *MNCM*, 'Stafford,' 1857, p. 401.

28 Ibid., 'Presentation to the Rev. W. Dunkerley,' 1858, p. 394.

CHAPTER 15

'Home' in Brighouse

'I felt quite at home on the *platform*, far more so
than I do in the *kitchen*!!'[1]

Catherine Booth

Brighouse

At the New Connexion Conference of 1857, it was decided, then, to remove William Booth from the travelling evangelistic ministry and place him in Brighouse in the Halifax South circuit in Yorkshire. The debate at the Conference on this was vigorous, but it went against Booth by 44 votes to 40.[2] However, according to that year's Minutes of Conference, it was decided that Booth, though appointed to Halifax South, would be free to 'visit two or three' other circuits during the year to minister as an evangelist, but the receiving circuit had to pay all expenses and supply a replacement for him[3], which did not encourage offers.

The Booths took the decision with mixed emotions. They both believed that William's ministry was, and should remain, as an itinerant evangelist, but travelling meant living in a succession of homes that were not their own, which presented many difficulties, especially for Catherine. That decision may also have hurt a little more as that Conference was held in Nottingham, Booth's hometown.

In the closing months of 1854 there had been a significant number of conversions in the New Connexion chapel in Brighouse, which led to a crowded chapel becoming too small for all those wishing to attend. So it was decided to enlarge it, which was done the following year. This increased the 'sittings' by almost 200. In addition, the circuit's officials purchased a cottage next door to the chapel, which was also enlarged, for the minister

---

1 'CBLP', Letter P108, 23 Dec. 1857, p. 150.
2 Ibid., Letter WBM4, possibly 8 June 1857, p. 126.
3 *MNCM*, 'Extracts from the Minutes… 1857,' 1857, p. 662, fn.

and his family.[4] On the surface, a posting to Brighouse may have seemed a good thing.

After arriving in Brighouse, Catherine gave a one-word address at the head of her first letter to her parents. That word was '*Home!*' underlined three times.

In that letter she expressed her mixed emotions concerning the change, saying,

> It is very nice to be in a home of one's own, and I think we shall be very happy & useful in the Circuit, tho' I shall never alter my opinion with reference to the spirit & motives that brought us here. Yet I do recognise the hand of God in it & am determined to reap the advantages it offers.[5]

Catherine's opinion of the New Connexion leadership had sharply declined.

William, meanwhile, was expecting that circuit ministry would be a rest, compared with the frenzied activity of evangelistic meetings. In that, he was to be disappointed. Circuit ministry had its own stresses and strains.[6]

For Catherine, being a circuit minister's wife was to prove a blessing in disguise, in that it led her into new areas of service. She had been very much in the background, while William conducted his frenetic campaigns. Now, as the wife of a circuit minister, she was to have more opportunities to serve and develop her talents.

The new baby

But service in the circuit would have to wait. Catherine was by this time at least eight months pregnant, and preparations needed to be quickly made for the arrival of the new baby. Eliza, the servant, was still with them and, at this stage, doing a satisfactory job. However, Catherine also employed 'a nice little lass to take care of Willie,' though she was to prove unsatisfactory. William's mother was also due to visit and stay for a while after the birth. In addition, William asked a doctor in Huddersfield to attend Catherine, though the medic seems to have been unwilling or unable to be present at the birth. However, he agreed to attend her afterwards. She told her mother 'on the whole I feel pretty well prepared. I shall, as my dear Mother says, be very thankful when it is safe over. It seems to be my only trouble just now.'[7]

---

4 Ibid., 'Brighouse Chapel,' 1856, p. 102.
5 'CBLP', Letter P92, 21 June 1857, p. 130.
6 Ibid., Letter WBM4, possibly 8 June 1857, p. 126.
7 Ibid., Letter P92, 21 June 1857, p. 130.

At the end of June, she told her 'precious Mother'

> I don't think I shall be long now. According to my *feelings*, I expect it
> every hour. I often feel very low about it, but I will hope *in God*, and
> when it safe over I will indeed praise him. I think I shall like Mrs B[ooth]
> to be with me. She is very kind and seems exceedingly anxious to do all
> in her power, but I cannot help often wishing for my own dear Mother.
> I know no one can feel like her. But it would be too much for you even
> if you were pretty well.[8]

Willie, meanwhile, was enjoying life. Catherine said,

> he is such a go-ahead that it is not safe to leave him a moment. He is
> up to all sorts of antics, climbing the stairs, pushing the chairs, rubbing
> the furniture, riding across the sofa pillows, getting up to the windows,
> dancing, etc., but amidst it all he gets more and more beautiful and
> interesting daily, everybody that sees him is charmed with him at once...

> My only fear is that they will spoil him while I am laid by. His grandma
> is of no use to him at all, she lets him do as he likes, and of course he
> shows off with the old lady in style, especially as she is the only one in
> the house he can master. It is quite amusing to see the difference in his
> manner to her, nevertheless she is getting very fond of him.[9]

The baby, a boy, was born, according to his birth certificate, on 7 July.[10]
Some sources say 28 July, but they must be incorrect. The Booths called him
Ballington, presumably after some of Catherine's ancestors.

A month or more after the birth, Catherine had recovered sufficiently to
write a colourful letter to her parents, telling them,

> I get as much support as I think needful, tho' my appetite is not very
> good, nor has not been since the end of the first week. I am dreadfully
> thirsty & as we get beautiful milk I drink a deal of it...

> I have still a great deal of milk. I began to wean the pup [Willie] the
> other day but am obliged to take to it again. Baby cannot take near all,
> tho' he is a famous sucker. He sleeps in a little bed by the side of ours.
> He is very good at night only he wants his titty often, generally three
> times, sometimes four, and when he has had a good fill out he goes to
> sleep. I never saw *anything* grow & thrive as he does in my life. I believe
> he is quite as big now as Willie was at two months, & he was only the

---

8 Ibid., Letter P93, 29 June 1857, p. 132.
9 Ibid., Letter P95, July 1857, p. 133.
10 Gordon Taylor has a copy of Ballington's birth certificate, which says 7 July.

skelleton [sic] of what he is now when he was born.[11]

But about five or six weeks later, Ballington had a bad attack of diarrhoea and, Catherine said, he was 'very ill indeed.' His appearance had altered dramatically 'in twenty-four hours' and he now looked 'like a little old man.' He seems to have been ill enough for Catherine to have feared for his life, though whether that was her anxious temperament getting the better of her or a realistic assessment we cannot know. Either way, the next day he had improved, 'tho' still very ill.'[12]

Catherine's extending ministries

Catherine first seemed to seriously consider public speaking soon after their arrival in Brighouse. She had taught children in a Sunday School in her days with the Reformers and was now again involved with a Sunday School class. She began leading a Methodist class of adults in Brighouse in the middle of October.[13] Each of these ministries required teaching skills and she seems to have met with success in both fields. But her timidity made the thought of standing up in front of adults and giving more direct teaching or even preaching a step too far.

The class she led was an already established one with 29 members, many of them elderly. She told her parents that she would have preferred a class of young people, but that was not to be. She accepted the situation philosophically, saying, 'It will be a beginning, and perhaps I shall gain confidence to undertake something more important in another circuit.' One must ask, what could be more important than leading a class of 29 people? Preaching?

That November she was asked to address the children at the local Band of Hope. The Band of Hope was a movement that aimed to steer children away from drinking alcohol. This was an issue dear to heart. Her father had been involved in temperance work before his decline into alcoholism, and as a child she had attended his meetings on the subject. She asked her father to send her some issues of the *Temperance Intelligencer*, which, apparently, he often read in earlier days, to give her some ideas.[14]

Early in December her thinking was clearly expanding. She wrote,

11 'CBLP', Letter P96, mid- or late August 1857, pp. 133–34.
12 Ibid., Letter P99, late September or early October 1857, p. 136.
13 Ibid., Letter P100, 9 or 10 Oct. 1857, p. 137.
14 Ibid., Letter P105, 22 or 29 Nov. 1857, pp. 145–46.

Thanks for your hints for the juveniles. I shall use some of them, but I want some *annecdotes* [sic]. Can't you get me some old publications? If I get on well and find that I really possess any ability for public speaking, I don't intend to *finish* with juveniles. I very *much desire to* earn some *money* some way, & I shall try this if I think there is any reason to hope for success. When we were in Cornwall, I went to hear a very popular female lecturer and felt much *encouraged* to try my hand, & Wm wants me to do. The lady I refer to is employed by the [Temperance] league, I believe, & I think gets 10/- per lecture. If I could do so, I could go with Wm evangelizing nicely. Now try & find me some old [*Temperance*] *Intelligence[r]s* etc., etc. at the book stalls. I only wish I begun years ago.

Then came the punch line: 'If I had been fortunate enough to have been brought up amongst the Primitives, I believe I should have been preaching now. You laugh! But I believe it.'

Preaching was now clearly on her agenda. To move her to the next step would not require a belief in the rights of women to preach, for she already had that; she would not even need a sense that she should be preaching. What she needed was the fortitude to stand up in front of a congregation and preach, but that would take time to develop.

But for now, she would give some temperance lectures. That would be a step in the right direction. In that letter she continued, 'The cares of a family and the bother of a house & *servants* now preclude any kind of labour that requires much study, but I don't think lecturing on Temperance would require much.'[15] She was probably right. She was already an authority on that subject.

Catherine was in action for the Band of Hope on Monday evening, 21 December, and two days later she excitedly told her parents that she 'got on far better than [she] expected.' Though she was addressing children, 'a few adults' also attached themselves to her audience, 'who seemed quite as much interested and pleased as the children.'

She added, 'I felt quite at home on the *platform*, far more so than I do in the *kitchen*!!'[16] Many women since have echoed that comment, but for Catherine it appears to have been a significant moment.

---

15 Ibid., Letter P106, 7 Dec. 1857, p. 147.
16 Ibid., Letter P108, 23 Dec. 1857, p. 150.

A meeting with Caughey

By February 1858 Ballington was seven months old and not yet baptised, which was strange for the son of a Methodist minister. The reason for this was that James Caughey, the American Methodist evangelist, was in England again, and the Booths hoped that he would conduct the ceremony. As has been seen, both William and Catherine had great admiration for Caughey.

Early that month the Booths went to Sheffield where Caughey was ministering, partly to hear and meet Caughey and partly to have him conduct the baptism. The day after they returned to Brighouse, Catherine excitedly told her parents,

> They had a very large meeting on Tuesday night. I suppose upwards of twelve hundred sat down to tea. We took tea with Mr Caughey at the same table, and Wm had some conversation with him. Then on Wednesday we dined with him where he is staying & enjoyed a rich treat in his society. He is a sweet fellow, one of the most gentle, loving, humble spirits you can conceive of. He treated us with great consideration & kindness, conversed with Wm on his present and future position like a *brother* and a friend, and prayed for us most fervently.

> On Thursday morn'g he called at Mr Wilkins' and baptised our boy...

She made her admiration for Caughey clear when she added, 'After almost adoring his very name for ten years past to be thus privileged was well-nigh to[o] much for me. I pressed one fervent kiss on his hand when he took leave of me & felt more gratified than if it had been Victoria's.'[17]

The Mumfords

It is difficult to establish with certainty the financial situation of John and Sarah Mumford, who were still living in London. The correspondence between the Booths and the Mumfords was almost entirely carried out by Catherine and Sarah, but it is, for the most part, Catherine's letters that have survived, which means that we only have one end of the conversation. The Mumfords always had a roof over their heads, for their address remained 7 Russell Street, Brixton, for years after Catherine had left the family home. But they did have financial problems, and John Mumford may have been out of work for a while or, more likely, had only part time work. They also,

---

17 Ibid., Letter P114, 5 Feb. 1858, p. 156.

as has been seen, took in lodgers, who were another source of income.

In these letters the Booths made suggestions about John making prams, one for the Booths and the rest for sale. John Mumford made at least two for the Booths (the first broke) and he seems to have made some to sell, though not many. As has been seen, there was also talk of John becoming an auctioneer, in this town or that town, but it came to nothing. Sarah Mumford also seems to have had a dream of running a shop selling 'Baby linen'. In one letter Catherine advised on that and said that William, in one of their richer moments, was prepared to put up the money for it. But that again did not materialise. By that time Sarah's dream seems to have faded.[18] There was also a frequent exchange between the two couples of 'we owe you' and 'you owe us', which gives the impression that the Mumfords were never poor, at least by Victorian standards. The Mumfords' financial and domestic situation was, however, an ongoing concern for the Booths.

Catherine was also continually concerned about her mother's health, which seems to have been fragile, like her daughter's. Catherine frequently told her mother not to do too much for the lodgers, but Sarah continued to wash and clean for them. Probably by her doing that the Mumfords received a little extra income.

In the middle of October 1857, Catherine wrote a letter to her parents, with suggestions for the family's future, some of which would come to pass, while other aspects would fade into nothingness. She said, 'Wm talks of us all having one home somewhere, and his being an Evangelist and me accompanying when able, & when unable staying at home with you & the children; & I expect it will come to that yet.' So, the idea was for the Booths and the Mumfords to live together, and for William to become an independent evangelist. Surely, they must have thought, what James Caughey and Reginald Radcliffe could do, William Booth could also do.

She continued,

> I am sure he will not continue a Circuit preacher, neither do I wish him. If you knew how every thing seems to go wrong with us in our present sphere, you would think, as we do, that the finger of God points in another direction. We, neither of us, are happy here. The people don't seem to take to us. The services don't succeed as we expected, and many things seems [sic] to indicate that Wm is out of his place. He has made up his mind to wait next Conference over & see what transpires & then

---

18 Ibid., Letter P226, 27 Feb. 1862, p. 304.

act accordingly, determined to do what he believes to be the will of God, even tho' he should have to risk every thing. Since this decission [sic] he has been much happier. 'No man hath forsaken houses or lands, husband or wife for my sake & the Gospel's, but he shall receive an hundredfold, even in this life and in that which is to come life everlasting.' We mean to prove the truth of this assertion if need be; the Lord help us.[19]

The Booths were now considering leaving the New Connexion and William becoming an independent evangelist. The mid-1858 Conference would be crucial. Would Booth be reappointed to Brighouse, sent to another circuit, or returned to his role as the denomination's travelling evangelist? A return to Brighouse would seem to be unacceptable for the Booths. Neither of them was happy there. Later Catherine said that she felt 'destitute of friends' while there and called it 'that hated Brighouse.'[20] The reasons why the people did not 'take to' them are unclear. Though the Booths did not seem to take to them either. It had clearly become a difficult situation. At this stage in their thinking, it sounds as though they might not even accept an appointment to another circuit. But Conference was still seven months away, so there was time to rethink.

In February, with nearly four months still to go to Conference, William seems to have met James Caughey again. The meeting was 'a blessing' to Booth. They discussed Booth's situation. Caughey 'was very cautious' but advised him to wait until he was ordained before making a decision. (Booth was still a minister on trial, so not yet ordained.) Caughey told Booth that he might eventually 'be compelled to "*cut loose.*"' If he did, Caughey said, 'there was plenty of room for him both' in Britain and 'in America', but, Catherine told her parents, she 'would not hear of *America*.' With all that in mind their thinking was for William to take another circuit for, perhaps, a year. They were still strongly against staying at Brighouse.[21]

Also that February Catherine wrote a letter to her parents, which must be seen as part of her developing social conscience, though what it does not say is striking. 'I think the time is fast coming when domestic servants will not ... be got at all,' she began. She was having trouble getting suitable servants at that time. She continued,

If you were to see the troops of young girls who turn out of these yorkshire factories & mills, with their blue smo[c]k pinafores, & red

---

19 Ibid., Letter P101, 26 Oct. 1857, p. 138.

20 Ibid., Letters P115, 8 Feb. 1858 and P128, 17 June 1858, pp. 157, 177.

21 Ibid., Letter P115, 8 Feb. 1858, p. 158.

handkerchiefs over their heads, and great wo[o]den-soled shoes on their feet, you would think so too. They begin to work as half-timers by [the time] they are seven or eight years old, and when they get to be pretty good hands can earn about eight or nine shillings per week. In a family of three or four girls, with perhaps a drunken father, this is a great temptation to the mother to let her girls go to the mill. Indeed, Parents seem to lose sight of the demoralising, unwomanising influence of the system altogether. I never met with such a 'pounds, shillings and pence' people in my life. They seem to loose [sic] sight of every thing – comfort, respectability, & every thing – for the 'brass,' as they call it. I know people, whom to look at & into their homes you would think as poor as rats, who are worth hundreds.

I was out for a little walk with Wm & a gentleman yesterday, when we met a troop of factory girls going to dinner. I observed that it augured discouragingly for the future of our Country, did this system of employing our young women in factories. What pityable [sic] wives & mothers they will make. Mothers! Alas! I should say bearers of children, for we have lamentable evidence that in everything desirable to the sacred relationship they are awfully deficient. I see no help for it but a *law* prohibiting young girls under twenty from working in factories before one o'clock at[22] noon. This would oblige them to attend to domestic matters in the fore noon, and in numbers of instances seek situations as household servants. What they would be able to earn not being sufficient to keep them. I wish some one would begin to agitate the subject in the news papers.[23]

While this can be seen as another aspect of Catherine's developing social ideas, at least with regard to women and girls, it is far from being ardent feminism. It is also noteworthy that she says nothing about schooling for children, which one would expect her to have done when she is talking about 'seven or eight years old' girls. This may reflect her mother's influence, though Catherine had earlier taught in a school. Compulsory schooling in Britain came about later through a sequence of Acts between 1870 and 1893.[24]

---

22 Presumably Catherine meant 'or' here.
23 'CBLP', Letter P116, mid-February. 1858, p. 160.
24 See https://www.bl.uk/collection-items/synopsis-of-the-forster-education-act-1870.

CHAPTER 16

Early Days at Gateshead

'Willie & Ballington get more trouble every day.
They almost weary me of life',

Catherine Booth to her parents.[1]

The Methodist New Connexion Conference of 1858 was held in Hull in Yorkshire and began on 24 May. Booth was ordained at this Conference and was appointed to minister at Gateshead, a fast-growing town in the north-east of England (an area now known as Tyne and Wear), where he was accompanied by an old friend, Andrew Lynn Jnr.[2] The Booths seem initially to have accepted the decision with resignation, though Catherine was disappointed that it was even further from London and the Mumfords than was Brighouse.[3]

The welcome

The people welcomed them gladly. In one letter soon after they arrived, she told the Mumfords, 'You could not conceive of a more marked contrast than that between our reception here & at Brighouse. In fact, it is all we can desire, and the leading men say & think that they have got the best appointment [i.e. William Booth] in the Connexion.' She added, 'The people here seem unanimous in their satisfaction & cordiality... They seem so intelligent & warm-hearted.'[4] Booth-Tucker described the move from Brighouse to Gateshead as 'like a transfer from the North Pole to the Equator.'[5]

---

1 'CBLP', Letter P135, 31 Aug. or 7 Sept. 1858, p. 186.

2 *MNCM*, 'Extracts from the Minutes … 1858,' 1858, pp. 666, 669.

3 'CBLP', Letter P126, 9 June 1858, p. 172.

4 Ibid., Letter P127, 15 June 1858, p. 175.

5 Booth-Tucker, *Catherine*, vol. 1, p. 224.

However, the house they were expected to live in was in a poor condition. It had little furniture and needed 'painting & cleaning from top to bottom.' Fortunately, the circuit stewards, the men responsible for such matters, were cooperative and quickly made some improvements, even though the circuit was in debt.[6] The Booths also bought some furniture at their own expense, the cost of which was offset by the fact that Mr Lynn was going to lodge with them and pay them rent.[7]

That welcome and acceptance by the people provided a firm foundation for what was to be a dynamic ministry. Preachers work best when their congregations work with them. The people work best when their leader can inspire them with earnestness and example. It also meant that their stay in Gateshead was likely to be of longer than a year's duration. It eventually lasted for three years, and, while important in its own right, it also proved to be a vital stepping-stone to the Booths' independent ministry and, eventually, The Salvation Army. Lessons learned in Gateshead were to bear fruit later, especially for Catherine.

Their New Connexion circuit was made up of several chapels in the Gateshead area, the main one being Bethesda, which seated more than a thousand, where Booth preached most frequently.[8] The circuit had hit difficult times and when the Booths arrived the congregation at Bethesda was small. However, under Booth's fiery and energetic preaching, the size of the main congregation increased quickly and considerably. One of William's early ventures was to hold a 'camp meeting' (really an extended outdoor service) on the nearby Windmill Hills.[9]

The growing family

Catherine, meanwhile, had her own difficulties. She had 'jumped into the cares & responsibilities of a large house and family all at once,' and she found that 'almost too much for' her. She was now the mistress of a 'family' of seven people; that is her, William, the two children, two servants and Andrew Lynn, 'and all want *cooking* for, etc.' It is striking that Catherine included the servants and Andrew Lynn in the 'family'. Fortunately, in those

---

6 'CBLP', Letter P127, 15 June 1858, p. 175.

7 Ibid., Letter P128, 17 June 1858, p. 176.

8 Ibid., Letters P128, 17 June 1858, and P152, 7 Feb. 1859, pp. 177, 206.

9 Hattersley, *Blood*, p. 100, quoting the *Gateshead Observer*, July 1858.

first few weeks in Gateshead her health was surprisingly good, considering all the organising and cleaning she had had to do. But there was one health issue that did cause her concern. She was pregnant again, about seven months. 'I do hope,' she said,

> that I shall get over my confinement better next time. I often feel ready to despair when I think of it and what has to follow it. If I could only hope to suckle my baby and be as well as I am now, I should indeed be thankful. But I dare not hope for it, and to give it the bottle will be very troublesome all the winter at nights. I don't feel any fear of it not *living*. It bids fair to be another rip[p]ing lad, I think.[10]

In that she was wrong. It proved to be a 'ripping gal'.

One Sunday morning in August she went to the chapel, 'but was obliged to go out directly the sermon was over.' It was only 'with difficulty' that she arrived home. At this stage she found 'it all but impossible to sit still for long together' and felt 'so restless & oppressed' that she decided that she would not go again until after the birth.

She engaged a doctor to be present at the confinement and a nurse to look after her afterwards. The doctor was 'a nice old gentleman, a quaker' who had a reputation 'for being very kind & gentle in such cases.' The only downside was he was 'one of the old School', not a homoeopathic doctor.[11]

But her family troubles were not only with the baby to come. 'Willie is not very well', she told her mother. 'He has scratched his heel, just at the back of his instep & it seems to be festering and getting very much inflamed & painful. I have applied poultice & hope it will soon be better.' At around this time, Willie, who was now getting on 'famously with his talking', looked at grandmother Mumford's portrait on the wall, remembered her from a previous visit, and said, 'Mamma, *come here*. Pilloo *ninnin*.' 'Pilloo' was his name for himself, 'Mamma' was grandma, and 'ninnin' was dinner, which he now wanted. Catherine thought that at this time he was becoming 'more of a mother's boy' and Ballington, who was now walking, was even more so.[12]

On a day in which she was 'both busy and poorly', she expressed her exasperation that 'There seems so many things that must be done before' the birth, but a lack of time, strength and help to do them. She was frustrated with her new servant, who did not manage the children well, and to whom

---

10 'CBLP', Letter P130, 11 July 1858, p. 179.
11 Ibid., Letter P133, 8 or 15 Aug. 1858, pp. 183–84.
12 Ibid., Letter P133, 8 or 15 Aug. 1858, p. 185.

Willie took a great dislike. Catherine admired the 'beautiful scenery' surrounding them but lamented the fact that she had only been able to go for 'two or three walks' because she was so busy. Thus, she was having to 'give up some of [her] darling notions about out of door exercise[13], a lament many mothers since have echoed. William, meanwhile, was busy and *very* poorly'.

About a week later she sounded even more desperate. She told her parents,

> I seem to get more & more unfit to struggle with the children. My nerves have been too much shattered in days gon[e] by to be capable of enduring much now, & really Willie & Ballington get more trouble every day. They almost weary me of life. It is next to an impossibility to keep Willie in the nursery & he is in all sorts of mischief the moment he gets out. He is so well & full of spirit there is no keeping him within bounds, & so masterful & determined that the girls can do nothing with him. I am obliged to be very severe with him myself, or he would soon be my master, and you know how it puts me about. I often wonder what I am to do with him. I feel so unfit to struggle with him. I believe he would be much better alone and more under my own care, but you know how nervous & impatient I am. I feel sometimes ready to lie down & die with dissatisfaction with myself. I fear I am not doing my duty to him as I ought.
>
> I don't know what I shall do when there is another...[14]

About two weeks later, on 18 September, the other was born. They called her Catherine.

William told the Mumfords, 'Baby is a little beauty, a perfect gem, healthy and quiet and is altogether all the fondest grandfather or grandmother could desire. I am sure you ought to send us a vote of thanks, passed unanimously, for conferring such an honour upon you.'[15] The original of this letter is lost, and this brief extract comes from Booth-Tucker. But, one suspects, that William must have said more than that, if only adding the baby's sex and name. A week or so later Catherine gave her parents a fuller description,

> I suppose you will think me like all mothers when I say she is a little *beauty*, tho' I don't think I ever said so of Ballington, because I did not think so. He was a much larger child but not near so pretty a baby, nor

---

13 Ibid., Letter P134, possibly 23 or 30 Aug. 1858, p. 185.

14 Ibid., Letter P135, possibly 31 Aug. or 7 Sept. 1858, pp. 186–87.

15 Ibid., Letter WBM6, September 1858, p. 190.

so fat, that is, when he was born. *Now* I consider him a fine, beautiful boy. Baby is more like Willie. Her hair is exactly the colour of mine & her eyes just the colour Willie's were. She has a nice nose & mouth, a fine forehead, & a plump round face.[16]

About two months later she reported to her parents the delights and trials of having three young children:

I am thankful to say I continue better, and if I were not so tired every day, I should enjoy life better than I generally do, but it is such a struggle with the children. They keep me going from morn'g till night, & then I cannot do as I would like for them. But they are three beauties, and I believe will grow up to be good & obedient. Baby is a real duck. I do wish you could see her. And such a *good* little creature. I often tell her that her grandma would almost worry her. She is the picture of health & happiness, and but for the wind sometimes I don't think she would cry once a week. Willie gets on famously with his talking. He can say almost any thing now. He prays every night for his grandma & grandpa. I wish it was practicable & consistent with your comfort & his welfare for him to come & stop with you a few months, but it cannot be.[17]

Thoughts of having one or more of the children live with the Mumfords for a while were to reoccur.

Catherine, like most mothers, wanted to dress her children in pretty clothes, something that was encouraged by her mother. But there was a problem, which she explained to Sarah Mumford,

You see, my dear mother, William speaks so plainly on the subject of dress, that it would be the most glaring inconsistency if I were to deck out my children as the worldlings do. And, besides, I find it would be dangerous for their own sakes. The seed of vanity is too deeply sown in the young heart for me to dare to cultivate it. I confess it requires some self-denial to abstain from making them as beautiful as they might be made to look. But oh! if God should take them from me, I should never regret it, and if He spares them, I trust that He will grant them the more of that inward adorning which is in His sight of great price.[18]

That said, Catherine, understandably, spent much of her letters talking about clothing material and clothes for the children, to be purchased or

---

16 Ibid., Letter P139, probably 25, 26, or 27, Sept. 1858, p. 191.
17 Ibid., Letter P146, 21, 28 Nov. or 5 Dec. 1858, p. 199.
18 Ibid., Letter P158, probably mid-April 1859, p. 214.

made either by her, her mother or by acquaintances. With the ever-growing family it was an ever-growing issue.

Catherine took on a Methodist class in Gateshead, as she had in Brighouse. However, the baby, other family duties and tiredness meant that she had to neglect her class on some occasions.[19]

That November or early December the church was preparing to hold a bazaar to raise funds for the church, and she, like all minister's wives, was expected to help. 'I am down to one of the stalls,' she told her mother, 'but am not able to do anything. I can *only beg*, & even in this department have not got much. I wish I was able to do something myself, but alas I cannot get my children's & husband's clothes mended, so I shall not attempt it.'[20] The bazaar proved successful in financial terms, raising £225, but neither Catherine nor William were happy with the 'dissipating, *godless* affair.'[21]

The accident

About four or five months into their ministry in Gateshead, Catherine had an accident, which could have been disastrous. 'I have not been out to day in consequence of feeling stiff & poorly from the effects of an accident, which befell me on friday evening,' she told her parents. '[W]hen I have described [it] to you I have no doubt you will join me in praising God that I am no worse.' William had been holding some evangelistic services in Sheriff Hill, about three kilometres from their home, and Catherine and the children went to the closing meeting, travelling in 'a very nice conveyance,' pulled by a pony. All went well on the journey there and they 'enjoyed the meeting.'

At about 6.30, they prepared to go home, but learned that the vehicle that brought them was no longer available, and instead they were to return in a gig, a smaller conveyance. So, Catherine sent Louisa, the children's nurse, home with the baby, accompanied by a young woman (it would have been dark by then), and prepared the boys for the ride home. Catherine's story continues:

> William stayed out of the meeting to pack us off all right. Young Scott was driving, Willie sat in the middle, and I with Ballington on my knee, all muffled and cloaked up, next to him. The moment we were all in I felt we were too light on the horse's back but did not say anything for fear

19 Ibid., Letter P128, 17 June 1858; Letter P141, possibly 8 Oct. 1858, pp. 177, 193.
20 Ibid., Letter P144, 5, 12 or 19 Nov. 1858, p. 196.
21 Ibid., Letter P146, 21, 28 Nov. or 5 Dec. 1858, p. 199.

of being thought ridiculous. We had not gon[e] many yards, however, before I felt sure we were not safe & said to young Scott, 'Oh, dear. I feel as though we were slipping backwards.' I had hardly got the words out of my mouth when the poney [sic], frightened by the riseing [sic] of the shafts, set off, and we were all thrown out backwards.

I fell flat on the back of my head, with Ballington on the top of me. I don't know how Willie fell, but, wonderful to say, they were neither of them hurt. Wm & all Mr Scott's family still stood watching us when it happened, and of course *flew* to our assistance, screaming as they came. Indeed, all the village was up in arms. The horse went off with the gig at full gallop & did not stop until he fell flat down & broke both shafts.

Wm took me in his arms and ran with me nearly all the way back. One and another took the children, and we all received the greatest care and kindness from the family, who were very much distressed indeed. I was very much shaken, and nearly all the sense [k]nocked out of me, but I trust nothing more. My back is the worse, but I think it is only sprained. I have had it well rubbed with Laudinum [sic] & laid in bed till dinner yesterday & to day, & I feel better this evening. Is it not a mercy that I am able to right [sic] to you? It seems wonderful to me that I have escaped so well, considering that I was rendered so helpless with the child on my knee & all muffled round so with wrap[p]ing. It was a terrible crash, such as I would not like over again, but, bless the Lord, we are all alive & the children are not a *bit worse*. What a mercy I had sent the baby home, was it not?

No one can account for the accident, but *I* think the harnessing was wrong. I am sure the horse was not to blame. It is a sweet thing & never did such a thing before, but the rising of the shafts frightened it… Another mercy connected with it is that we had *just* got over some very large and sharp stones, recently laid down, & had got onto an even road. If it had happened on the stones, I think my head would have been laid open.[22]

It was, indeed, a mercy, in fact, more than one.

A domestic disturbance

The problems with the servants were ongoing, especially with Louisa, whom Willie called 'Weedy.' Early in the new year, Catherine told her parents,

One little incident which occurred before Louisa left, I have wanted to

---

22 Ibid., Letter P145, 14, 21 or 28 Nov. 1858, pp. 197–98.

tell you ever since, but have never had time… One day Willie was crying very bitterly in the nursery and I thought it sounded as if Louisa was shaking him, & knowing she was in a bad temper I felt very much vexed & did what I seldom do, spoke very angrily to her. I called out up the kitchen stairs, 'If you shake him, I will shake you.' She denied it & it passed over without further notice, but in about half an hour afterwards, Willie came down into the kitchen, and with the air of a little lord and a look of *indescribable* dignity & injured innocence he said, 'If Weedy *shake Pilloo, Pilloo shake Weedy.*' I could not help smiling to myself at the majesty he assumed. Nevertheless, I felt sorry I had carelessly taught him a lesson of revenge & saw more than ever the necessity of watchfulness.[23]

---

23 Ibid., Letter P148, 3 Jan. 1859, p. 202.

CHAPTER 17

Revival at Gateshead

'Not only have our own people been revived and quickened and brought into the most delightful union of heart and effort in this work, but many, very many stout-hearted sinners have been broken down and with weeping eyes have cried for mercy',

John Firbank.[1]

Revival in America and Ireland

A dramatic event lies behind the Booths' ministry in Gateshead, which needs to be explored briefly. A remarkable revival took place in the USA in the years 1856–57, which then jumped the Atlantic, exploded in Ulster and to a lesser extent in Scotland and Wales in the years immediately following.[2] (Here it needs to be understood that the term 'revival' is being used in the sense of a significant and powerful outpouring of the Spirit of God, which led to many conversions. It is not being used in the sense of an evangelistic mission.) However, it has been argued by John Kent that 'the much desired major English revival of 1859–60 did not take place.'[3]

There is some support for Kent's view in reports in the press at that time. In October 1859, the editor of the *Carlisle Journal*, a northern newspaper thought that 'The efforts ... to spread the [Irish revival] epidemic in England and Scotland appear to have totally failed.'[4] Also that October, in a similar vein, the *Sheffield Independent* said, 'There are at present few signs that the revival excitement has made any progress in England. In Newcastle it is confined to Methodists, among whom it has been imported from

---

1 Firbank, 'Revival in Gateshead', *MNCM*, 1859, p. 224.
2 The literature on these revivals is voluminous, but see (USA) Long, *The Revival of 1857–58: Interpreting an American Religious Awakening*; (Ulster) Gibson, *The Year of Grace: A History of the Ulster Revival in 1859*; (Scotland) Jeffrey, *When the Lord Walked the Land: The 1858–62 Revival in the North East of Scotland*; (Wales) Evans, *Revival Comes to Wales*.
3 Kent, *Holding the Fort: Studies in Victorian Revivalism*, p. 32, see also p. 71.
4 *Carlisle Journal*, 'The Irish Revivals', 7 Oct. 1859, p. 5.

America'[5], which was presumably a reference to Phoebe and Walter Palmer.

Yet on the last day of 1859 another northern newspaper, the *Rochdale Observer* in its 'Review of the Year', said, 'In religious matters the most important feature of the year has been the revival of religion in Ireland, and, to a smaller extent, in our own country.'[6] In other words, the editor of that English newspaper was aware that there had been a movement of the Spirit in England, but it was nothing like as powerful as the one in Ireland. And that is how it seems to have been.

Catherine Booth, who ministered in those years, also later agreed. She said in an address recorded in the *War Cry* on 23 December 1880, 'I shall never forget how my heart ached when the wave of revival was sweeping over America and Ireland a few years ago. We had united prayer-meetings all over this land to pray for it, and it did not come.'[7] While the revivals being considered were 20 years before she said that, which might be seen to stretch Catherine's 'few years', there can be little doubt that her comments refer to the late 1850s and early 1860s.

In other words, the evidence seems to indicate that while there were authentic and powerful revivals in Ulster, Scotland and Wales, there had been no major revival in England at that time. However, while powerful movements did occur in a few parts of England in that period, Catherine Booth's comment needs to be understood as from one who was hoping for a nation-wide movement rather than a local one, for one of those favoured areas was Gateshead, when they were there. Certainly, the Booths' three years in Gateshead during this period saw much successful ministry, in which many were converted, and it is tempting to consider it a genuine revival. If that is so, why the revival occurred there but not in most other parts of the country is not clear, though it could be that it was situated just south of Scotland and it caught the breeze from there, or perhaps it may have been because that town had a man on the spot to capitalise on a movement of the Spirit of God. That man was William Booth. The ministry of William and, later, Catherine Booth in Gateshead (1858–61) needs to be seen against that background.

---

5 *Sheffield and Rotherham Independent*, 'Metropolitan Gossip', 1 Oct. 1859, p. 7.

6 *Rochdale Observer*, 'Review of the Year', 31 Dec. 1859, p. 2.

7 Booth, 'Some Objections to the Salvation Army Answered', *The War Cry*, 23 Dec. 1880, p. 2, col. 1.

The Gateshead 'Revival'

This is not the place to give a full account of the Gateshead revival, if such it was, as William Booth was used in that more than Catherine. However, it is impossible to ignore, as she was not only on the spot at that time, it is also where and when she first began preaching.

A lengthy account of 'The Great American Revival' appeared in the New Connexion Magazine in 1858, so the Booths and their people would have been well aware of it.[8] It is also likely that they would have heard of encouraging events in Ulster and Scotland in 1859.

The Gateshead circuit, as has been seen, was at a low ebb when the Booths arrived. However, under Booth's fiery and energetic preaching, the size of the main congregation increased quickly and considerably. Booth moved into top gear early in 1859. For at least five weeks he held two services on Sunday at Bethesda and four evening meetings during the week.[9] Leaflets were printed to advertise the meetings and Catherine helped to distribute them. She said in one letter dated 1 February,

> I have undertaken a district in which to distribute bills like the enclosed, which are to be carried by members of Society to every house in Gateshead, & verbal invitations given where practicable. My district contains about a hundred & fifty houses. On Thursday there is a public prayer-meeting at the chapel commencing at 7 o'clock in the morn'g, to be continued till 10 at night. Of course, we shall not stay *all* day, but it will suit everybodies [sic] convenience. You will see by this we have plenty of work on hand of one sort or another.

After finishing that letter, she hurried off to the prayer meeting.[10] There were 400 people present at some Sunday afternoon prayer-meetings.[11]

When Catherine had visited her 150 houses, she helped some of the other visitors with theirs, and seems to have finally visited over 300. That was a remarkable effort for a woman who was nearly always 'poorly' and with 3 children to care for, and it was seemingly a new ministry for her. But more was to come.

The meetings began with a bang on 6 February. On the first night the 'Chapel *well filled* ... such a sight as they have not seen since Wm was here

8 Cartledge, 'The Great American Revival', *MNCM*, 1858, pp. 295–318.
9 Firbank, 'Revival in Gateshead', *MNCM*, 1859, p. 224.
10 'CBLP', Letter P151, 1 Feb. 1859, pp. 205–206.
11 Firbank, 'Revival...', *MNCM*, 1859, p. 224.

three years ago,' Catherine told her parents, 'a capatol [sic] prayer-meeting & *five cases*, bless the Lord. I trust we are going to have a glorious work.' The next evening Catherine said,

> I understand there is a good congregation to night. I am too tired to go. I must pray for them at home, & besides, Wm will make me work so when I am there, & I don't feel equal to it. Last night week he called on me to pray at the close of the sermon before a crowded chapel at mount pleasant. I carn't [sic] stand that, tho' many have spoken of it as a good season & I believe it was.

Clearly William was encouraging his wife to engage in public ministry, but Catherine's timidity again was standing in the way. 'If I only had more grace, I could do any thing', she added, and then ruefully, 'But what avails superior light, without superior love. Oh, for an indwelling Christ.'[12]

During this campaign Bethesda was frequently packed, with sometimes, it is claimed, as many as 2,000 squeezed into the chapel.[13] John Firbank, a leading layman in the circuit, said, 'Not only have our own people been revived and quickened and brought into the most delightful union of heart and effort in this work, but many, very many stout-hearted sinners have been broken down and with weeping eyes have cried for mercy.' Firbank estimated that there had been about 200 conversions in that campaign up until mid-March.[14] These 'conversions', at least most of them, appear to have been genuine. Catherine thought, 'We never were in any work where the cases were of so good a character & so satisfactory. Nearly all are adults, & many intelligent, educated, & respectable.'

The campaign continued. Later in March Catherine said, 'The congregations keep up *amazingly*. In fact, they keep improving. Vast numbers of strangers come every night, so that the material does not fail. I think to night [William] preaches his 36th sermon since the services began.' That means that Booth had preached about 36 sermons in seemingly the same chapel in six or seven weeks. That was an astonishing and demanding schedule, especially when one considers that each of those sermons would have had to undergo at least some fresh preparation.[15] Catherine was greatly

---

12 'CBLP', Letter P152, 7 Feb. 1859, p. 206.
13 Williamson, 'William Booth and Revival on Tyneside.'
14 Firbank, 'Revival...', *MNCM*, 1859, p. 224.
15 These special services began on Sunday 6 February, see Firbank, 'Revival...', *MNCM*, 1859, p. 224.

concerned and no wonder. She thought that was 'a task ... probably never undertaken before by a *resident* minister under such circumstances... The people want him to go on & go on, but I tell them they are unmerciful in their requirements. I know such labour must tell in time. I fully believe he is shortening his days.'[16]

It was probably on the first Sunday in April that the congregations at Bethesda were 'the best' Booth had had, with '21 cases' at the evening service. Inevitably, by that time, William was 'very poorly, completely done up.'[17]

Late in April, Catherine, though unwell, 'ventured to the "public recognition service"', in which

> persons brought to God in the last connexional year were admitted *by ticket* into the body of the chapel, & *they only*, while the old members and the public occupied the gal[l]ery. It would have done your soul good to have seen the bottom of that large chapel almost *full* of new converts, most of them people in middle life, & a great proportion *men*. Wm gave them an address composed of various counsels respecting their future course, which if they adopt, they will *do* something for this poor world of ours.[18]

It is not surprising that Bethesda Chapel became known as 'the Converting Shop.'

One new feature Booth introduced was to precede the evening service with a parade. The procession marched to the chapel, its members singing as they went. Several times they would stop, and someone would give a brief gospel message and invite the listeners to the service.[19]

A week later they held a tea meeting, which commonly marked the closure of a campaign. Unfortunately, 'it was a dreadful day for *wind* & rain', which made it impossible for those from more distant parts to attend. But despite that there were still between 500 and 600 present. Catherine proudly told her parents that William 'spoke nearly an hour & a half to the evident satisfaction & delight of the audience. In fact, he was obliged to check the cheering all the way through. But when he had done, my word, they gave vent & made the chapel ring again for several minutes.'[20]

The membership of the whole Gateshead circuit when the Booths

---

16 'CBLP', Letter P155, 20 or 27 Mar. 1859, pp. 211–12.
17 Ibid., Letter P156, possibly 4 Apr. 1859, p. 212.
18 Ibid., Letter P159, 24 Apr. 1859, pp. 214–15.
19 Booth-Tucker, *Catherine*, vol. 1, pp. 224–25, 229.
20 'CBLP', Letter 160, 26 Apr. 1859, p. 216.

arrived in the middle of 1858 was 270. A year later, after the just detailed campaign, it was 407, with an additional 129 on probation[21], a significant rise in 12 months. Total attendances at the 11 chapels scattered around the area at any one time would have been much higher than the membership figures. Bethesda's membership alone increased from 92 to 224 in eighteen months, from mid-1858 to January 1860.[22] The New Connexion's magazine did not give membership figures for 1860 and 1861, but the later volume records that in Gateshead there had been 'considerable accessions and some remarkable conversions' during the 1860–61 year.[23] And Catherine had been preaching during that later period.

But the Booths were never satisfied with circuit work. As early as the end of March 1859, while the evangelistic campaign in Gateshead was continuing, Catherine told her parents,

> I have fully & formally consented to let William go as an Evangelist on condition of his working a district & coming home once a week, and he now thinks of writing to the annual committee & making certain proposals to them, & asking their advice how to proceed next Conference. If they decline to employ him as before, he will ask to be allowed to retain his standing amongst them & left at liberty to accept invitations whereever [sic] they may offer, & get his salery [sic] as he can. If they refuse this (which he thinks they will not), he will then most likely cut loose altogether.[24]

In other words, the plan was to suggest to the Annual Committee that Booth return to his work as the denomination's fulltime evangelist. If it or the Conference declined, he would then ask to be allowed to keep his standing as a New Connexion minister, but to accept invitations from any denomination. If that was not accepted, he would probably sever his link with the New Connexion and go out as an independent evangelist and trust the Lord for income. And Catherine had 'fully & formally consented' to that. One suspects that she thought that any of those alternatives would be easier for her husband than preaching 36 sermons in less than two months. However, it does not seem that William wrote to the Annual Committee about it, at least, not at that time.

---

21 *MNCM*, 1858, p. 671; *MNCM*, 1859, p. 688. The 1858 record did not give probationers.
22 Walker, *Pulling*, pp. 22 & 253, n.73; she is quoting from the 'Gateshead Society Members' Class Register', which one would expect to be accurate.
23 *MNCM*, 1861, pp. 155–56.
24 'CBLP', Letter P155, 20 or 27 Mar. 1859, p. 211.

More trouble with the servants

In the first half of 1859 Catherine was having servant trouble again. She told her mother, 'The lass I have got as nurse' for the children 'has turned out good for *nothing*. She came a month on trial fortunately, so I sack her on Wednesday, when I intend to do *without* one, while my present servant stops. For if I have a dozen, she will ruin them.' Catherine had a strong suspicion that the girl was stealing 'bacon, Tea, [and] Sugar' from the household supply, so Catherine kept a closer watch on her. This 'annoyed' the girl, and 'made her very disagreeable, & she has managed to bring the others over to her side.'[25]

Sometime later she wrote,

I am still without a nurse and intend to be as long as I can do at all. I have more to do but I am a deal happier in mind. I have not half as much to try me as I had with two of them. I keep the servant [named Ann] untill [sic] May... I told her that when the nurse left that I intended to try to do without one & offered her £10 wages if she would help me with the extra work. She seemed pleased and said she would try, and she has done *well* so far as the work is concerned. She is as *strong* as a poney [sic] & a good manager. She gets up by half past 5 in a morn'g & gets half her work done before the children gets [sic] up. I put part of the washing out & on the whole I am far more comfortable than with two eternally gossiping & chattering together. If I could only put confidence in Ann & she could get rid of her propensities, I would sooner give her £12 than let her go. But [and there was nearly always a but when it came to the servants] I have not a bit of confidence in her conscientiousness.[26]

Ann's lack of conscientiousness continued and when she was about to leave, Catherine hired another girl. 'My new Servant has been here a week,' she told her mother. 'She seems a good natured, willing girl & is very kind to the children, but I am disappointed in her as a *Servant*.' It appears that the girl was 'not near so efficient as Ann'. Because Catherine was still trying to cope without a nurse for the children, it had 'been very heavy upon' her during the last few weeks. Catherine's back was troubling her again and her 'nerves [were] quite unstrung.' She had sat down and 'cried many a time from exhaustion & worry.' The youngest members of the family caused

25 Ibid., Letter P156, possibly 4 Apr. 1859, p. 212.
26 Ibid., Letter P157, 15 Apr. 1859, p. 213.

plenty of problems. 'The children are such rips', she said. 'They *never rest* from morn'g to night, nor will they let any body else who is with them.'[27]

Outreach and care

There is a sequence of events that Catherine spoke about in one of her addresses years later, which was then recorded in a book, that was both remarkable and crucial for her development. It appears to have taken place in Gateshead in 1860, probably at about the time she had first preached.[28] She said,

> On a certain Sabbath, some years ago, I was passing down a narrow, thickly-populated street on my way to hear a much-honoured minister of Christ, anticipating an evening's enjoyment for myself and hoping to see some anxious ones brought into the kingdom, when I chanced to look up at the thick rows of small windows above me, where numbers of women were sitting, peering through at the passers-by, or listlessly gossiping with each other. It was suggested to my mind with great power, 'Would you not be doing God more service, and acting more like your Redeemer, by turning into some of these houses, speaking to these care-less sinners, and inviting them to the service, than by going to enjoy it yourself?'

This thought 'startled' and 'greatly agitated' her, and she felt 'very guilty' for her neglect of such people. She 'looked up to heaven' and prayed and took what was for the timid Catherine Booth a giant step. She went up to 'a group of women sitting on a door step' and spoke to them. They gave her 'a patient and respectful hearing with a promise from some of them to attend the house of God.' Much encouraged, Catherine 'went on to the next group standing at the entrance of a low, dirty court. Here, again, [she] was received kindly, and promises were given.' At that point, she said, she 'began to realise that my Master's feet were behind me; nay, before me, smoothing my path and preparing my way.'

Her confidence increasing, she

> ventured to knock at the door of the next house, and when it was opened, to go in and speak to the inmates of Jesus, death, judgment,

---

27 Ibid., Letter P161, possibly 1 or 8 May 1859, p. 217.

28 The dating of these events depends mainly upon 'CBLP', Letter P177, p. 234. In that letter, probably dated 6 or 13 July 1860, she mentions what appears to be some of the later stages of these activities.

and eternity. The man, who appeared to be one of the better class of mechanics, seemed to be much interested and affected by my words, and promised with his wife to attend the revival services which were being held at the chapel farther on. With a heart full of gratitude and eyes full of tears, I was thinking where I should go next, when I observed a woman standing on an adjoining doorstep, with a jug in her hand. My Divine Teacher said, 'Speak to that woman.' Satan suggested, 'Perhaps she is intoxicated;' but after a momentary struggle, I introduced myself to her by saying, 'Are the people out who live on this floor?' observing that the lower part of the house was closed.

'Yes,' she said, 'they are gone to chapel;' and I thought I perceived a weary sadness in her voice and manner. I said, 'Oh, I am so glad to hear that; how is it that *you* are not gone to a place of worship?' 'Me!' she said, looking down upon her forlorn appearance; 'I can't go to chapel; I am kept at home by a drunken husband. I have to stop with him to keep him from the public-house, and I have just been fetching him some drink.'

Catherine expressed her sympathy with the woman and asked to see her husband. This seems to have taken the woman by surprise and she protested, explaining that he was drunk, and thus not likely to receive a visitor kindly. Catherine, no doubt thinking of the times her father had been drunk, said that she was not afraid and that she still wanted to see him.

'Well,' said the woman, 'you can come if you like; but he will only abuse you.'

Catherine responded, 'Never mind that.'

So, the woman went up the stairs and Catherine followed her. Catherine later recorded that at that time she 'felt strong ... in the Lord, and in the power of His might, and as safe as a babe in the arms of its mother. I felt that I was in the path of obedience, and I feared no evil.'

Catherine continued,

The woman led me to a small room on the first floor, where I found a fine, intelligent man, about forty, sitting almost double in a chair, with a jug by his side out of which he had been drinking that which had reduced him beneath the level of the beasts that perish. I leaned on my heavenly Guide for strength and wisdom, love and power, and He gave me all I needed. He silenced the demon, Strong Drink, and quickened the man's perceptions to receive my words. As I began to talk to him, with my heart full of sympathy, he gradually raised himself in his chair and listened with a surprised and half-vacant stare. I spoke to him of his present deplorable condition, of the folly and wickedness of his course, of the interests of his wife and children, until he was thoroughly waked up and aroused from the stupor in which I found him.

During this conversation his wife wept bitterly, and by fragments told me a little of their previous history. I found that she had once known the Lord, but had allowed herself to be dragged down by trouble, had cast away her confidence, and fallen into sin. She told me that her husband had a brother in the Wesleyan ministry, who had done all that a brother could do to save him; that they had buried a daughter two years before, who died triumphantly in the Lord, and besought her father with her dying breath to leave off drinking, and prepare to meet her in heaven; that she had a son, then about eighteen, who, she feared, was going into a consumption; that her husband was a clever workman, and could earn three or four pounds per week as a journeyman, but he drank it nearly all, so that they were compelled to live in two rooms, and often went without necessary food.

Catherine read to him the parable of the prodigal son, 'while the tears ran down his face like rain.' She prayed with him and promised to come back 'the next day with a temperance-pledge book, which he promised to sign.'

'Exhausted in body, but happy in soul,' Catherine went to the chapel, 'just in time for the conclusion of the service, and to lend a helping hand in the prayer-meeting.'

The next day she visited that man again and he signed the pledge. In the following weeks, she visited other homes and managed to get 'ten drunkards to abandon their soul-destroying habits, and to meet me once a week for reading and expounding the Scriptures, and prayer.'[29] She found it easy to find these other men, for she 'used to ask one drunkard's wife where another lived. They always knew.'[30]

She told her parents

I have commenced my opperations [sic] amongst the men. I wish I could give you *particulars*, but I cannot spare time, so it must suffice to say that I have been quite as successful as I expected and have met with nothing but the greatest civility & attention. I have visited two evn'gs this week and have attended two cottage prayer meetings at which I have given addresses & had four penitents. The rooms were very full and hot, and of course I felt rather [k]nocked up the next day. But by laying down

---

29 Booth, *Practical Religion*, pp. 121–25.
30 Booth-Tucker, *Catherine*, vol. 1, p. 238.

in the afternoons I don't think I am any the worse.[31]

Then in her next letter she reported, 'I continue my visitations amongst the men. Our first weekly meeting is to be on Thursday ev'ng at 8 o'clock, in a room at Lampton Terrace. I have ten *pledged* men to begin with, most of whom have been much addicted to drink for years, but who have now kept the pledge above a fortnight.'[32]

In her report about this years later, she added, 'We held three or four blessed little meetings, and I doubt not our numbers would have increased more and more, but, in the inscrutable workings of Divine Providence, my health gave way, and I was most reluctantly compelled to abandon my happy and promising sphere of labour.'[33]

How genuine these men were and how long their commitments to abstinence lasted we cannot know, but this was a significant step for Catherine Booth. Indeed, it was probably more than one step.

On another occasion when she was visiting homes, probably in Gateshead, she entered a hovel and found 'a poor woman lying on a heap of rags. She had just given birth to twins, and there was nobody of any sort to wait upon her.' Catherine said years later, 'I can never forget the desolation of that room. By her side was a crust of bread, and a small lump of lard.' When Catherine looked at her sparse meal, the woman said to her, 'I fancied a bit o' bootter and my mon, he'd do owt for me he could, bless 'm—he couldna git me iny bootter, so he fitcht me this bit o' lard. Have you iver tried lard instead of bootter? It's rare good.' Waves of guilt swept over Catherine as she thought of the many times she had enjoyed 'bootter' on her bread, but not lard. She did her best to make the woman more comfortable and she washed the babies in a broken pie-dish. As Catherine departed the woman looked at her and, Catherine said, 'the gratitude of those large eyes, that gazed upon me from that wan and shrunken face, can never fade from my memory.'[34]

What happened to that poor woman and her family can only be guessed, and the guessing does not produce good results. And that family was one of many like it, scattered throughout England. Soon after Catherine had to stop her visitation because of her health, but this sad encounter made a deep impression upon her, which would bear much fruit later.

---

31 'CBLP', Letter P177, probably 6 or 13 July 1860, p. 234.
32 Ibid., Letter P178, 23 July 1860, p. 235.
33 Booth, *Practical Religion*, p. 125.
34 Booth-Tucker, *Catherine*, vol. 1, p. 238.

CHAPTER 18

Mrs Booth and Mrs Palmer

'More than any other woman Catherine Booth brought home to the conscience and heart of the Church the value of women's work,' Rev. John Hugh Morgan.

(In an obituary in the Wesleyan Methodist Magazine.)

Catherine Booth had ably demonstrated her belief in woman's equality with man in letters to her then fiancé and to Rev. David Thomas. But she had not taken that as far in practice as one would have expected. Most significantly, she was still not preaching in 1859, nor have we seen anything more than hints that she thought she ought to be.

Phoebe and Walter Palmer in England

Catherine's next step towards this occurred in 1859. It was prompted by the arrival in England that June of the American holiness teachers Walter and Phoebe Palmer. As far as public speaking and other forms of Christian ministry were concerned the Palmers were equal, but one was more equal than the other: in the public favour Phoebe quite clearly had the pre-eminence over her physician husband.

Phoebe Palmer had first risen to prominence in New York City, where in 1836 she had begun a regular meeting for women, known as 'The Tuesday meeting', with the intention of promoting holiness. The meeting took on new dynamics when it was opened to men at the end of 1839. From then she became noted as a holiness speaker, evangelist and writer, and according to Thomas Oden had a wide-ranging influence over many people, including leading Christian speakers and seminary professors.[1] She was, in fact, first and foremost a teacher of holiness rather than an evangelist, and she was to have a marked influence on the Booths in the area of holiness.

It is probable that Catherine heard Mrs Palmer speak in 1859. In some

---

[1] Oden, *Phoebe Palmer: Selected Writings*, pp. 1–12.

letters to her parents in the second half of September and October that year she mentioned that Phoebe Palmer was conducting a series of meetings in Newcastle, near where they lived, for the Wesleyans, speaking 'every night to a crowded chapel', with '30 & 40 of a night up to the communion rail.' Catherine stated at least twice in her correspondence that she intended to go to hear her, but there are a number of her letters from this period missing and it is not clear whether she did or not. But she certainly followed the American woman's ministry with interest and sympathy.[2]

The Palmers' meetings in England were usually led by a local minister, and after hymns and a prayer Dr Palmer would preach. This was followed by a brief address from the local man, which was then followed by another hymn. At this point, strangely, but significantly, those who wished to leave were invited to do so. Few if any ever did, for the meeting's climax was yet to come. Phoebe Palmer would then move behind the communion rail, but not enter the pulpit, and deliver her holiness address. At the conclusion her husband would come forward again to invite people to the communion rail. It seems that generally Mrs Palmer's addresses were not referred to as sermons, and she usually 'talked' or 'spoke' rather than 'preached'. Officially she did not seek that women should preach as such, though what she advocated, and indeed what she usually did herself, was so close to preaching that it made such a distinction almost meaningless. Presumably these practices and terms were designed to remove the prospect of criticism, as much as possible. Not that it removed it altogether.[3]

Catherine Booth defends Phoebe Palmer

Criticism came, and the most noted appeared at the end of 1859 from the Rev. Arthur Augustus Rees, a Congregational minister. Rees preached a sermon to his 1000-strong congregation attacking the Palmers' meetings, and this address was turned into a booklet entitled, *Reasons for Not Cooperating in the Alleged Sunderland Revivals*. The primary reason outlined in the pamphlet was Phoebe Palmer's ministry, whether called preaching or not.

When Catherine Booth read Rees's pamphlet, she was very angry. She later told her parents, 'I am determined that fellow shall not go unthrashed.'

2 'CBLP', Letters P166, P167 & P169, 16 and 26 Sept., and possibly 14 Oct. 1859, pp. 222–24; Green, *Catherine*, p. 104.

3 Carwardine, *Transatlantic Revivalism*, pp. 183–84; Oden, *Palmer*, p. 5; Walker, *Devil's Kingdom*, p. 23, quoting from the *Wesleyan Times*, 3 Oct. 1859, p. 644.

It is striking that when Booth-Tucker quoted this section he changed 'unthrashed' to 'unanswered', thus softening it.[4] But Catherine was in a mood to thrash Rees, not just to answer him. And she wrote that on Christmas Day, the day of 'goodwill to all men.'

The primary tool she used to thrash Rees was the pen. She wrote a small booklet late in 1859, originally called, *Female Teaching: or the Rev. A.A. Rees versus Mrs Palmer, Being a Reply to a Pamphlet by the Above Gentleman on the Sunderland Revival*. This pamphlet was revised and enlarged to 32 pages by Catherine in 1861, and in 1870 altered and republished, omitting the specific references to the original controversy, under the title, *Female Ministry: Woman's Right to Preach the Gospel*. No copies of the first edition have been found so all quotations here are from the 1861 publication.[5] In the 1861 edition Catherine Booth referred to a book by Phoebe Palmer called *The Promise of the Father*. Palmer's book was published in 1859[6]; it is unlikely that Catherine had read Palmer's book when she wrote the first edition of her pamphlet, but she had when she wrote the 1861 edition.

Even in the original title of her booklet it was clear that Catherine Booth viewed this as a battle to be fought. It was 'the Rev. A.A. Rees *versus* Mrs Palmer', and that had now become Mrs Palmer and Mrs Booth versus Rev. A.A. Rees.

There were also now no longer half measures for Catherine. She did not just want to gain women the right to 'talk' or 'speak' at church meetings, she wanted them to be able to 'preach', and not to fear calling it such. In that she went further than Phoebe Palmer.

Her booklet had two principal arguments, each dealing with the main points in Rees's booklet, supported by other material. The first concerned the common confusion of what was natural with that which was merely to do with custom. To Catherine Booth there was nothing in nature that forbade women preaching. The second dealt with the biblical arguments Rees used against women's pulpit ministry, and then looked at those passages of Scripture that indicated some women in both Testaments

---

4 'CBLP', Letter P174, 25 Dec. 1859, p. 231; Booth-Tucker, *Catherine*, vol. 1, p. 243. The words 'shall' and 'not' in the original could be 'sharnt', which is a contraction she uses later in this letter. These words or word are squeezed in at the end of a line, so are hard to read. But 'unthrashed' is definite.

5 Booth, *Female Teaching: or The Rev. A. A. Rees versus Mrs. Palmer*. For comparison see the further revised edition, *Female Ministry: Woman's Right to Preach the Gospel*.

6 Palmer, *The Promise of the Father: Or a Neglected Speciality of the Last Days*.

exercised speaking and leadership roles. She then drew the conclusion that if the Bible approved of women preaching and teaching, who dare forbid it?

In the first part she argued that Rees was 'labouring under a very great but common mistake', in that he confounded 'nature with custom.' For 'Use, or custom, makes things appear to us natural, which, in reality, are very unnatural, while … novelty and rarity make very natural things appear strange and contrary to nature.' She then conceded that a woman preaching is a 'novelty', but that does not make it in any sense 'unnatural or immodest'. Indeed,

> God has given to woman a graceful form and attitude, winning manners, persuasive speech, and, above all, a finely-toned emotional nature, all of which appear to us eminent *natural* qualifications for public speaking. We admit that want of mental culture, the trammels of custom, the force of prejudice and the assumptions of the other sex with their one-sided interpretations of Scripture, have, hitherto, almost excluded her from this sphere; but, before Mr Rees dogmatically asserts such a sphere to be unnatural, he must prove either that woman has not the *ability* to teach or to preach, or, that the possession and exercise of that ability unnaturalises her in other respects; that, so soon as she presumes to step on the platform or into the pulpit, she loses the delicacy and grace of the female character–in fact, ceases to be a woman.

She knew that Rees could not do this, for it is evident that women can teach and preach and in doing so do not in any sense lose their femininity. Catherine then asked a crucial question, why has God 'endowed' her 'with powers he never intended her to employ'?[7] To Catherine that did not make sense, though, no doubt, Rees would have responded that those 'powers' were given to teach other women and children.

In the second, longer section she dealt with the biblical case for women's ministry, quoting various scholars in support, including once more Adam Clarke. In the letters to her fiancé and David Thomas on this subject, though she had made use of the Bible in her arguments, she had noticeably not referred to the Scriptures that appeared most strongly against what she believed. The relevant verses from 1 Corinthians chapter 14 and 1 Timothy chapter 2 had been blatantly ignored. But in this section of the booklet she immediately deals with the verses from 1 Corinthians 14 and the passages related to them. Concerning, these related verses she quotes

---

7 Booth, *Female Teaching*, pp. 3–4.

a 'talented writer', who was none other than Phoebe Palmer. Having now read Palmer's *Promise of the Father*, she had moved a step or two further in her understanding of the issue. She was now competent and confident enough to engage the learned in debate on these texts that she once seemed to avoid discussing.

The first Scripture she looked at in detail was 1 Cor 11:4-6, verses that she rightly saw as being related to 1 Cor 14:33-34. Those verses in chapter 11 state that when a woman is prophesying or praying she should have her head covered (whatever that may mean). She first quoted Phoebe Palmer and Adam Clarke on these verses, who both argued that this passage clearly takes for granted that women were allowed to speak in meetings in the New Testament church to edify, exhort and comfort believers, but, according to Palmer, did not in so doing assume 'personal authority over others.' Catherine then summarised their opinions by saying that

> the view above given is the only common-sense interpretation of this passage. If Paul did not recognize the *fact*, that women did actually pray and prophesy in the primitive churches, his language has no meaning at all; and if he does not recognize their right to do so, by dictating the proprieties of their appearance while so engaged, he talks jargon.[8]

She then related that passage to 1 Cor 14:33–34 ('Let your women keep silence in the churches…') by saying, 'Now let it be borne in mind that this is the same apostle, writing to the same church, as in the above instance' and then proceeded to argue that it would be totally illogical for Paul to describe in what manner women should speak in one place and then a few verses later say that they were forbidden to do so. What is forbidden therefore must be a specific kind of speaking, namely, speaking 'to its political and disciplinary assemblies.'

Basically, then, her argument on 1 Cor 14:33–34 was, if women were allowed to prophesy according to 1 Cor 11:4–6 and Acts 2:17 (and both Catherine Booth and Phoebe Palmer equated prophesying with preaching or teaching)[9], then the speaking that is forbidden in 1 Corinthians 14 must be of some other type, which cannot possibly be normal preaching or teaching because that has already been approved. Therefore, it is in order for women to preach and teach.

With regard to the verses in 1 Timothy 2, Catherine stated that what was

---

8 Ibid., pp. 7–8.
9 Ibid., p. 13.

being forbidden was the kind of teaching that 'involves' female 'usurpation of authority over the man', not preaching and teaching *per se*. To her that usurpation was indeed forbidden, but that did not mean that women should not be allowed to preach.[10] This argument is common today, yet one cannot help asking, from that perspective should a woman be allowed to become the General of The Salvation Army? Is a woman occupying that position an 'usurpation of authority' over at least some men? But that was later, and long after Catherine had died. Yet suitable women were theoretically 'eligible for any office' in the Christian Mission as early as 1870.[11] If that is anything to go by, Catherine's views may have been later extended to allow women to lead Christian organisations. However, even the revised, 1870 edition of her booklet, reprinted in 1975 and 2001[12] still included that clause, which would seem to forbid it.

She then used various Old Testament instances to support her case in a similar fashion to that in her letter to her husband. In addition, she used what appears to be a new argument for her. She mentioned the text 'The Lord gave the word; great was the company of those that published it' (Ps 68:11), and then states, 'In the original Hebrew it is, "Great was the company of woman publishers, or woman evangelists."' This part is lifted word for word from Palmer's book.[13] She then returned to the New Testament and examined various other texts suited to her purpose.[14]

But Catherine was not all sweetness, light and logic in the pursuing of her theme. She gave Mr Rees the sharp end of her tongue, or rather pen, in more than one place, showing that it was not just her logical reasoning that made her a formidable adversary. At one point, she quoted Rees as saying, 'Of course it is not disputed that many individuals of the female sex are, in every respect, far superior to many individuals of the male sex.' Such condescension stirred Catherine's anger. 'Truly', she responded, 'the ladies of Mr Rees's congregation must have felt themselves highly complimented

---

10 Ibid., pp. 7–16, 31.

11 'The Constitution of the Christian Mission', Section 'XII, Female Preachers', from the Mission's Minutes of Conference, 1870, courtesy of the Heritage Centre of The Salvation Army, Sydney.

12 This latest printing of *Female Ministry* appears in *Terms of Empowerment: Salvation Army Women in Ministry* (NY: Salvation Army, 2001), pp. 1–32. See page 17 in that work for this reference.

13 Booth, *Female Teaching*, pp. 17–18.

14 Ibid., pp. 18–22.

by this very gracious admission, which simply amounts to saying that a refined, intelligent and Christian female is, after all, superior to a course, besotted, ignorant vagabond of the opposite sex, notwithstanding that she is a woman!'

It appears that Rees went on, 'Nay, I hold that a good woman is the best thing in the world.' That comment once more stirred Catherine's anger.

> We do not doubt for a moment the truth of this assertion; a *thing*, and not a *being*, is what Mr Rees has been labouring to make a woman appear in all the way through his remarks; and if he can only find one good, after his own model, we have no doubt he will exalt her above all other good things. Even then, however, she must be in her 'right place', which, according to Mr R., is amongst many other good things–'in the kitchen.'[15]

A modern-day feminist could have hardly put it more pointedly.

Towards the end of the booklet she asserted, 'Whether the church will allow women to speak in her assemblies or not can only be a question of time; common sense and public opinion will force her to examine honestly and impartially the texts on which she grounds her prohibitions.' She then closed the pamphlet with the brief stories of various women who had been used by God in the modern era in the spreading of his word. In this section she acknowledged the influence of Phoebe Palmer, but some of the examples she used here were the same as those used in her earlier letters to William Booth and David Thomas.[16]

Although Catherine was strongly advocating woman's right to preach and minister in the church alongside man, it needs to be noted that she seems to have continued to believe that the man was the head in the home. In the letter to her husband that expressed so strongly woman's right to preach, she could still say, 'I would not alter woman's domestic position (when indeed it is scriptural), because God has plainly fixed it', and in that same letter she also expressed that she would 'promise to *obey*' her husband.[17]

In addition, towards the end of the 1861 edition of *Female Teaching* she made the quite surprising concession that though a woman had 'the

---

15 Ibid., p. 23.

16 Ibid., pp. 26–30.

17 Booth, *Letters*, Letter CM122, 9 Apr. 1855, pp. 283 & 285–86; Booth, *Letters CD*, pp. 283, 285.

right' to preach 'independently of any man-made restrictions, which do not equally refer to the opposite sex,' there was one exception. That was when 'as a wife, silence is imposed upon her by her own husband.'[18] In other words, there was only one man who could legitimately stop a woman preaching, and that was her own husband. Significantly, though not surprisingly, that concession was omitted from the 1870 edition of this booklet, even though the wording of the rest of that section is word for word the same as its predecessor.[19]

It seems, then, that she had undergone some change in her thinking on this issue, but that change does not appear to have extended very far. Apart from the above omission, we have not come across any evidence that she later changed her views on wives' submission to their husbands. Indeed, a few months after she began preaching, she asked for her husband's approval before accepting an appointment outside their circuit[20], though it could be argued that this was because he was the circuit superintendent and she was substituting for him while he was ill.

Andrew Eason agrees that Catherine never applied this belief in woman's equality with man to her domestic situation, at least to any degree. He says, 'While she felt justified in pursuing a public life of preaching, she continued to support the Victorian pillars of domesticity: feminine submission in marriage and maternal obligation in the home.'[21]

To preach or not to preach

But even after having written that booklet Catherine Booth did not immediately begin preaching. She later admitted that she had felt called to preach for some time before she took that step, but, it seems, her timidity was too strong for too long to permit it. She had led classes, prayed at prayer meetings, and, as far back as 1857, even given temperance lectures. She had even now written a pamphlet defending women's right to preach. But for her to preach seemed a step too far. Yet there appears to have been a bigger problem here than her timidity. Perhaps it was the uniqueness of preaching, the special role it played in the church that deterred her. After all, giving a temperance lecture to, say, 20 or 50, is almost as likely to frighten a timid

---

18 Booth, *Female Teaching*, p. 30.
19 Ibid., p. 19; *Terms of Empowerment*, p. 31.
20 Booth, *Letters*, Letter CB153, 17 Sept. 1860, pp. 332–33; Booth, *Letters CD*, pp. 330–31.
21 Eason, *Women in God's Army*, p. 113.

person as preaching to hundreds in a chapel.

In September 1859, at about the time she was writing the pamphlet defending Phoebe Palmer, she told her parents, 'I received a unanimous invitation from our Leaders' meeting the other night to give an address at the special prayer-meetings this week, but of course I declined. I don't know what they can be thinking of.' And she said that just after mentioning Mrs Palmer.[22] From our perspective, knowing what she later achieved, that is a remarkable and surprising comment. Perhaps she was feeling overwhelmed by the responsibilities already placed upon her.

Catherine Booth gave a detailed account of her call to engage in public ministry, especially preaching, in a lecture delivered in the West End of London one evening in 1880, which was later published in her book *Papers on Aggressive Christianity*. It contains some clear errors of memory. For example, she said that William 'had been trying to persuade' her to preach 'for ten years' before she decided to do so. She began preaching in the middle of 1860, but they had not even met in 1850, and William seems to have had doubts about her preaching as late as 1855. In this lecture, she, judging by her diary, even gets her age at her conversion wrong. However, there is no reason to doubt the main points of her account.

She began, 'I had long had a controversy on this question in my soul. In fact, from the time I was converted, the Spirit of God had constantly been urging me into paths of usefulness and labour, which seemed to me impossible.' We earlier noted that she had had an intense struggle over witnessing to people one on one. That had seemed to her impossible, but she eventually did it.

She continued,

Perhaps some of you would hardly credit that I was one of the most timid and bashful disciples the Lord Jesus ever saved. For ten years of my Christian life my life was one daily battle with the cross—not because I wilfully rejected, as many do, for that I never dared to do. Oh, no! I used to make up my mind I would, and resolve and intend, and then, when the hour came, I used to fail for want of courage. I need not have failed. I now see how foolish I was, and how wrong; but, for some four or five months before I commenced speaking, the controversy had been signally roused in my soul which God had awakened years before, but which, through mistaken notions, fear, and timidity, I had allowed

---

[22] 'CBLP', Letter P167, 26 Sept. 1859, p. 223.

almost to die out.[23]

It is striking that in addition to the barriers of 'fear, and timidity' she adds another, 'mistaken notions,' indeed, she puts it first. What these notions were is unclear. In her 1855 letter in the *New Connexion Magazine*, she clearly wanted Methodist women 'to engage in prayer, speak in love-feasts and meetings, or in any public manner bear testimony for their Lord.' But then she said, 'Mistake me not, I am not advocating female preaching, but female efforts in other ways, especially for the benefit of their own sex.'[24] Perhaps this limitation was one of her 'mistaken notions'.

She continued,

> I was brought to very severe heart-searchings at this time. I had not been realising so much of the Divine presence. I had lost a great deal of the power and happiness I once enjoyed. During a season of sickness, one day it seemed as if the Lord revealed it all to me by His Spirit. I had no vision, but a revelation to my mind. He seemed to take me back to the time when I was fifteen and sixteen, when I first gave my heart to Him. He seemed to show me, all the bitter way, how this one thing had been the fly in the pot of ointment, the bitter in the cup, and prevented me from realising what I should otherwise have done. I felt how it had hindered the revelation of Himself to me, and hindered me from growing in grace, and learning more of the deep things of God. He showed it to me, and then I remember prostrating myself upon my face before Him, and I promised Him there in the sick room: 'Lord, if Thou wilt return unto me, as in the days of old, and re-visit me with those urgings of Thy Spirit which I used to have, I will obey, if I die in the attempt. I care not; I will obey.' However, the Lord did not revisit me immediately. He let me recover, and I went out again.
>
> About three months after that I went to the chapel of which my husband was a minister, and he had an extraordinary service. Even then he was ever trying something new to get the outside people. They were having a meeting in which ministers and friends in the town were taking part, and all giving their testimony and speaking for God. I was in the minister's pew, with my eldest boy, then four years old, and there were some thousand people present. I felt much more depressed than usual in spirit, and not expecting anything particular, but, as the testimonies went on, I felt the Spirit come upon me. You alone who have felt it know

23 Booth, *Aggressive*, pp. 135–36.
24 C[atherine] M[umford], 'How to Train', *MNCM*, 1855, p. 321.

what it means. It cannot be described. I felt it to the extremities of my fingers and toes. It seemed as if a voice said to me, 'Now, if you were to go and testify, you know I would bless it to your own soul as well as to the souls of the people,' and I gasped again, and I said, in my soul, 'Yes, Lord, I believe Thou wouldst, but I cannot do it.' I had forgotten my vow—it did not occur to me at all.

All in a moment, after I had said that to the Lord I seemed to see the bedroom where I had lain, and to see myself as though I had been there prostrate before the Lord promising Him that, and then the voice seemed to say to me, 'Is this consistent with that promise?' and I almost jumped up and said, 'No, Lord, it is the old thing over again, but I cannot do it,' and I felt as though I would sooner die than do it. And then the Devil said, 'Besides, you are not prepared to speak. You will look like a fool, and have nothing to say.' He made a mistake. He overdid himself for once. It was that word settled it. I said, 'Ah! this is just the point. I have never yet been willing to be a fool for Christ, now I will be one;' and without stopping another moment, I rose up in the seat, and walked up the chapel. My dear husband was just going to conclude. He thought something had happened to me, and so did the people. We had been there two years, and they knew my timid, bashful nature. He stepped down to ask me, 'What is the matter, my dear.' I said, 'I want to say a word.' He was so taken by surprise, he could only say, 'My dear wife wants to say a word,' and sat down. He had been trying to persuade me to do it for ten years. He and a lady in the church, only that very week, had been trying to persuade me to go and address a little cottage meeting, of some twenty working people, but could not. I got up—God only knows how—and if any mortal ever did hang on the arm of Omnipotence, I did. I felt as if I were clinging to some human arm—and yet it was a Divine arm—to hold me. I just got up and told the people how it came about. I confessed, as I think everybody should, when they have been in the wrong and misrepresented the religion of Jesus Christ…

I said, 'I dare say many of you have been looking upon me as a very devoted woman, and one who has been living faithfully to God, but I have come to know that I have been living in disobedience, and to that extent I have brought darkness and leanness into my soul, but I promised the Lord three or four months ago, and I dare not disobey. I have come to tell you this, and to promise the Lord that I will be obedient to the Heavenly vision.'

... There was more weeping, they said, in the chapel that day, than ever there had been before. Many dated a renewal in righteousness from that very moment, and began a life of devotion and consecration to God.[25]

She seems to have preached for the first time on Whitsunday, 27 May 1860.[26] The congregation liked what they heard. Word about her preaching quickly travelled. Soon Catherine Booth was fielding invitations from their own circuit for her to preach in the different chapels. Her life was changing, and it was about to change even more.

Substituting for William

William Booth became sick. Towards the end of August, he went to Smedley's Hydro in Matlock to recover. The leaders in the circuit were now faced with a major problem. Who would take William Booth's numerous preaching appointments? So, 'A deputation' from the circuit approached Catherine to take his place. Years later Catherine said that she told them, 'I could not think of such a thing... They must not ask me—and away they went.' But

> They came back again to know if I would take the nights, they implored and importuned me until I promised ... I was obliged, and I did it with four little children, the eldest then four years and three months old... While I was nursing my baby, many a time I was thinking of what I was going to say next Sunday, and between times noted down with a pencil the thoughts as they struck me. And then I would appear sometimes, with an outline scratched in pencil, trusting in the Lord to give me the power of His Holy Spirit.[27]

One of her letters to her mother at the end of that August illustrates perfectly what her new life had become. She told her mother,

> I have scarce time to write to day. I have to go out directly to visit, and I have been writing all the morn'g preparing for Sunday. I am published for anniversary sermons at Felling Shore, morn'g & night... On Sunday week I am at the *Teams* anniversary, morn'g & night, and the Sunday after they want me to take *Bethesda* again, and the Sunday after that they want me at Sheriff Hill for their anniversary, & then they want me at

---

25 Booth, *Aggressive*, pp. 136–39.
26 Bramwell-Booth, *Catherine*, p. 185.
27 Booth, *Aggressive*, p. 140.

Gateshead Fell. So you see, I have plenty of work cut out. I am anxious to do as much as I can while Wm is away, as they esteem me as a competent supply for him, & this will prevent disappointment.

She then added, 'but I don't intend to do so much when he returns.'[28] And who could blame her? At Felling Shore on 2 September she worked with another female preacher, a Mrs Dixon, who appears to have lived in Sheriff Hill.[29]

A woman preaching was still sufficiently newsworthy for newspapers around Britain to report her new venture. The *Court Journal* said,

The Rev. W. Booth having been laid aside by indisposition for the last week or two, Mrs Booth officiated for him on Sunday last, in Bethesda Chapel, Newcastle. The lady grounded her discourse on 'Strive to enter in at the straight gate,' etc., and the large audience which had congregated to hear sat with evident interest, listening to her chaste and fervid eloquence for upwards of an hour. The service was a very effective one.

This was copied in numerous other papers scattered around the country.[30]

As her ministry progressed the people continued to come to hear her. 'Whenever I spoke,' she said, 'the chapel used to be crowded to its utmost capacity, and numbers were converted. Not to me but to God be all the glory. Shame to me that I did not begin sooner. It was not I that did this, but the Holy Ghost, the Holy Spirit of God.'[31]

It is easy to forgive her for not beginning sooner, for on 8 January 1860 she had given birth to her fourth child. They called her Emma Moss Booth.[32] With Catherine's poor health and anxious temperament, she had found it difficult looking after her family to her satisfaction when she had three children. Now there was a fourth child and she had taken on the responsibilities of preaching, and that often. How would she cope?

---

28 'CBLP', Letter P181, 31 Aug. 1860, p. 240.

29 *Newcastle Guardian and Tyne Mercury*, 'Lady Preachers', 8 Sept. 1860, p. 5, col. 6.

30 This item seems to have first appeared in the *Court Journal*, but was picked up, with slight variations by newspapers around the country, including *Hartlepool Free Press*, 25 Aug. 1860 p. 3, col. 6; the *Cheltenham Chronicle*, 28 Aug. 1860, p. 3, col. 5; the *Cornish Telegraph*, 29 Aug. 1860, p. 3, col. 5; the *Whitehaven News*, 30 Aug. 1860, p. 4, col. 2; the *Coventry Standard*, 31 Aug. 1860, p. 2, col. 3; and the *Elgin Courier*, 31 Aug. 1860, p. 4, col. 2.

31 Booth, *Aggressive*, p. 139.

32 Green, *Catherine*, p. 94.

John Mumford and Wreckington

That October John Mumford visited the Booths in Gateshead. On the 21ˢᵗ of that month Catherine preached at the chapel at Wreckington and her father went to hear her. Catherine knew later that something had happened to her father that day but was not sure what. In a letter to both parents written after his return to London, she told him, 'I cannot express my gratitude that your visit has been in any way made a blessing to you. I do hope that it may lead to the glorious result you refer to, but *don't procrastinate*. Time is flying. Death is striking, and eternity is full in view. May the Lord help you to press into the Kingdom.'[33]

Was John Mumford converted at that time, or was that experience a recommitment to the faith, or did he have some other spiritual experience? A year later John Mumford must have explained how he understood it, for his daughter responded, 'I do wish you could both spend the day with us. It would be better than "Wreckington", I fancy. I did not know before, that my dear Father regarded that as the day of his decision for Jesus.'[34]

Two matters need to be mentioned at this point. First, it has been common to regard this experience of John Mumford's as happening in Cornwall, when visiting the by then travelling Booths late in October 1861. However, Wreckington is in the north-east of England, not in Cornwall in the south-west, and Catherine's letters make it clear that it occurred in 1860 not 1861. Secondly, we must ask the question what happened to John Mumford after this? Did he continue in the faith or did he backslide? It is probably fairest to say that life continued to be a great struggle for him. He did at times help his daughter and son-in-law with their work[35], but later he seems to have once more fallen under the influence of the 'demon drink'. No wonder Catherine hated alcohol.

---

33 'CBLP', Letter P187, 31 Oct., or 1 or 2 Nov. 1860, p. 247. See also letter P186, 10 Oct. 1860, p. 246.
34 Ibid., Letter P220, 18 Oct. 1861, p. 293.
35 Bennett, *General*, vol. 1, pp. 298–99, 334.

CHAPTER 19

Holiness to the Lord

'I don't fear anything but lack of spiritual power',
Catherine Booth.[1]

It appears to have been in January 1861 that the Booths became greatly concerned about the issue of holiness. In one letter, the original of which is now lost, Catherine said,

My soul has been much called out of late on the doctrine of holiness. I feel that hitherto we have not put it in a sufficiently definite and tangible manner before the people–I mean as a specific and attainable experience. Oh, that I had entered into the fulness of the enjoyment of it myself. I intend to struggle after it. In the mean time we have commenced already to bring it specially before our dear people.

Though this letter was written by Catherine the change from 'I' to 'we' is significant. It was not just her desire but William's too.[2] This is proved by what follows.

The climax

It was probably a little later that she wrote to her parents, saying, 'I hope you have not thought me unkind in not writing earlier. I was unusually occupied last week… I have been for sometime past in a very low, miserable state of mind, partly, perhaps, arising from physical causes & grievous temptation, but chiefly from unbelief and unfaithfulness. I seemed to reach a climax on

---

1 'CBLP', Letter P100, 9 or 10 Oct. 1857, p. 138.

2 Ibid., Letter P194, possibly 14 Jan. 1861, p. 254. This does not appear in the Booth Papers, but is drawn from Booth-Tucker, *Catherine*, vol. 1, p. 271. Though Booth-Tucker often paraphrases these letters, it does not seem likely that he would have changed 'I' to 'we', so it was presumably that way in the original. The dating is, though, uncertain.

Thursday.' That Thursday was her thirty-second birthday, which, no doubt, was a time of reflection. She continued,

> I felt as if the Devil was in personal contact with me. I was almost driven to dispare [sic].
>
> On friday morn'g[3], however, Wm tried to encourage [me], & after a long & agonising struggle together at the throne of grace I was enabled afresh to cast my self on Jesus, and since have realised a complete deliverance from the peculiar temptations under which I was labouring. I have peace with God through our Lord Jesus Xt & I have pledged myself to seek till I find holiness of heart. Oh, I see what an enemy *unbelief* has been to me all the way through my religious life. It is *faith* that brings power, not merely praying & weeping & struggling, but *believing*, dareing [sic] to believe the written word with or without feeling. Oh, I do hope I have turned over a new leaf in my experience & that henceforth I shall be content to let Jesus save me without trying to save myself.
>
> I shall be eternally thankful that I ever read Mrs Palmer's books. They have done me more good than any thing I ever met with.

Catherine then urged her parents to buy a copy of Phoebe Palmer's *Faith and its Effects*, giving them publication details and the price.[4] They did that and Catherine then advised them not 'to read it all at once. Just find some portion that suits your case and apply it and pray over it, and ask the Lord to help you to receive all the light it is fitted to impart, and then act according to it.'[5]

By this time, it appears, the Booths were presenting the doctrine of holiness to their people in a more 'definite and tangible manner', for, she continued,

> Our services are going on delightfully. We had about 35 cases on the week and 13 last night, eight of the whole number for Holiness. It is more eminently a work of the Spirit than any we have had in Gateshead. The church is coming better up to the mark, seeking a higher life. Many of the cases are very remarkable ones, middle aged *men* of intelligence & respectability. We had a special prayer-meeting yesterday afternoon. I

---

3 Bramwell-Booth, *Catherine*, p. 201, has 'driven to despair on Friday morning. However William…' While this is possible, Catherine has a comma after 'dispare,' and with Catherine commas often function as full stops. The original has no punctuation marks after 'morn'g' or 'however'.

4 'CBLP', Letter P195, 21 Jan. 1861, pp. 254–55.

5 Ibid., Letter P196, 4 Feb. 1861, p. 257.

went & lead [sic] it & gave an address to save Wm the extra service. I had a very good time; a rich melting influence was present.[6]

Bearing in mind what had already occurred in Gateshead under their ministry, to call this 'more eminently a work of the Spirit' than what they had previously experienced in that town, suggests that this was an outstanding time.

In another letter that is only in the biographies, probably written about two weeks after the one just quoted, she said,

I spoke a fortnight since at Bethesda on holiness, and a precious time we had. On the Sunday following two beautiful testimonies were given in the love-feast as to the attainment of the blessing through that address. One of them, an old gray-headed leader, is perhaps the most spiritual man in the society. He had never before seen it his privilege to be sanctified. Others have claimed it since. William has preached on it twice, and there is a glorious quickening amongst the people. I am to speak again next Friday night and on Sunday afternoon. Pray for me. I only want perfect consecration and Christ as my all, and then I might be very useful, to the glory, not of myself, the most unworthy of all who e'er His grace received, but of His great and boundless love. May the Lord enable me to give my wanderings o'er and to find in Christ perfect peace and full salvation.

I have much to be thankful for in my dearest husband. The Lord has been dealing very graciously with him for some time past. His soul has been growing in grace, and its outward developments have been proportionate. He is now on full stretch for holiness. You would be amazed at the change in him. It would take me all night to detail all the circumstances and convergings of Providence and Grace which have led up to this experience, but I assure you it is a glorious reality, and I know you will rejoice in it.

'The evangelistic question'

But holiness was not the only issue facing them. Catherine put it this way, 'As has always been the case with every quickening we have experienced in our own souls, there has been a renewal of the evangelistic question, especially in my mind.' In other words, should they leave the New Connexion and

---

6 Ibid., Letter P195, 21 Jan. 1861, p. 255.

launch out as independent evangelists? While that is what they both desired, if they did that, there was no guarantee of a salary, and with four children now and perhaps more later that was a significant problem and a major test of faith. She continued,

> I felt as though that was the point of controversy between me and God. Indeed, I know it was. And on the day I referred to in my last letter to you, I determined to bring it to a point before the Lord, trusting in Him for strength to suffer as well as to do His will, if He should call me to it. I did so. What I went through in the conflict I could not, if I would, describe. It seemed far worse than death. Since that hour, however, although I have been tempted, I have not taken back the sacrifice from the altar but have been enabled calmly to contemplate it *as done*.
>
> Such an unexpected surrender on my part of course revived William's yearnings towards the evangelistic work, though in quite another spirit to that in which he used to long for it. In fact, now I think the sacrifice will be almost as great to him as to me. He has got so much more settled in his habits, and so fond of home. But he feels as though the Lord calls him to it. So, we are going to make it a matter of daily prayer for a week, and then decide, leaving all consequences with the Lord. He says that we shall not lack any good thing if we do His will, and if He puts us to the test, we are going to trust Him with each other, life, health, salary, and all.

Catherine then asked her parents to pray for them that they might know the will of God on the matter. Yet Catherine knew that knowing it was one thing, having the courage to do it was another. So she prayed that the 'Holy Ghost [would] apply the words of God … to our waiting, anxious hearts on this momentously important subject.' Then in a mixture of faith and self-criticism, she said,

> The Lord will order all things if we only do His will and trust Him with consequences. 'Them that honour me I will honour.' Oh, what a fool I have been! How slow, how backward, how blinded, how hindered by unbelief. And even now some bolts and bars are round me, which my foolish heart will not consent to have broken down. O unbelief, truly it binds the hands of Omnipotence itself. 'He could not do many mighty works because of their unbelief.' May the Lord increase our faith![7]

---

7 Ibid., Letter P196, 4 Feb. 1861, pp. 256–57.

A deeper experience of God

Yet the issue of whether they should become fulltime evangelists was put on hold, while they sought for that deeper relationship with God. Their next step is again recorded in Catherine's own words. On 11 February, she reflected, 'If I am only fully the Lord's, He has unalterably bound Himself to be the portion of my inheritance for ever. This I have felt, & a week last Friday,' that is 1 February, 'when I made the surrender refer[r]ed to in my last, I was made to feel in order to carry out my vow in the true spirit of consecration I must have a *whole* Christ, a perfect Saviour, & that every moment. I therefore resolved to seek till I found that 'pearl of great price" – "the white stone, which no man knoweth, save him that receiveth it."'

She had been reading a book, probably H.E. Boardman's *The Higher Christian Life*, from which she perceived that she

has been in some degree of error with reference to the nature, or rather *manner* of Sanctification, regarding it rather as a great and mighty work to be wrought in me *through* Christ, than the simple reception *of Christ* as an *all sufficient* Saviour, *dwelling in* my heart, and thus cleansing it every moment from all sin. I had been earnestly seeking to apprehend Him as my perfect Saviour all the week but on Thursday & Friday I was totally absorbed in the subject & laid aside almost everything else & spent the chief [part] of the day in reading and prayer & trying to believe for it. On Thursday afternoon at Tea time I was well nigh discouraged. I felt my old besetment, irratability [sic], and the Devil told me I should *never* get it, & so I might as well give it up at once. However, I knew him of old as a lier [sic] and the father of lies, and pressed on; tho' cast down, not destroyed.

On Friday morn'g God gave me two precious passages. First, 'Come unto Me, *all* ye that *labour* and are *heavy laden*, & I *will* give you rest.' Oh, how sweet it sounded to my poor, weary, sin stricken soul! I almost dared to believe He did give me rest from inbred sin, the rest of perfect holiness. But I staggered at the promise through unbelief, & therefore failed to enter in. The second passage was these thrice blessed words: 'Of him are ye in Christ Jesus, *who* is made unto us wisdom, Righteousness, *Sanctification*, & redemption.' But *again* unbelief hindered me, altho' I felt as tho' getting gradually nearer.

I struggled on through the day untill [sic] a little after six in the even'g, when Wm joined me in prayer. We had a blessed season. While he was saying, 'Lord, we open our hearts to receive Thee,' that word was spoken to my heart, 'Behold, I stand at the door & knock. If any man hear my voice, and open unto me, I *will* come in and sup with him.' I felt sure He had long been knocking, and oh, how I longed to receive him as perfect Saviour. But oh, the inveterate habbit [sic] of unbelief! How wonderful that God should have borne so long with me.

When we got up from our knees I lay on the Sofa, exhausted with the excitement & effort of the day. William said, 'Don't you lay all on the alter [sic]?' I replied, 'I am sure I do!' Then he said, '& isn't the altar holy?' I replied in the language of the Holy Ghost, 'The altar is *most* holy, & whatsoever toucheth it is holy.' Then said he, 'Are you not holy?' I replied with my heart full of emmotion [sic] & some faith, 'Oh, I think I am.' Immediately the word was given me to confirm my faith, '*Now* ye are clean through the word which I have spoken unto you', & I took hold, true, with a trembling hand and not unmolested by the tempter, but I held fast the *begin[n]ing* of my confidence, & it grew stronger, & from that moment I have dared to reckon myself 'dead indeed unto sin, & alive unto God, through Jesus Xst, my Lord.'

I did feel much rapturous joy[8] but perfect peace, the sweet *rest* which Jesus promised to the heavy laden. I have entered into the apostle's meaning when he says, 'We who *believe* do enter into *rest*.' This is just discriptive [sic] of my state at present. Not that I am not tempted, but I am allowed to *know* the devil when he approaches me, and I look to my deliverer Jesus, & he still gives me rest. Two or three very trying things occur[r]ed on Saturday, which at another time would have excited impatience, but I was kept by the power of God through faith unto full salvation. & now what shall I say? 'Unto Him who hath washed me in His own blood, be glory & dominion forever and ever', & all within me says, 'Amen!'

Oh, I cannot discribe [sic], I have no words to set forth, the sense I have of my own utter *vileness*. The rebel[l]ion of my heart against God has been *awful* in the extreme. It is because his mercy endureth *foreve[r]* that I am not in hell.[9]

---

8 Booth-Tucker, *Catherine*, vol. 1, p. 273 and Bramwell-Booth, *Catherine*, p. 204, have 'I did *not* feel much rapturous joy', presumably because they thought the word 'not' was required because of the following 'but'. However, the original does not contain the word 'not'.

9 'CBLP', Letter P197, 11 Feb. 1861, pp. 257–58.

It is striking that at this point Booth-Tucker in his record has changed 'vileness' to 'unworthiness' and has omitted the two sentences about Catherine's rebellion 'against God' and her deserving hell.[10] This is an example of how he often softens her words and thoughts. But Catherine, here, is not moderate in her language. She said 'vileness' and meant vileness; she described herself as a rebel deserving hell and she meant it.

She continued,

> Satan met me continually with my peculiarly ag[g]ravated sins, black as hell itself, & I admit it *all, all*. But then I said the Lord has not made my salvation to depend in any measure on my own worthiness or unworthiness, but on the worthiness of my Saviour. He 'came to seek and to save that which was lost.' 'Whe[r]e sin hath abounded, grace doth much more abound', & now, my dear parents, will you let it abound towards you? 'Whosoever will, let him come & take *freely*.'[11]

At this point what still remains of the original letter ends, yet it is clear that she had more to say. Booth-Tucker also ends his record of this letter at this point, which may suggest that the final page(s) has long been lost.

Here the Booths' understanding of this experience is in line with Salvation Army doctrine. Or perhaps it would be better to say that Salvation Army doctrine is here in line with the Booths' experience. For the Booths and Salvationists generally, an initial conversion experience and a later holiness encounter are, as Booth-Tucker described them, 'the twin doctrines' at 'the forefront of The Salvation Army Zion.'[12]

Hartlepool

That Easter, both William and Catherine Booth went to Hartlepool, on the coast about 50 kilometres to the south of Gateshead, to conduct the anniversary services at the New Connexion Chapel. The chapel in Hartlepool was in the same New Connexion District as Gateshead, but in a different circuit. They arrived on Thursday and Catherine preached on Good Friday morning on Acts chapters one and two to a full chapel. The congregation 'listened with the most marked attention', though the

---

10 Booth-Tucker, *Catherine*, vol. 1, p. 273.

11 'CBLP', Letter P197, 11 Feb. 1861, pp. 258–59.

12 Booth-Tucker, *Catherine*, vol. 1, pp. 273–74.

New Connexion's magazine hinted that not all were happy about a woman preaching.[13]

William preached on Sunday morning and Catherine in the afternoon. The 'Chapel was packed' that afternoon, with many on the 'aisles & pulpit stairs, & many went away unable to get in.' William preached again in the evening, when once more the chapel was full. They had 'a good prayer meeting & a few cases.' According to the magazine, 'twelve persons found peace' that evening.

This may have been the first time that the Booths had ministered together in this way other than in their own circuit. If so, it was to be the first of many times. William returned to Gateshead, leaving Catherine to take another service on Monday night. She intended to return to Gateshead probably the next day. That Monday morning she told her parents, 'There were many under conviction last night, whom I hope to see converted to night. The Lord has been very graciously present with me hitherto & given me great liberty & influence. I am trusting him again for to night.' Then significantly she added, 'I am just in my element in the work. I only regret that I did not commence *years ago*. Oh, to live for souls! It is a dark, sinful world, & a comparitively [sic] dead and useless Church. May God pour out his Spirit!'[14]

In another letter written probably the following Monday Catherine said that things had not gone to plan. They had gone far better than the plan. She was still in Hartlepool.

> You will be surprised to find I am still here, but so it is. I told you I had to stay on Monday eve'ng. Well, the Lord came down amongst the people so gloriously that I dare not leave, so the friends tellegraphed [sic] to Wm and I stayed. I preached again on Tuesday eve'ng, chapel full, & bottom crowded to the prayer-meeting. I gave an invitation, and the Lord helped as I think he never did before. When I had done speaking there was a general move all over the chapel, and the rail was filled with penitents again and again and *again* during the eve'ng. The second time it was filled I never saw such a sight before. They were all men, with two exceptions, & most of them great, fine fellows of mature years. All glory to Jesus! He hath 'chosen the *weak* things to confound the mighty.'
>
> Suffice it to say, I preached on the Wednesday and Friday ev'ngs also, & gave two addresses, one in the morn'g & afternoon on holiness, & the

---

13 *MNCM*, 'Hartlepool', 1861, pp. 261–62.
14 'CBLP', Letter P200, 1 Apl. 1861, pp. 261–62; *MNCM*, 'Hartlepool', 1861, p. 262.

Lord has been very graciously with me, & above a hundred names were [taken] on the week, besides members, & I think we have had quite half the members up to seek a clear sense of their acceptance.

Rev. J.W. Williams arrived on Saturday to help her and they 'had a glorious fellowship meeting.' She added, 'Oh, it would have rejoiced your hearts to have heard one after another bless God for bringing your feeble and unworthy child to Hartlepool. I shall never forget that meeting, on earth or in heaven.' Rev. Williams preached on Sunday morning to a 'very good congregation.' Catherine was due to preach at night and she later said that a quarter of an hour before the service was due to commence,

the chapel was wedged so full that the people were drifting away again, so it was announced to the crowd outside that Mr Williams would preach in the School room under the chapel at the same time. It is a splendid room, cappable [sic] of holding nearly 500. It was soon filled to overflowing, & then, they tell me, numbers went away unable to get in. I preached on the 'Judgment' & enjoyed great liberty. The people listened as tho' they already realized the dread tribunal. Oh, it was indeed a solemn time! For some time we carried on both prayer-meetings, then we amalgamated, allowing the people to remain in the gal[l]ery, which they did till nearly 10 o'clock. We had upwards of 40 cases altogether. To God be all the praise! ... Our Jesus can do wondrous things, and that by the feeblest instruments...

It was all most exciting, yet she added, 'there is one great blessing: we have no wild fire, no violent shouting & raving. It is a calm, solemn, deep work of the Sp[iri]t. May God preserve the fruit unto eternal life.'

She seems to have addressed the new converts the next night; 140 'found pardon' according to the *MNCM*, and she returned to Gateshead on Tuesday. In addition, they sold 100 copies of her booklet on women's ministry.[15]

She returned to Hartlepool towards the end of April. They 'had a splendid day' on the last Sunday of the month. The chapel was 'wedged at night & numbers went away unable to get in, a good prayer-meeting & 17 cases. It was like beginning over again after three weeks cessation of special effort.' Not surprisingly 'The friends expressed themselves as very highly gratified, even more so than on any former occasion.' She also 'heard a great deal of gracious and heart cheering intelligence with reference to

15 'CBLP', Letter P201, probably 8 Apl. 1861, pp. 263–64; *MNCM*, 'Hartlepool', 1861, p. 262.

those brought in during my former visit. They reckon to get 80 good & permanent members for their own church & have handed the names of 40 to other denominations.'

It is not only bad news that travels fast. Good news does too. She told her parents, 'The news of the Hartlepool work has spread far & near & is bringing me fresh invitations.'[16]

When her parents read these accounts, they must have asked themselves, 'Is that our Kate? How could she, that poor "frail thing", do all that?' Catherine anticipated the questions. She answered in one letter,

> And now I know what you are thinking about, viz., that I shall be [k]nocked up. If you knew how I have laboured, talking to penitents as hard as I could for two hours every night after preaching, you would not believe that it could be *me*. I scarcely can believe it myself, but hitherto the Lord hath helped me, & tho' often almost finished & scarcely able to speak or walk, he has wonderfully restored me, & the next night I have felt able for the work again. But I feel very poorly this morn'g.[17]

It is probably no coincidence that these remarkable, though brief, campaigns in Hartlepool came soon after that deep encounter with God earlier in the year. Through that the Spirit of God had empowered her for this work.

---

16 'CBLP', Letter P204, 1 May 1861, p. 267.
17 Ibid., Letter P201, probably 8 Apl. 1861, p. 264.

CHAPTER 20

The Resignation

'Am I, or am I not, to resume the work of an evangelist?'
William Booth to Rev. James Stacey.[1]

The Booths' resignation from the Methodist New Connexion was, in the strictest sense, an issue for William Booth, not Catherine. He was an ordained minister of that denomination. Catherine was a lay preacher and class leader, but otherwise seems to have held no official position. Consequently, most of this chapter must focus on William, although Catherine was involved in this matter in every way that was open to her. The possibility of William resigning was very much a joint issue, a joint decision. It is also an event that has been mythologised and is much misunderstood.[2] It must also be realised that if the Booths had not left the New Connexion there would have been no Salvation Army, so this is an important incident.

Preparation for the 1861 Conference

The New Connexion Conference for 1861 was due to be held at the end of May. The Booths knew that this Conference was crucial to their future. Would it reappoint William to the specifically evangelistic ministry or would it make him continue in circuit work? There was never any thought of appointing Catherine to an official position. The choice for the Booths was that if the Conference appointed William to the evangelistic ministry, they would stay in the New Connexion, if it did not, then the Booths would leave

---

1 See Booth, 'Resignation of The Rev. W. Booth,' which contains this letter and his later letter of resignation.
2 For a fuller account of the resignation, which seeks to strip away the mythology, see Bennett, 'William Booth's resignation from the Methodist New Connexion', *AJSAH*, vol. 4, iss. 1, pp. 25–39.

and become independent evangelists, trusting God for their material wants.

With that in mind William Booth wrote a letter to Rev. James Stacey, the then President of the Conference, on 5 March, more than two months before Conference.[3] In the letter Booth referred to the time he had joined the New Connexion and his studying (if that is not too strong a word) under Dr Cooke. He then added, that after that period, 'the Annual Committee, and afterwards the Sheffield Conference [1855], without any solicitation on my part, appointed me to that sphere [that is, the role of evangelist]. After being engaged in it for two years and a half, the Nottingham Conference [1857], by a small majority, decided that I should take a circuit.' The claim that he had earlier been officially appointed to the role of the denomination's evangelist is significant, because at the 1861 Conference some officials argued against such a role being created. Yet it had previously existed.

Booth then made it clear that after four years of circuit work he desired to be appointed to the evangelistic role once more, and asked Stacey the key question: 'Am I, or am I not, to resume the work of an evangelist?' That question would have to be answered by the 1861 Conference, under its new President, not James Stacey.

The quarterly meeting of the New Connexion Gateshead Circuit was probably held late in April 1861. It proposed to the Newcastle District, of which it was part, that that District recommend to the upcoming Conference that William Booth be employed as the denomination's evangelist. The District meeting, held on 6 and 7 May, tabled a resolution for the Conference, which read:

> That owing to the spiritual necessitive of this District, calling, as they do for the employment of some extraordinary agency to supply them, this meeting earnestly requests the conference to *appoint the Revd Mr. Booth, to labour as an Evangelist in this District* for the next year residing at Newcastle on Tyne[4] (emphasis added).

There are two key points in this Newcastle District proposal that became

---

3 There has been disagreement over the date of this letter, different parties opting for 5 and 15 March 1861. The printed form of the letter, which was later produced by William Booth for distribution to his friends, says 5 March. See Booth, 'Resignation of The Rev. W. Booth,' which contains this letter. The quotations here are from that edition of the March letter, not Frederick Booth-Tucker's version. (A copy of this resignation document is in the International Heritage Centre, London.)

4 Extracts from the minutes of the Methodist New Connexion Newcastle District meeting, 6 and 7 May 1861, Part 15, 2nd and 3rd sections.

significant later. The first was that William Booth should be set aside 'as an Evangelist'. The second was that he should be based in Newcastle and serve in that area for at least a year.

The 1861 Conference

The Conference was held at the Bethesda Chapel in Liverpool (not Gateshead) and the opening services were held on Sunday 19 May.[5] A writer in the *Staffordshire Advertiser* thought that the Conference was 'a harmonious, prosperous and generally highly encouraging gathering.'[6] However, it was not always harmonious, and it is likely that many were discouraged rather than encouraged. The matter of William Booth's future arose more than once as the Conference progressed and was hotly debated. Catherine was present for most, if not all, of the Conference.

The Conference first discussed Booth's case on Thursday afternoon 23 May. The Newcastle District tabled 'a series of resolutions' advocating that William Booth be used as an evangelist. The one original resolution of the District Meeting now became three, but, as shall be seen, they fairly reflected the spirit of the original.[7] Roy Hattersley says that this was for legal reasons and that whether there was to be an evangelistic 'agency', a specific position had first to be decided.[8] Yet, as has been seen, such an agency had previously existed and William Booth had been the agent.

The first resolution formally 'recognized the value and importance of evangelical agency.' The second proposed that 'the Rev. W. Booth be employed as an Evangelist.' The third 'recommended that for the next year he, in that capacity, should be located at Newcastle-upon-Tyne.'

The discussions on those resolutions resulted in 'a very long, anxious, and spirited debate.' The legal position was discussed that Thursday and the two lawyers present 'like doctors … differed.' One said that the denomination's Poll Deed 'interposed neither let nor hindrance' to such an appointment, while the other said 'that it did'. After considerable 'tedious' discussion, the Conference decided 'by a large majority' that it was 'compatible with the Deed Book to employ, *if found necessary*, a special agency for carrying on

---

5 *MNCM*, 'The Recent Conference at Liverpool', 1861, pp. 324–25.

6 *Staffordshire Advertiser* 'The Methodist New Connexion Annual Conference', 1 June 1861, p. 5, col. 5.

7 *MNCM*, 'Recent Conference', 1861, p. 330.

8 Hattersley, *Blood*, pp. 119–20.

the work of God among us'[9] (emphasis added). That seems to have ended the debate for that day.

So, there was no legal complication that would stop the appointment of Booth as the denomination's evangelist. But it remained to be decided on a later day if that appointment was 'necessary' and, what appears to have been the real issue, if it was desirable.

The next stage of the debate about appointing Booth as evangelist took place on Saturday 25 May. The first point was, according to the *MNCM*, to decide 'the *desirability* or otherwise of establishing such an agency' (emphasis added), that is, the position of an evangelist. This issue, again according to *MNCM*, 'gave rise to a discussion, which, while eliciting some diversity of sentiment ... was yet, on the whole, distinguished by intelligence, sobriety, and straightforwardness.'[10] Not that Catherine Booth saw it that way, as shall be seen. It also appears that during this part of the debate, the chairman invited Booth to read the letter that he had sent to James Stacey in March.[11]

Then, when some in the Booth camp were sensing victory[12], though that was far from assured, unexpectedly Rev. William Cooke moved an amendment, which appears to have been an attempt at a compromise. It stated, 'The Conference declares that any circuit, with the consent of the superintendent preacher, is at liberty to make such arrangements with any of our ministers and their respective circuits, as may be found needful for holding revival services among them.' Suddenly the issue of an appointment of an evangelist had flown out the window, and William Booth had become just one 'of our ministers' who would serve in a circuit and might be called upon to conduct a series of evangelistic services elsewhere. The amendment thus meant that any evangelistic ministry that Booth might exercise would be part time by arrangement. This was not what he or Catherine wanted.

Then, after what appears to have been a break (perhaps for lunch) the third and final stage of the debate was launched. The delegates then 'elicited much kindly feeling towards Mr Booth and his earnest measures.' (Whether William Booth saw it that way is doubtful, and it can be guaranteed that Catherine did not.) However, the Conference decided that now was not

---

9 *MNCM*, 'Recent Conference', 1861, p. 330.

10 Ibid., pp. 332–33.

11 Booth-Tucker, *Catherine*, vol. 1, p. 289.

12 See Catherine Booth's account in Booth-Tucker, *Catherine*, vol. 1, p. 287. See also Booth-Tucker, *Catherine*, vol. 1, p. 289.

the time to originate 'the agency discussed', perhaps in the future, but not now.[13] It was presumably then that the amendment was put to the vote and it was approved by, according to Booth-Tucker, 'a large majority.'[14] The appointment of an evangelist, then, seems to have been deemed neither necessary nor desirable, at least at that time. The Booths and their supporters had lost. The Conference directed that William Booth was to take the Newcastle circuit and arrange evangelistic meetings in other circuits as time and commitments to his own circuit allowed.

Rev. J. Stokoe, the writer of the report in the *MNCM*, concluded by saying that it had been 'a good Conference. At times there had been sharp-shooting, but in the end it turned out to be with blank cartridges. No one, unless sensitive to a high degree, was wounded.'[15] But two people had been 'wounded', William and Catherine Booth.

Catherine gave an account of some of the discussions in the debate, which paint a different picture from Stokoe's. She later recalled,

> At length our case came on for consideration. As we anticipated, the proposal for our restoration to the evangelistic sphere met with brisk opposition, although the reasons advanced for it had undergone a complete change. In fact, it was necessary for Mr Wright and his friends to invent some fresh pretexts for their action, inasmuch as we had completely cut the ground from beneath their former objections. Nevertheless, there was every reason to believe that nearly half the ministers and the majority of the laymen present were in favour of the proposal, and we trusted that with their help we should be able to carry the day. Nothing surprised me, however, more than the half-hearted and hesitating manner in which some spoke, who had in private assured us most emphatically of their sympathy and support. I believe that *cowardice* is one of the most prevailing and subtle sins of the day. People are so *pusillanimous* that they dare not say 'No,' and are afraid to go contrary to the opinions of others, or to find themselves in a minority.

On three separate occasions the subject of our appointment was brought forward for discussion and was successively adjourned, the debate occasioning considerable excitement throughout. Every imaginable and unimaginable objection was resorted to by the opposition, which was

---

13 *MNCM*, 'Recent Conference', 1861, p. 333.
14 Booth-Tucker, *Catherine*, vol. 1, p. 289.
15 *MNCM*, 'Recent Conference', 1861, p. 336.

headed, as before, by the Rev. P. J. Wright. It so happened, moreover, that Dr Crofts, who had been largely instrumental on the first occasion in relegating us to circuit work, was this year appointed as President of the Connexion. There can be little doubt that this nomination exercised an important influence upon the events that followed.[16]

Catherine's account is vivid and emotive, though not necessarily inaccurate. The phrase 'relegating *us*' also needs to be noted. It was not just William Booth being relegated; it was Catherine too.

Catherine wrote to her parents at this time, giving them the news. At the end of that letter she instructed them to 'burn the first part of this letter.' Sadly, they seem to have done so, for the top of the first two pages (one sheet) are missing. The remaining letter begins:

> … been triumphant & we should have had a majority, but for his empty & foolish ressolution [sic].[17] P. J. Wright only laughed at it, & no man of any perception could do any other. Mr Cook[e] sold our cause, & I find it very difficult to rid myself of the opinion, & so do others, that he offered up my husband on the altar between *two parties*, in order to procure for himself a reap[p]ointment to the Editorship.[18] If it was so, the bait took admirably & verily he has his reward. But God lives & *justice* & *judgment* are the…[19]

But however the Booths felt about it, the Conference had appointed William Booth to the Newcastle circuit, which was at least what the Newcastle District had requested, and he had permission to conduct evangelistic meetings in other New Connexion circuits by arrangement.

A myth exposed

It is with regard to the Booths' response to this decision that mythology often seems to take over from fact, especially with regard to events at the Conference. Booth-Tucker recorded it this way: Mrs Booth 'had been sitting at a point in the gallery from which she and her husband could

---

16 Booth-Tucker, *Catherine*, vol. 1, pp. 287–88. This seems to follow on from a passage on page 286 that Catherine wrote 'in later years'.

17 That is, Rev. Cooke's amendment.

18 A move had been made to remove Cooke from the editorship of the magazine.

19 'CBLP', Letter P207, late May 1861 p. 270. As the top of this letter is missing, it is not dated. However, it sounds as though it was written soon after the vote on William's role in the denomination, which was on Saturday, 25 May.

interchange glances.' When the decision was announced, 'Rising from her seat and bending over the gallery, Mrs Booth's clear voice rang through the Conference, as she said to her husband, "Never!"'

Booth-Tucker continued:

Every eye was turned towards the speaker in the gallery. The idea of a woman daring to utter her protest, or to make her voice heard in the Conference, produced little short of consternation. It was a sublime scene, as with flushed face and flashing eye, she stood before that audience... Her 'Never!' seemed to penetrate like an electric flash through every heart...

Mr Booth sprang to his feet, and waved his hat in the direction of the door. Heedless of the ministerial cries of 'Order, Order,' and not pausing for another word, they hurried forth, met and embraced each other at the foot of the gallery stairs, and turned their backs upon the Conference, resolved to trust God for the future...

Accompanying Booth-Tucker's text is an illustration of the scene. In this Catherine is standing in the second row of the crowded gallery, with her arm raised. William is standing amidst the delegates in the lower part of the chapel, with one hand holding his hat, lifted high, and the other hand pointing towards the chapel door. The message is clear. The Booths were not just leaving the chapel, but there and then they were leaving the New Connexion.

It is all detailed, dramatic and vivid. But is it true?

The simple answer to that is 'No.' However, we will not detail the evidence here, except to give the Booths' subsequent words and actions, which, in themselves, are enough to deny the account.[20]

According to William Booth, after the Conference decision had been made, he 'informed the Stationing Committee and afterwards the Conference, both orally and by letter, that I could not take the responsibility of the Newcastle appointment, but still the Conference persisted in it.' He thought of resigning there and then but decided to wait until he could see what arrangement could be made with the Newcastle circuit.[21]

There is no reason to doubt that Booth did what he claimed here. But it is surprising that the New Connexion leaders did not ask for his

---

20 For a detailed examination of this see, Bennett, 'Booth's resignation', *AJSAH*, vol. 4, iss. 1, pp. 32–39.
21 Booth, 'Resignation of The Rev. W. Booth', p. 2.

resignation at that time or take some conciliatory action. It was clear that if they took Booth's words seriously, the Newcastle Circuit was likely to be without an effective superintendent. After the Conference the Booths did not immediately leave the Connexion to become travelling evangelists, as some seem to suppose. The Booths went to Newcastle to take up their appointment, however reluctantly and with whatever reservations. But their intention was very different from what the Conference had laid down.

Indeed, it appears that even before they arrived in Newcastle the Booths were looking elsewhere. In a letter that was clearly written soon after the Conference decision, presumably late in May, Catherine told her parents, 'Wm is writing to day to Mr Caughey & Reginald Radcliffe', which strongly suggests that they were already seriously considering independent evangelism. Then she added,

> If an arrangement should be come to with Newcastle so that we get the House, would my dear Mother come & keep house for me for three or four months, & so let me go & hold services in some adjacent places? But I want Wm to begin in London. Can you get us any information about the committee who appoints the preachers for the Halls & theatres in London?[22]

This letter indicates that the Booths were hoping to live in Newcastle for some time and that Catherine desired to conduct missions in 'adjacent places', though whether only in New Connexion chapels is not clear. Yet William, with the support of his wife, was already looking further afield and clearly hoping to conduct missions outside the New Connexion, and apparently on an independent basis.

A little later Catherine told her parents,

> Our position alltogether [sic] is about as trying as it well could be. We have reason to fear that the Annual Committee will not allow even this arrangement with the Circuit to be carried out, & if not, I don't see any honourable course for us but to resign at once & risk all, if trusting in the Lord for our bread in order to do what we believe to be his will, ought to be called a *risk*.

> If the arrangement *is* allowed to work, which I fear will not be the case, it involves all sorts of difficulties. This Circuit is the worst to be managed in the whole connexion & Wm will get nothing by his connection with

---

22 'CBLP', Letter P207, late May 1861 p. 271.

it but trouble & vexation. This I have seen from the beginning & have opposed his coming as far as I could. I am sick of the New Connexion from *top* to *bottom*...[23]

In this letter Catherine does not make clear what was the 'arrangement with the Circuit', though it appears to have been made at the circuit meeting held on a Monday, either 3 or 10 June.[24] However, the arrangement seems to have been quite different from that which the Conference had made with the Newcastle Circuit, and it favoured more mobility for Booth and more absences from the circuit. While the Conference had in mind the Newcastle Circuit first and evangelising in other New Connexion circuits second, the arrangement with the circuit seems to have been evangelising anywhere and with whoever was willing first, and the Newcastle circuit second. It is astonishing that a circuit would have agreed to that, but that appears to have been, at least, how the Booths understood it. What is most strange is that, according to the Booths, the Newcastle Circuit had approved this arrangement 'unanimously'.[25]

Towards the end of June, William Booth went to London and met some people engaged in independent evangelism, with, it would appear, the intention of conducting missions in halls and theatres.[26] While there he met an evangelist named Hammond, probably E.P. Hammond an American, who told Booth, 'Cut the denomination and go to work for Jesus, and He will open your way.'[27]

Booth returned to Newcastle and in the first week of July, he seems to have fulfilled part of his obligation to the New Connexion. He ministered in nearby Alnwick, presumably in a New Connexion chapel.[28]

However, Booth's visit to London's evangelistic agencies was clearly contrary to what the Conference had decided. So, the New Connexion officials had no option but to take action. On 16 July, Rev. H.O. Crofts wrote to Booth accusing him of 'not taking [his] circuit, according to the rules and usages of the body, nor according to the resolution of Dr Cooke.' Frankly,

---

23 Ibid., Letter P208, probably mid-June 1861, p. 272.

24 I have tried to obtain the minutes of the relevant circuit meeting but have been unsuccessful.

25 Booth, 'Resignation of The Rev. W. Booth', 2; 'CBLP', Letter P210, 5 July 1861, p. 275.

26 Booth, *Letters*, Letters (WB129) probably 19 or 20 June, (WB130) probably 22 June, and (WB131), probably 24 June 1861, pp. 343–46; Booth, *Letters CD*, pp. 333–35.

27 Ibid., Letter (WB129) probably 19 or 20 June 1861, p. 343; ibid., p. 333.

28 'CBLP', Letter P210, 5 July 1861, p. 275.

however much Booth might have argued otherwise, that charge seems fair. Yet he had warned them at the close of Conference that he did not wish to take on the 'responsibility' of the Newcastle Circuit. Booth responded to Crofts' letter on 18 July and resigned from the New Connexion, so about seven weeks after the Conference.

On 20 August 1861 and after, Booth sent to an unknown number of friends a printed document that contained the letter that he had sent to Rev. Stacey in March and his letter of resignation from the New Connexion that he had sent to Rev. Crofts on 18 July. The Booths plainly intended to make their position clear.[29]

Catherine also wished to write her criticism of the Conference decision for one of the Methodist journals. But, according to her, William 'will not consent.' He may have feared that strong words from Catherine would restrict their future usefulness, especially as she seems to have been keen on making a stern criticism of Rev. William Cooke.[30] William was more cautious.

Another matter needs to be considered on the resignation. Was opposition to Catherine preaching one reason for rejecting William Booth from being the denomination's evangelist? Were some afraid that they would have an evangelistic team, one of them a woman, preaching on behalf of the New Connexion? While that thought may have dwelt in the minds of some, it does need to be borne in mind that the New Connexion Conference of 1857 had originally decided against reappointing William Booth as the denomination's evangelist, and that was more than two years before Catherine had begun to preach. In addition, since then Catherine had been accepted as a legitimate preacher by at least two northern New Connexion circuits, and many members of the New Connexion had gone to hear Phoebe Palmer.

---

29 Booth, 'Resignation of The Rev. W. Booth', pp. 1–2.
30 'CBLP', Letter P219, probably 9 Oct. 1861, p. 292.

CHAPTER 21

Cornwall on Fire

'Never forget to pray for us,'

Catherine Booth to her parents.[1]

In August 1861 William and Catherine Booth launched out as an independent evangelistic team; that is, two evangelists working together, but without denominational ties. This meant they were unlike most independent evangelists, who were mainly men who functioned alone. There was, of course, Phoebe and Walter Palmer, but their emphasis was more on encouraging people to have a holiness experience than on evangelism, and most of their time was spent in America. The Booths were committed to England and had no thought at that stage of spreading their wings overseas.

There had been husband and wife preachers before, such as John and Mary Fletcher and Zechariah and Mary Taft of the Wesleyans, and John and Sarah Harrison of the Primitive Methodists. But the Booths had shed their link with the New Connexion and had not sought formal association with any other body. This gave them freedom, but it guaranteed neither cooperation nor an income. As Catherine reflected a little later, 'We can go where we like & where the people *want us*. We can stay as long as we like, and we can receive what the people like to give us.'[2] Their early campaigns were to be mainly with various shades of Methodism.

Hayle and Camborne

Rev. Shone of the New Connexion church in Hayle, on the northern coast of Cornwall, sent the Booths an invitation to conduct a mission in his town,

---

1 'CBLP', Letter P224, late January 1862, p. 301.

2 Ibid., p. 300.

which they accepted. Booth-Tucker says that Shone had been converted during Booth's campaign in Chester, and he had been a colleague of Booth's in Gateshead from 1859–60.

According to Booth-Tucker, the Booths received Shone's letter of invitation 'at the breakfast-table.' Catherine was delighted with it. She said, 'The earnest way in which I had been included in the invitation, and the evident appreciation and value put upon my labours seemed to me as the cloud like a man's hand on my horizon', which would lead to the Booths ministering together.[3] While Shone probably left Gateshead soon after Catherine had begun preaching and may never have heard her preach, he must have known her well, realised what she was capable of, and had heard about her successful ministry. He therefore deliberately included her in the invitation.

So, William and Catherine arranged for their children to stay with the Mumfords, sending Mary Kirton, the latest children's nurse, with them to help with their care, and then went to Hayle. If an invitation from a New Connexion minister seems strange, in that Booth had just resigned from that denomination, he was technically still a New Connexion minister, as his resignation could not officially be accepted until the Conference the following year. It needs to be understood, though, that the Booths were intending to minister to specific towns or areas, not to particular denominations. In other words, they were happy to preach for any denomination that offered them a pulpit, and they favoured remaining in one district until they felt their work was done in that area.

Yet the Booths do not seem to have been expecting a long stay in Cornwall. They began in Hayle 'in good earnest' on Monday 15 August at the New Connexion chapel which seated about 420. William preached that Monday and Tuesday and Catherine on Wednesday and they had 21 'cases'. When each sermon had concluded, Catherine occupied herself by 'going to the people in the pews', but that work proved difficult because of the noise. 'I never saw people cry & shout as they do here', she told her parents. 'The place is full of conviction, & I doubt not we shall have a glorious work.'

The Mumfords appear to have been a little concerned that the Booths might not receive sufficient invitations from churches to make their work viable. They need not have worried, for the Booths were already receiving

---

[3] Booth-Tucker, *Catherine*, vol. 1, pp. 307–308; *MNCM*, 'Extracts from the Minutes…', 1859, p. 686.

numerous invitations and they found it '*perplexing*' trying to decide which to accept. Some of these invitations, perhaps most, were from other parts of Cornwall, which made them consider 'a much longer stay' in that county than they had originally planned.

One invitation was from Rev. Samuel Dunn in nearby Camborne, who had been William's minister at Wesley's Chapel in Nottingham. He was now an independent Methodist, having left the Wesleyans over the Fly Sheet affair. They visited Dunn and arranged for Catherine to preach for him on Sunday and two or three weekday evenings if she was well enough. If that proved successful, the Booths would 'work' Hayle and Camborne 'at the same time, interchanging with one another, according to circumstances.'[4]

So, Catherine went to Camborne and had 'a glorious beginning', with a 'packed' chapel.[5] At the same time the work in Hayle got 'better & better'. Then they received an invitation from St Ives, not far from Hayle, but their mission in Hayle was going too well to leave. It was going so well that the local Wesleyan minister opened his chapel for the work on two nights and William preached in that one Sunday night, and it was 'crammed to suffocation'. Catherine preached in the New Connexion chapel, apparently on the same night, and it was also '*well filled*'. That night they had 30 cases at the Wesleyan chapel and 20 at the New Connexion. This was a significant development for the Booths as they were now involved with two denominations.

After less than a month in their new work, they were sufficiently confident of success to begin forming plans. It was clear that their stay in Cornwall was going to be longer than originally thought, so Catherine began making arrangements for the children to join them. She was also confident that an extended mission in Cornwall would greatly improve her husband's reputation, and, though she did not say so, improve hers too. She hoped that what was happening on Cornwall would be repeated elsewhere so that they could 'work a district or a County', while being based in 'one centre', where they could establish a home and stay for a year or so, instead of being always on the move.[6]

On Wednesday 4 September, William preached in Copper House Wesleyan Chapel in Hayle. This, according to Catherine, was only about

---

4 'CBLP', Letter P215, 15 Aug. 1861, p. 287.
5 Ibid., Letter P216, probably late August 1861, p. 289.
6 Ibid., Letter P217, 2 Sept. 1861, p. 290.

a mile from the other Wesleyan chapel, which gives an indication of the strength of Methodism in Cornwall. Large as this chapel was, it was still 'cram[m]ed out into the street', with an estimated 1800 people. Catherine told her parents that she had 'never witnessed such a scene in [her] life as the prayer-meeting presented' that night. 'The rail was filled in a few minutes with great strong men, who cried alloud [sic] for mercy, some of them as though the pains of hell had got hold upon them. Oh, it was a scene! No one could be heard praying & the cries & shouts of the Penitents almost overpowered the singing.' The Booths did not get away until 10 o'clock, and they still left people in the chapel.[7]

They did very little socialising while in Cornwall, and, indeed, in other places that they visited later, despite getting many invitations. There were two reasons for that. Firstly, it was time consuming. Secondly, if they said yes to one invitation, but no to another they were likely to offend.

While they were apart from their children, Catherine wrote at least two letters to Willie, who was now five. Just after they had arrived in Cornwall, Catherine wrote to him saying,

> I have been thinking a great deal about you, my dear boy and about Ballington, Katy, and Baby, too; but most about you, because you are the oldest and biggest, and I know if you are good and do as you are told, they will most likely be the same. I do hope you are praying to the Lord every day to help you, and are trying to do as Grandma and Mary tell you. If you are, I know this letter will find you happy and joyous, because when little children are *good* they are always *happy*…

> I want to tell you, too, about a children's meeting which we have here. Papa tells all the little children to come to the chapel at six o'clock of an evening and such a lot come, half the chapel full. And then either papa or I speak to them about Jesus and teach them to sing pretty little hymns… When I look at them all singing so merrily, I do wish my Willie was amongst them.

Then in a later letter, she told him that she understood that he must be missing them, but 'you see we cannot always do just what we would like. We have to wait until the Lord lets us, and we may always be sure that He knows best.'[8]

---

7 Ibid., Letter P218, 7 Sept. 1861, p. 291.

8 Booth-Tucker, *Catherine*, Letters dated 15 Aug. 1861 and 'A month later', vol. 1, pp. 310–11.

In the middle of September, the Mumfords visited the Booths in Cornwall, bringing the children and Mary Kirton with them. They seem to have stayed for about three weeks before returning to London, leaving the children and Mary with the Booths. Now that the Booths' mission was reasonably stable, they were able to rent accommodation for the whole family. The children adapted quickly to Cornish conditions. 'The fresh air on the sea beach agrees with them first rate', Catherine told her parents.[9] 'They go off directly after breakfast & stop till 11 o'clock, then again at 2 & stay on the sands till 5. They each have a spade, with which they dig tunnels, mountains, brooks… They never had such fun in their lives before. You would be delighted to see them running away from the waves & then back again to their brooks, which the retreating wave has filled with water.'[10]

Mary, who appears to have suffered from epilepsy, was 'very kind' to the children. She also assisted at some of the services, going 'about every other night' and rendering 'efficient help in sp[e]aking to young persons & inviting them to the communion rail.'[11]

In what appears to have been the first letter Catherine wrote to the Mumfords after the latter's return to London, she urged them not to be uneasy about her working so hard. She said, this 'life is not more trying to *me* at *present* than a regular preacher's, & *much* more *agreeable*.' She was in her element, and so was William. He 'is happier' than she could recall him ever being.[12]

St Ives

They moved to St Ives, a fishing town, probably early in October. A few days after they arrived Catherine wrote, 'The work brok[e] out with glory on Sunday night, such a scene as I never beheld; chapel crowded, gal[l]ery and all till near 10 o'clock. There have been about 80 names taken on the two nights.' However, this work was proving 'dreadfully heavy' for William. 'The people are so *curious* & require so much managing.' But despite the confusion he was able to keep order. And 'amidst it all, the Lord is present & is hewing out of nature's Quarry some beautiful stones for his spiritual temple.'[13]

---

9 'CBLP', Letter P219 probably 9 Oct. 1861, p. 293.

10 Ibid., Letter P220. 18 Oct. 1861, p. 294.

11 Ibid., Letters P207, late May 1861, and P219, probably 9 Oct. 1861, pp. 271, 293.

12 Ibid., Letter P219, probably 9 Oct. 1861, p. 292.

13 Ibid., Letter P219, probably 9 Oct. 1861, p. 292.

On what appears to have been the second Sunday of their time in St Ives, Catherine preached and the chapel was 'packed and hundreds went away unable to get in.' During the following week Catherine held some meetings in the mornings, presumably for women, and on the Friday the lower area of the chapel was 'nearly three parts full. In addition, the chapel was 'well filled' every night, when, presumably, William preached.[14]

It is striking that during all this busyness Catherine seemed generally in better health, at least she says she is 'poorly' much less often. Perhaps she was in better health, though it may have been a case of not having time to think and write about her ailments. But even if her health had improved, she was never strong, and her condition may have been a triumph of faith and determination over physical limitations.

An invitation from Phoebe Palmer

Early in November they received a letter from Phoebe Palmer. The Palmers were in Liverpool and Walter had been 'taken so ill with a severe cold, which threatened to settle permanently on his lungs' that the Palmers had cancelled some of their appointments. Mrs Palmer suggested in the letter that the Booths take over from them in Liverpool, while Walter recovered.[15] Catherine was keen on responding favourably to the suggestion. She thought 'that the very fact of [William's] succeeding Mrs Palmer will give him status with thousands who would never think any thing of him otherwise. Of course,' by that she meant 'as increasing his *influence for good*.' And she had a point. This could lead to greater fame for each of them, which, while that is unlikely to be what they sought, would lead to wider opportunities for evangelism. In addition, clearly the Palmers were grateful for Catherine's earlier defence of Phoebe and her letter indicates that she had a high opinion of the Booths and their work.

William's automatic reaction to this was to send a reply saying 'No!' After all, their work in Cornwall was being greatly blessed, the family was settled, so why travel a long journey north to a ministry that might not be as successful. But Catherine persuaded him to consider it carefully before deciding. Catherine says, '*we* wrote' (emphasis added) a tentative response,

---

14 Ibid., Letter P220, 18 Oct. 1861, pp. 293–94.
15 Booth-Tucker has what seems to be the whole of this letter in *Catherine*, vol. 1, pp. 320–21.

neither rejecting nor accepting the offer.[16] However, in the end it came to nothing, as the people in Liverpool hosting the Palmers seem to have lost interest in possible substitutes. It is also likely that William Booth was no longer prepared to be anyone's replacement.

More at St Ives

The work in St Ives continued 'gloriously', though Catherine was not involved in it as much as she would have liked, for she was unwell for a lot of this time. Yet, by mid-November, 800 names of those seeking salvation had been taken, and then they moved to the Primitive Methodist chapel for a week or so. In addition, the Wesleyans, 'Trustees, Leaders and people, without a *disentient*' were all 'very anxious to have W[illia]m in their chapel' but the Superintendent minister 'stood in the way.' Catherine was not surprised by that one-man roadblock, because she had 'no faith in Parsons'. In one of her more military moods, she added, 'The *people* of *all* denominations and of no denomination at all are exceedingly anxious to keep us. I cannot speak, however, for the Priests, neither do I care much whether they are anxious or not.'[17] It appears, though, that William, at least, was allowed to preach in the Wesleyan chapel.

The January issue of the *Methodist New Connexion Magazine* excitedly reported, 'At St Ives and Hayle numbers have been added to the Lord.' However, it did not mention the Booths as being the human agents.[18]

According to the *Cornish Telegraph*, the St Ives' Methodists held a 'Farewell Tea Meeting' in the 'Wesleyan Day Schools, and the New Connexion Chapel' for the Booths on Thursday 16 January 1862, with 1200 in attendance. Remarkably, that afternoon the town 'bore quite a holiday appearance', with a lot of the shops closed, showing the impact the mission had had on that town. That newspaper said that there had been 1026 adult converts (Booth-Tucker says 1028 over the age of 14), plus children, during the St Ives mission, including '23 ... captains of vessels' (Booth-Tucker says 28), three mine agents and two ... members of the Corporation.'[19] Catherine

---

16 'CBLP', Letter P221, possibly 7 or 8 Nov. 1861, p. 295.

17 Ibid., Letter P222, 18 Nov. 1861, p. 297.

18 *MNCM*, 'Connexional Progress', 1862, p. 40.

19 *Cornish Telegraph,* 'Farewell Tea Meeting to Rev. W. Booth' 22 Jan. 1862, p. 2, col. 4.; Booth-Tucker, *Catherine*, vol. 1, pp. 321–22. The differences in the figures may be because of difficulty in reading someone's handwriting.

called the tea meeting a 'glorious finish up'.

In November 1862 an official from the St Ives circuit of the New Connexion wrote a letter that was published in the *Methodist New Connexion Magazine* that year. It said, 'In 1861', presumably at conference time, 'the number of members' in the circuit 'was 229', while at the 1862 Conference 'the number returned was 700'.[20]

On 14 December 1861, while the St Ives campaign was at its height, an event occurred that saddened all England. Albert, Prince Consort, the husband of Queen Victoria, died. The Queen went into perpetual mourning, and for a while the nation mourned with her.[21] The January 1862 issue of the *New Connexion Magazine* published an eight-page tribute to him, with a black border around each page.[22]

St Just

Late in January, the Booths arranged to move to St Just, a mining town, further to the south in Cornwall. There a wealthy Wesleyan layman was preparing the way for them. He and his wife had promised to furnish a home for them for the duration of their stay. By that time Catherine was pregnant again and 'poorly'.[23]

According to William Booth, St Just had plenty of churches and chapels for its 10,000 inhabitants and had been well-evangelised in the past. The Booths began there at a Bible Christian chapel on Sunday 26 January; the New Connexion chapel (if there was one) was probably too small to hold the expected crowds.[24] The Bible Christians were a Methodist offshoot, strongest in Cornwall and Devon. The Booths had 'a splendid beginning'. At that Sunday morning service 'the bottom of the chapel [was] well filled'. Catherine spoke 'for nearly an hour' and 'The people wept all over the place'. When she 'invited the Lord's people forward to make a fresh consecration,

20 *MNCM*, Letter from J. Harker, 11 Nov. 1862, pp. 755–76.

21 Longford, *Victoria R. I.*, pp. 298–300.

22 *MNCM*, 'Memoir of the Prince Consort', 1862, pp. 33–40.

23 'CBLP', Letters P223, mid-January 1862, and P224, late January 1862, pp. 298–99.

24 Booth-Tucker, *Catherine*, vol. 1, p. 325, quotes William Booth's list of churches and chapels in the town, which includes a New Connexion chapel, but other evidence may suggest that this is a Booth-Tucker addition to Booth's list. See 'Methodist Church in Cornwall', and the *MNCM*, 1859, p. 688, which says that there were three chapels in the Truro circuit (the New Connexion's only circuit in Cornwall), and these seem to have been in Truro, St Ives and Hayle.

[they] had the rail nearly filled, 3 or 4 of them being penitents.'[25]

William preached in the evening. He later wrote, 'At night the place was literally besieged with people, and it was calculated that some two thousand were turned away unable to gain admission.'[26]

It appears to have been on the following Thursday that the work became explosive. William Booth recalled it this way,

> On Thursday much prayer had been offered, and at half-past nine that night the answer came. The windows of Heaven were opened and a shower of blessed influence descended upon us. The effect was electrical. It was sudden and overpowering. The sinners could restrain themselves no longer. Hearts were breaking, or broken, in every direction. The chapel was filled with glory. The meeting was continued until midnight, and numbers found peace.[27]

The campaign moved to the nearby Free Methodist Church on Wednesday 5 February, which 'led to a temporary check in the progress of the work.' At first the church members were not enthusiastic, particularly about some of the methods used, and little of value seems to have occurred. However, on Sunday evening 'the clouds began to break, and the powers of darkness yielded in all directions, and by midnight a multitude had been saved.'[28] It is unclear how much Catherine was involved in this part of the mission. She was still struggling with the early stages of her latest pregnancy, but it is amazing how often she rose above her struggles and illnesses.

Significantly, some of the leading local Wesleyans had played truant from their own church on that first Sunday morning in St Just and went to the Bible Christian chapel, hoping to invite the Booths to preach for them. William and Catherine had seen the local Wesleyan chapel and she described it as 'immense', a good place to house the large number of people eager to hear them. Most of the Wesleyan circuit leaders and people were in favour of the Booths preaching at their chapel, but they were expecting opposition from Mr Hobson, the Superintendent minister of the circuit, who was also the District Chairman. He, it seems, had recently 'declared it contrary to their *rules & usages* for *Females* to speak in their chapels.'[29]

---

25 'CBLP', Letter P224, late January 1862, p. 300.

26 Booth-Tucker, *Catherine*, vol. 1, p. 326, quoting from the *Wesleyan Times*.

27 Ibid., vol. 1, p. 329, quoting from the *Wesleyan Times*.

28 Ibid., vol. 1, p. 331, quoting from the *Wesleyan Times*.

29 'CBLP', Letter P224, late January 1862, pp. 300–301.

Eventually the Booths were invited to preach for the Wesleyans. Catherine told her parents that at one of her services

> I had Mr Hobson ... hearing me, & also the second preacher who opened the service for me. I did not know Mr Hobson was there till after; he sat right under the Platform. But the presence of the other preacher did not embar[r]ass me in the least. I am wonderfully delivered from all fear after I once get my mouth open. When I came down from platform, Mr Hobson received me most kindly, took my hand in both his, like a father, & told me he should often be coming to see us *now*. Does it not seem wonderful how 'the rough places are made smooth & the crooked places straight' before us? This is the Chairman who sent word to Hayle, in answer to the enquiries of the Super[intendent] there, as to whether I might go into their chapel at the wish of their people, that it was contrary to their *rules* & *usages*!! Rules & usages can be twisted wonderfully when folks have a mind; where there's a will there's a way, & Mr Hobson's perception of the lift we may give to his darling Methodism has changed his *will*, & behold the result.

> Well, the Lord rules & overrules both men & rules & usages, & I trust this is of the Lord's doings. At any rate, it enables my dear husband to *get at the* people, which was partially impossible in the small chapels, besides almost killing him every night with the crush & the heat. The Wesleyans have the large chapels, and for any thing I see they take better care of the converts than the liberal Methodists... I am utterly sick of New Connexion parsons, and what is church polity compared with successful action? The people are all right every where, but the preachers are awfully wrong in most instances. I shall never be content untill [sic] we have had a fair try in some Hall or public building, thoroughly apart from any denomination, and we shall get it before long.[30]

Catherine the timid had become Catherine the bold. By this time, once in a pulpit or on a platform and speaking to a crowd, however large, she seems to have become devoid of fear and uncertainty. God was with her, she was sure, and He would bless her efforts. Why should she fear those who might oppose her? For she knew that there would always be opposition. It is claimed that when Catherine preached on Sunday afternoons during the mission in St Just, people from distant parts, wishing to hear her, began the long trek to St Just early in the morning and on the way home walked into the night.[31]

---

30 Ibid., Letter P225, 25 Feb. 1862, pp. 302–303.
31 Booth, *Reminiscences*, p. 54; *Reminiscences CD*, p. 13. This claim is on a supplementary

She, and William too, had decided that the best solution to reach the lost, many of whom would not set foot in a church or chapel, was to hire secular buildings and preach in them. That too would attract people from different denominations. Preaching in, say, a Wesleyan chapel would draw in those associated with the Wesleyans and some strays from other Methodist denominations, but many, perhaps, loosely connected with the Church of England, the Baptists or the Congregationalists, would not readily go to a Methodist chapel of any kind. And many of those outside the churches would not enter any church or chapel. But if the Booths ministered in a public hall, it was likely that many more people would feel free to attend.

Catherine's letters to her parents were less frequent during this period. She told them in one of her rare missives, 'It will appear strange to you, but it seems easier to go & give an address at the chapel than to sit down to write a long letter. Excitement carries me through the former and drives away for a time the horrible nausea I am so much troubled with, but in the latter I find no such relief. I hope on this account you will excuse my seeming neglect.'[32]

The Booths' mission in St Just continued right through March. They were to have concluded on the 28th of that month, 'but a deputation of *all the officials*, a large vestry full, waited on Mr Hobson … & wrung from him consent for another week.' The Wesleyans held some missionary services that weekend, which gave William, who was not well, a break, before he brought the campaign to a close early in April.[33]

St Buryan, Pendeen and Lelant

The Booths carried out brief missions in nearby St Buryan and Pendeen, and then moved to Lelant, which is near Hayle and St Ives. One encouraging aspect of the mission in Lelant was that, being so close to towns in which that had already ministered, some of the converts of the earlier work supported the new ministry.

They began there on Sunday 18 May. On each of the first two Sundays the chapel was packed, and many had to go away disappointed. The third Sunday was, according to William Booth, a 'powerful day.' William preached

---

page and was not made by Catherine.
32 'CBLP', Letter P225, 25 Feb. 1862, p. 302.
33 Ibid., Letter P228, 2 Apr. 1862, pp. 308–309.

in the morning and Catherine in the afternoon. The latter he described as 'a mighty time'. William took to the pulpit again that evening. Well before he had finished his sermon, there were so many people in the congregation 'shouting and weeping' that he had to stop speaking. So, he invited 'the wounded to come forward'. Booth said that there were nearly 40 'seeking mercy' on this occasion and, he thought, 26 found it that night.[34]

By the end of their time in Lelant, William was unwell and Catherine was far into her latest pregnancy, so they decided to have a break. It was probably late in June or early in July that they returned to London, where they stayed with the Mumfords. They left the children in Cornwall in the care of Mary Kirton. The Booths had had a long succession of servants, most of whom had been in varying degrees unreliable, but Mary was able, trustworthy and, now, greatly devoted to the Booths and their mission.[35]

Penzance and Mousehole

They returned to Cornwall and late in July went to Penzance, a larger coastal town to the east of St Just, hoping to conduct a mission there. Catherine said, 'There is a very strong & universal desire amongst the people of this town for us to labour here. Mary carn't [sic] go into a shop or speak to an individual but they want to know when Mr Booth begins in Penzance. The people, saints, & *sinners*, are ripe for a glorious work. And what hinders?' she asked. Her answer: 'Nothing on earth, or in *hell*, but two or three parsons! And shall they not be held accountable for the blood of these souls, yea verily; and I would tell them so as soon as not if I had the opportunity.'[36] Catherine was often highly critical of 'parsons', sometimes fairly, sometimes not, but she seemed to forget that her husband was also a parson.

Not finding openings in Penzance, from 2 August, William preached in the quaintly named Mousehole (pronounced Mowzal), a small village a little further to the south. As Catherine put it, 'Mousehole is only a very small place & a small cause, and is taken now just as a make shift to suit other & more important places further on in the season.' That is, if there were to be any 'more important places'. Catherine, eight months pregnant, was unable to help with this mission. Catherine later said, that this campaign was made

---

34 Booth-Tucker, *Catherine*, vol. 1, pp. 340–41.
35 Ibid., vol. 1, pp. 345, 349.
36 'CBLP', Letter P229, probably early August 1862, p. 311.

more difficult because it was a fishing community, and many of the men were, at that time, 'off on the Irish coast or in the North Sea.' Despite that there were still about 80 'professed' conversions.[37]

It certainly was not one of their more successful missions. One visitor to the area soon after was told by a local, 'If you are going over to Mowzal, me Cappen, I hope you will find they have mended their ways, as they have had a Mr Booth there and converted a passel of 'em.' The visitor went to Mousehole and said he found little evidence of the results of Booth's mission, though he did not stay long enough to make a thorough check.[38]

The three Conferences

But bigger trouble was brewing, major opposition was mounting. The New Connexion Conference that year formally accepted William Booth's resignation on 11 June, hoping that 'he may continue to be useful as a minister of Jesus Christ.'[39] While this was precisely what Booth wanted, it did mean that he was no longer a New Connexion minister, which led to some ministers in that Connexion being reluctant to use him.

The Wesleyan Methodist Conference that year was held in the Cornish town Camborne in early August. Inevitably, bearing in mind the location, one of the topics was to be the Booths and their ministry. Indeed, it appears that the Wesleyan District of Cornwall had already expressed opposition to them. This opposition, it needs to be borne in mind, was mainly from the ministers, 'the parsons', as Catherine continued to point out. Most lay Wesleyans loved the Booths and wanted to hear them.

According to the *Western Times*, when the practice of using 'Revivalists' was discussed at the 1862 Wesleyan Conference, it was claimed that this practice had 'led to much disquiet in many places.' That newspaper added that the President of the Conference, Rev. Charles Prest, said, 'that ministers must learn to say "No!" to applications' from these travelling preachers. He told the story of how in one of his circuits some of his laymen had approached him about having 'an American revivalist', probably James Caughey, 'occupy a chapel for a month.' He told them that, as long as he was

---

37 Ibid., Letter P229, pp. 310–11; Booth, *Reminiscences*, pp. 51–52; *Reminiscences CD*, pp. 10–11.
38 *Royal Cornwall Gazette*, 'Penzance and its Western Villages', 21 Nov. 1862, p. 6, col. 1.
39 *MNCM*, 'The Dudley Conference', 1862, p. 451.

Superintendent, that man 'should not place his foot in any of the pulpits.'[40] The President also spoke sarcastically of 'the perambulations of the male and female' in reference to the Booths, and it came as no surprise that the Conference decided to ban itinerant preachers such as the Booths and the Palmers from its pulpits.[41] That Conference was concerned about 'sound doctrine and godly order' and, presumably, thought that these evangelists contributed to neither.[42] This was a severe blow to the Booths, after a year of highly successful labour. While such bans are not always totally effective, it was to close many of the largest Methodist chapels to the Booths.

More bad news was to come. The Primitive Methodists at their Conference passed a resolution urging their churches 'to avoid the employment of revivalists so-called'.[43] While this may not have been a total ban, it did make many Primitives, who had their own travelling evangelists, reluctant to use the Booths.

It would be a mistake, however, to regard all Methodist ministers, of whatever faction, as being opposed to the Booths. Most of them seem to have been, but not all. But it must be asked, why did so many Methodist clergy oppose the Booths? Those who opposed them did so, probably, for various reasons. Many of the clergy were understandably afraid that a nondenominational preacher might lead their people away from their church. After all, some must have wondered: 'the Booths had left the New Connexion, so would they encourage others to do so?' Others, most probably, liked to have some control over what was taught in their church, which they were in danger of losing with an outside preacher. Some had also refused to cooperate with James Caughey in earlier times.

It is also possible that some were against the Booths' use of what is known as the altar call or public invitation. Both Catherine and William used this, and some clergy may have objected to that practice. When the Booths first went to Cornwall, the people were rather hesitant about it, but they later accepted it. By this time, however, it was a fairly common practice in most, if not all, shades of British Methodism.

Lorenzo Dow, the American evangelist, had introduced it to the Primitive Methodists in the early years of the nineteenth century. William Bramwell

---

40 *Western Times*, 'The Wesleyan Conference at Camborne', 16 Aug. 1862, p. 8, col. 1.

41 Booth-Tucker, *Catherine*, vol. 1, pp. 345–46.

42 'Minutes of the Methodist Conference', 1862, vol. xv, p. 362, para 4; quoted in Stead, *General Booth*, 56.

43 Booth-Tucker, *Catherine*, vol. 1, p. 346.

of the Wesleyans was using it by 1817, perhaps before, and he may have been following the example of at least one Wesleyan minister who had been to America, where the practice had already become common in some Methodist circles. American evangelists, such as James Caughey, Calvin Colton, Edward Kirk and Charles Finney (first British visit 1849-51) all used it, though in Finney's case not frequently.[44] In other words, by the 1850s the practice was fairly well known in Britain, especially in Methodism, though there was opposition to it, mainly in the Calvinistic churches. The use of the altar call, then, may have been a reason why some Methodist ministers objected to the Booths, though it is unlikely to have been a major one.

Battling against the odds

So, many of the Methodist chapels, up until now the Booths' main scenes of activity, were being closed to them. There were still the Methodist Reformers, the Free Methodists and some other smaller sects in the Methodist tradition, but by mid-1862, a year after they had begun independent ministry, doors were closing. As Catherine put it many years later, 'the road' they now had to travel, 'if not entirely blocked, was narrow and dark, and in consequence more rugged and difficult to tread.'[45]

Catherine, meanwhile, was in search of someone to be on hand for the birth of their next baby. Early in August she told her parents that she had 'spoken to a nurse', who had 'several times' acted as a midwife, and as 'She is highly recommended' and there were no local midwives available, Catherine decided to employ her.[46] This nurse was presumably on hand when Herbert Henry Booth was born on 26 August. Soon after the Booths changed that to Herbert Howard Booth.[47]

Towards the end of the Booths' time in Penzance the Free Methodist Church did invite William to conduct a mission there, which he accepted, but they, according to Catherine, were 'an insignificant, and not very notable society' and their chapel was 'very small' only 'holding 500 people.' It is worth noting at this point, that when Catherine called a chapel 'small' it was not necessarily what we might call 'small'. Any chapel that held 500 people, however tightly packed, would seem to have had the potential to

---

44 Bennett, *The Altar Call: Its Origins and Present Usage*, pp. 117–27.
45 Booth, *Reminiscences*, p. 51; *Reminiscences CD*, p. 10.
46 'CBLP', Letter P229, probably early August 1862, p. 310.
47 Ervine, *Soldier*, vol. 1, p. 261.

hold a significant mission field.

Catherine, meanwhile, having just given birth, was unable to help. The Conference edicts from the other Methodist denominations were also beginning to bite. 'The Wesleyans' in Penzance, she told her parents, 'have behaved shamefully,' and 'for fear of their preachers they nearly all stand aloof [sic]', while leaving her husband 'to struggle on with a few lads to help him'. All this made William anxious, and when he was anxious so was Catherine. Once more she blamed 'the *parsons*'. The Booths were again thinking that the way ahead was to hold their meetings in secular buildings.[48]

Three weeks after the birth of Herbert, and still in Penzance, Catherine told her parents,

You will be glad to hear that I continue to improve. I went out for a drive yesterday and have had two short walks to day. Of course, I feel weak at present but considering all things I am wonderful. The suckling affects my back very much, and I experience many of my old feelings of weakness & despondency. I often wish my dear Mother was within reach. If we were going to stop here any time, I should be anxious for you to come a bit, but we expect to leave for Redruth next week and we don't know how we may get fixed there.

They also had financial problems. The larger churches were being closed to them, so, inevitably, their income, which was mainly from church collections, was less than the previous year. They also now had five children to dress and feed plus two servants to pay. Catherine reflected, 'if needs be, we must be willing to suffer for our master's cause as well as to labour'[49], and it was looking as though they may have to do that.

At the end of September, they moved to Redruth, which was in the northern part of Cornwall nearer Camborne. The work in Redruth was held in the Free Methodist chapel, seating, Catherine thought, 900, though it held 1100 or 1200 'at a push.' This mission, which lasted about two months, progressed wonderfully, though Catherine was unable to play her part in it in the first fortnight. In some of the later weeks she took one of the Sunday services and spoke at two or three meetings during the week.[50]

---

48 'CBLP', Letter P230, 16 Sept. 1862, p. 312; Booth, *Reminiscences*, p. 52; *Reminiscences CD*, p. 11.

49 'CBLP', Letter P230, 16 Sept. 1862, p. 312.

50 Booth, *Reminiscences*, p. 53; *Reminiscences CD*, p. 12.

At one evening service a young man, as Catherine put it, 'yielded to the Spirit's call, and gave himself up to God.' He was a regular at the local pub and the news quickly reached his friends at the hostelry, where they were playing cards. When they heard it, they hurried to the chapel and found their friend rejoicing in God. Some of them, too, it is believed, later became Christians.[51]

'We *know*', she told her parents during the later stages of the mission, 'that we are instrumental in gladdening the hearts & homes of hundreds whom he has redeemed with his most precious blood. The movement here has stirred the whole Town & for miles round. The chapel was open almost all day yesterday, untill [sic] 12 o'clock last night. The people could hear the cries of the penitents as they lay in their *beds*. Glory to Jesus.' Catherine had been due to preach the previous Sunday, and some had come 'a great distance' to hear her, but she was too unwell to speak. She had also been unable to take a morning meeting during the following week. But she was due to preach again the following Sunday and she hoped to be able to do so by then.[52]

She was able to take a mid-week women's meeting soon after and 'the chapel was very full'. She 'had a good time: 10 conversions & several for holiness'. Their final services in Redruth were to be on 7 December, with Catherine preaching in the morning and William in the evening. The chapel was 'packed to suffocation' in the morning and 'many hearts were pierced'. After the evening service 'there was a rush to the front ... and about 40 professed to find salvation.' The Booths were optimistic that the closing tea meeting on the following Tuesday would raise some much-needed money for the family.[53]

It appears to have been in November, while they were still in Redruth, that the family had several health problems. Willie had been ill, and when he began to get better Catherine was taken ill and recovered only slowly. Then Ballington became unwell with a chesty cough, and they had to send to Penzance for the doctor. Catherine feared that that might lead to consumption. Fortunately, 'Baby [Herbert] thrives amazingly.'[54] Herbert was baptised in Redruth, with his mother preaching and his father conducting

---

51 Ibid., pp. 55–56; ibid., p. 14.

52 'CBLP', Letter P231, probably mid-November 1862, p. 314.

53 Ibid, Letter P232, 25 Nov. 1862, pp. 315–16; Booth, *Reminiscences*, p. 57; *Reminiscences CD*, p. 15.

54 'CBLP', Letter P231, probably mid-November 1862, pp. 313–14.

the ceremony.[55]

One local reflecting on this time in Redruth years later said, that of the converts in those two months, 'A great many' became 'ministers and local preachers'.[56] After Redruth the Booths made a return visit to Camborne, which lasted from mid-December into the new year. At Camborne 442 'professed to find salvation'.

When the Booths began their work in Cornwall in August 1861 they had no intention of staying long. But their work there grew powerfully and spread through a large part of the county. It was not until denominational opposition raised its head that they decided to move on. It has been claimed that there had been 7000 conversions through the Booths' ministry in the nearly 18 months that they were in the county.[57]

---

55 Booth, *Reminiscences*, pp. 56–57; *Reminiscences CD*, p. 15.
56 Ibid., p. 56; ibid., pp. 14–15.
57 Ibid., pp. 57–58; ibid., p. 16; Booth-Tucker, *Catherine*, vol 1, p. 355.

CHAPTER 22

The Booth Family

'The children are well. Willie gets very interesting but is still very
troublesome. I think I never felt as I do now the responsibility
of being a mother & the need I have of wisdom & grace for
the task before me. Oh, how unfit I feel for it. Pray for me',

Catherine Booth to her parents.[1]

A miscarriage

Towards the end of June 1861, Catherine wrote a letter to her 'very dear
Husband', in which she said, 'It is beyond a doubt now. I am just in the old
fix, but I think worse than with either of the two last, sick, languid & spiritless
in the extreme.'[2] Catherine was pregnant again, or thought she was.

In the middle of January the next year, she told her mother,

I fear you will think me long silent, but I know you will forgive me when
I tell you that I have been so poorly that I could not command nerve to
sit to write. I don't know what is the matter with me, but I am sick and ill
all day long, just as tho' it was the first three months with me. Sometimes
I think I miscarried when I was so ill and that I am now beginning again,
and sometimes I think the child is dead and that is what is making me
so poorly. William much wants me to see some doctor, but I cannot
consent. I don't see any good in it. If I am so, it will come at the time, I
suppose, and if I miscarried before, I am so again, so I don't see what
good a doctor could do, and I have the greatest aborhance [sic] of a
doctor quising [sic] about *me*. I must just wait with as much patience as
I can summon and try to hope for the best. I am certainly larger than
my natural size, but not more than I ought to be at 4 or 5 months, so
what to think I don't know, but I have quite given up the idea of a *living*
child. That is impossible… I hope all will be well. What I feel most is the

---

1 'CBLP', Letter P137, 5 or 12 Sept. 1858, p. 189.
2 Booth, *Letters*, Letter CB161, 21 June 1861, pp. 343–44, Booth, *Letters CD*, pp. 340–41.

useless life I am living. I do hope it is not a fresh beginning. I am ready to die at the prospect of another such a nine months as the past. Pray for me; I need patience.[3]

Catherine was clearly not only unwell she was confused about what was happening to her. Was she pregnant back in June or just unwell? Was she pregnant then and miscarried? Was she 'beginning again' in the following January? Herbert was not born until late in August 1862, so Catherine was either mistaken about the June 1861 experience or, more likely, she miscarried, but by the following January she was about two months pregnant.

The Booth children

Catherine and William Booth eventually had eight children, though by the time we have reached they had five, Willie, Ballington, Catherine, Emma and Herbert. Even with the help of servants, looking after them while accepting multiple speaking engagements and being engaged in other church activities and grappling with poor health, was, for Catherine, at the good times difficult and at the bad times a nightmare. Catherine Booth was, in modern terms, 'a working mum' and a very busy one. It is also probably true to say that Catherine did not take easily or naturally to motherhood.

It is not intended to speak about the Booths' sexual relationship. That is for the most part a closed book. But three months after the birth of Herbert, Catherine told her mother, William 'is very considerate for me or there would probably have been another on the way by this time'.[4] She also said something similar back in November 1857[5], four months after the birth of Ballington, though the meaning there is less clear.

When she was expecting Willie, she had to move from home to home because of William's itinerant ministry. She was not always happy in these places, and at times that was because of unruly resident children. She told her parents in one letter, 'We are to have a *very nice* home in Leeds, where there are no children (quite a recommendation, seeing how they are usually trained).' Then she added the rather startling, 'I hope if I have not both sense & grace to train mine so that they shall not be nuisances to everybody near them, that God will in mercy take them to heaven in infancy.' However, in

---

3 'CBLP', Letter P223, mid-January 1862, p. 298.

4 Ibid., Letter P232, 25 Nov. 1862, p. 315.

5 Ibid., Letter P105, probably 22 or 29 Nov. 1857, p. 145.

these homes, good and bad, she was 'learning a few useful lessons from *observation*.'[6]

Catherine loved her children. But she was strict. She was a firm believer in stern discipline. In one of her lectures she said, 'wise parents universally recognise, whether they make any pretensions to Christianity or not, the necessity of family government and careful training in order to check, counteract or eradicate, as the case may be, these tendencies to evil... A child left to itself brings its mother to shame.'[7]

'The Lord help', she told he mother. 'I have had to whip [Willie] twice lately severely for disobedience, and it has cost me *some tears*. But it has done him good, and I am reaping the reward of my self sacrifice already.' One rather suspects that it cost Willie some tears too and that the sacrifice was not all Catherine's. It needs to be noted that 'whip' here refers to a severe spanking, not whipping in the normal sense. Willie would have been about 20 months at this time. She added in that letter, 'The Lord help me to be faithful and firm as a rock in the path of duty towards my children.' In that same letter she said, 'The children' (Willie and Ballington) 'are well & two *beauties*. Oh, I often feel as though they cannot be *mine*. It seems too much to be true that they should be so beautiful & so *healthy* when I am such a poor thing, but it seems as if the Lord has ordered it so.'[8]

Her physical condition caused her many frustrations. She told her parents in the first half of 1858, 'I must say I am almost weary of it, and sometimes feel that if it were not for the children it would be nice to lay this troublesome, crazy body down... It is much harder to suffer than to labour, especially when you have so many calls on your attention.' She compared her present situation with her unmarried state, saying, 'It is so different lying ill in bed now, with two children, perhaps one crying against the other, to what it used to be with no responsibility or care, and a kind, loving mother to anticipate every want. But enough! The cup which my Father hath given me shall I not drink it? Especially seeing it is so much better than I have merited.'[9]

A little later that year she said,

The children are well. Willie gets very interesting but is still very troublesome. I think I never felt as I do now the responsibility of being a

---

6 Ibid., Letter P27, probably, 21 Nov. 1855, p. 48.
7 Booth, *Popular Christianity*, p. 30.
8 'CBLP', Letter P103, 28 Oct. or 4 Nov. 1857, p. 143.
9 Ibid., Letter P118, probably the first half of 1858, p. 146.

mother & the need I have of wisdom & grace for the task before me. Oh, how unfit I feel for it. Pray for me. I have felt very deeply on the subject of late. I often fear that Willie does not get so much of my attention & supervision as he requires, but I am so engaged & my nerves are so irratable [sic] that I cannot be long with him at a time. He wears me out with his incessant activity & prattle.[10]

The children had their distinctive ways and at times said memorable things. On one occasion Mary Kirton was telling Emma to be quiet when she was talking to her mother. Emma responded, 'Me not peakin to ou, me peaking to Mama!' While Katie, her mother said, 'is a *beautiful* girl and Papa says she inherits her grandma's dignity, at any rate she inherits somebody's, for she moves about like a little Princess and would grace Win[d]sor Castle itself.'[11]

When Ballington was six he went through a difficult phase, which Catherine found hard to deal with. She described him at that time as 'most dreadfully unstable. We are obliged to keep him entirely out of the nursery. He [k]nocks the little ones down without mercy.'[12] Fortunately, it does not seem to have lasted long. A week later she said, 'I think Bal'ton is better in some respects.' In some respects, perhaps, but it appears not in all. The previous day Ballington had set up a pile of chairs and placed Emma at the top. The chairs collapsed, down came Emma and 'cut her lip almost through. She was picked up streaming with blood' and the experience 'made her very poorly.'[13] A few weeks later, to everybody's relief, Ballington was 'much better.'

It was probably early in November that Catherine had told her parents that Herbert, now 14 months old, had started walking. However, he did not seem too keen on the idea, and would start walking and then fall down on his bottom and laugh at those watching him. Yet he would not 'sit still for a moment.'[14]

Play and school

Catherine believed in encouraging children to play. That may not seem significant, but in the first sixty years or so of the nineteenth century

---

10 Ibid., Letter P137, 5 or 12 Sept. 1858, p. 189.
11 Ibid., Letter P232, 25 Nov. 1862, p. 315.
12 Ibid., Letter P251, 12 Oct. 1863, p. 340.
13 Ibid., Letter P252, 20 Oct. 1863, p. 341.
14 Ibid., Letter P254, 12 Nov. 1863, p. 344.

childhood was not a time of innocence, fun and play in most families. As A.N. Wilson says, such things were 'virtually non-existent for the majority' of them. 'Millions of children in the nineteenth century had the experience of working in a grown up world' when as young as ten.[15] But the Booth children had the opportunity to play and were encouraged to do so.

William was often in the thick of it. When Willie was only five months old he greeted his father's arrival on the scene with enthusiasm, which was quickly reciprocated. 'When his father first comes in sight', Catherine told her parents, Willie 'is fit to fly; they play all sorts of games, such as tossing, rolling, jumping, walking'. Catherine meanwhile was 'in a ferment all the time for fear of an accident.'[16] Later, when the family had increased, he played Fox and Goose with the children, and, according to his eldest son, the father 'was always the fox', the one doing the chasing.[17]

Catherine played with the children too, but, usually nursing her health, her games were more docile. She used the toys in the nursery to teach lessons from the Bible. They had a model of Noah's Ark, with toy animals, which was used to teach that story.[18] While in Gateshead Catherine and Willie visited a neighbour, and the neighbour's children had a rocking-horse. Willie, inevitably, had a ride and loved it. Now he wanted one. But Catherine thought they were too expensive for them to buy, so she asked her father to make one, and offered to pay for any expenses incurred.[19] He seems to have done so, at any rate the Booths acquired one. On one occasion, Willie mounted the rocking-horse and with great enthusiasm told Ballington and their nurse how Joseph had ridden on a 'gee-gee' when he went to collect his father to bring him to Pharaoh.[20]

Belinda Youseff says, 'Toys were important to the spiritual development' of the Booth children. They 'used their toys to learn and mimic their parents' ministry... Imitation of behaviour through the use of toys meant that the children were unwittingly using the toys to prepare themselves for the future that God had in store for them.'[21]

In an intensely Christian home, with both parents preaching, it was

---

15 Wilson, *Victorians*, p. 260.
16 'CBLP', Letter P56, probably 29, 30, or 31 Aug. 1856, p. 91.
17 Quoted in Wilson, *General Evangeline Booth of The Salvation Army*, p. 33.
18 Booth, *Practical Religion*, p. 24.
19 'CBLP', Letters P149, 14 Jan. 1859, and P150, probably 28 Jan. 1859, pp. 203–205.
20 Booth, *Practical Religion*, p. 24.
21 Youseff, 'Toys Relating', *AJSAH*, vol.3, iss.1, p. 23.

inevitable that the children would play church and later mission. The older children often led these impromptu services and preached to the younger and their collection of dolls and animals. When Ballington was eleven, he was preaching in the nursery to Kate and Emma, and possibly Herbert. The girls had 'trouble keeping their dolls quiet.' Not pleased with the interruption, 'Ballington demanded, "Take those babies out of the meeting." But his sisters refused to go, reminding him, "Papa would not have told us to leave; Papa would have kept on preaching."'[22]

Catherine recognised that children were children and not small adults, which was not the opinion of everyone in the Victorian era. She also appears to have been more positive about schools than her mother, but not by much. She first thought of sending Willie to school when he was three and a half. In a letter to her parents she said,

> Willie is not very well. Has a sore tongue & throat, not sufficient, however, to keep him from using it, which he does without ceasing. He gets more & more old fashioned every day. Every body say[s] they never heard such remarks from such a child before, & yet *he is* a *child*, not a premature man, a species of precocity which you know I dislike & could not tolerate. I fear we are neglecting him now, so far as any book learning goes. I would send him to school... I dread the influence of other children on him, especially of rude & ill-mannered children, such as the majority are.[23]

Eight months later, so when he was still only four, they sent him to a school in Gateshead and he seemed to like it.[24] A little over nine months later he was still attending, presumably, the same school, and was getting on 'nicely.'[25] However, that was soon to end when the family moved to Newcastle, before leaving the New Connexion and their travelling evangelists phase. However, even in their brief time in Newcastle Catherine was looking for a school there for both Willie and Ballington[26], who was now almost four.

A few days later, as it became likely that they would engage once more in an itinerant lifestyle, Catherine thought of sending the children to live with the Mumfords. Willie and Ballington 'could go to school', she told her

---

22 Ibid., p. 23, quoting from Troutt, *The General was a Lady: The Story of Evangeline Booth*, p. 25.
23 'CBLP', Letter P171, 14 Nov. 1859, p. 227.
24 Ibid., Letter P178, 23 July 1860, pp. 236–37.
25 Ibid., Letter P204, 1 May 1861, p. 268.
26 Ibid., Letter P210, 5 July 1861, p. 277.

parents, while 'the others both go to bed every day for nearly 2 hours, & they all go to bed at 7 at night & sleep well.' This would all be made easier for the Mumfords, she said, because she would send with them their children's nurse, Mary Kirton[27], who was still proving a useful and faithful servant to the Booths.

At the end of August 1861 William and Catherine went to Cornwall, and the children were sent to the Mumfords. While in Brixton, Willie, at least, attended a school, for it appears that he did not like to go unless he knew his spelling. Sarah Mumford seems to have suggested that he do some homework to help with that, but Catherine, wisely, said no. 'I would not have the book made a *bore* to him for a hundred pounds', she told her parents.

All these schools were probably small, some perhaps run by just one person. In reference to that school in London, Catherine referred to Willie's 'Governess'[28], which suggests that she was the only teacher. When the family was reunited in Cornwall, the two boys went to a school, run by 'a very nice young lady' who had been converted during the Booths' mission in St Ives.[29] This once more sounds like a one-teacher school.

The constant moving about was clearly not ideal for the children's education. Each teacher, no doubt, had their own rules and their own way of teaching. One example of that was a school they 'thought was a first rate one, but the master took nearly all [Willie's] books away & put him into babyish spelling which he learnt 3 years ago & let him sit doing nothing nearly all his time.' In addition, Catherine found that when she sent him to a new school the teachers tended not to pay much attention to him 'when they know he is only going for a few weeks.'[30]

Facing these problems, Catherine thought it would be better in future to have a live-in governess.[31] Though the Booths had no guarantee of an income in their new area of service, when church leaders see people won to Christ and their churches grow, they can be very generous, and while the people in Cornwall were not generally rich, so the Booth income was not great then, it improved later, so that they could afford to employ a governess. However, Catherine never saw eye to eye with the governesses that she employed, and

27 Ibid., Letter P211, 9 July 1861, p. 278.
28 Ibid., Letter P217, 2 Sept. 1861, p. 289.
29 Ibid., Letter P221, possibly 7 or 8 Nov. 1861, p. 296.
30 Ibid., Letter P257, 24 Nov. 1863, p. 346.
31 Ibid., Letter P221, possibly 7 or 8 Nov. 1861, p. 296.

so that experiment was a failure. In her Reminiscences she said, 'As a rule they are a total delusion so far as education is concerned... They often have no notion of training children... The schools are a damnation one way and governesses a failure the other.'[32]

Catherine was most uneasy about sending children to boarding schools, though for a brief while in 1863 she did consider it for the two eldest boys. She decided against it, as she was 'afraid of evil contamination' in such schools, and she felt as though she '*dare* not think of it.'[33] She believed that if children were sent to such places, they should not be sent 'before their principles are formed or their characters developed.' To Catherine 'a school is a little world where all the elements of unrenewed human nature are at work with as great variety, subtlety, and power as in the great world outside', and consequently as dangerous, more so, when away from the influence of home.[34]

Roy Hattersley gives a rather negative and unfair account of life in the Booth family, and makes the children sound repressed.[35] However, the Booth children probably had happier lives than most children in the Victorian age, including those from wealthy homes, many of whom would have been sent off to the boarding schools Catherine justly disliked.

Bramwell (Willie) Booth years later gave a striking insight into the Booth family life, particularly concerning the relationship of his parents. He said that sometimes when Catherine was hassled by her many domestic and other responsibilities, William would come home, immediately assess the situation, take her by the hand and say, 'Kate, let me pray with you.' He would then send the children out of the room, while they knelt and prayed. 'Then a little while after,' said Bramwell, 'the skies were blue again.'[36]

Were the Booths vegetarians?

It has been claimed that Catherine was a vegetarian and that 'The eight Booth children were reared in a vegetarian home.'[37] However, this, for the most part, is not true, though Catherine may have become a vegetarian

32 Booth, *Reminiscences*, p. 95; *Reminiscences CD*, p. 51.
33 'CBLP', Letter P237, possibly 26 Mar. 1863, p. 324.
34 Booth, *Practical Religion*, pp. 31–32.
35 Hattersley, *Blood*, pp. 170–73.
36 Booth, *Echoes and Memories*, p. 7.
37 Green, *Catherine*, p. 26.

late in life. Her eldest son certainly became a vegetarian, probably in the 1880s and wrote articles promoting it published in Salvation Army and vegetarian publications.[38] Catherine seems to have considered becoming a vegetarian as early as 1852.[39] Yet there is an abundance of evidence to prove that meat was commonly on the table in the Booth home from the mid-1850s to at least the mid-1860s. For example, in one letter in 1862 Catherine told her mother,

> You did not say whether I must put the sugar over the ham at the *time* I put it in salt or afterwards, so I salted it as you directed but have not put the sugar on yet. How long should I let it lay in pickle? It weighs 13lbs & ½. You know I never cured one before. We give 6½^d & 7^d per pound for pork, beef & mutton, best parts for 7^d. I sometimes pot a bit of beef by a recipe of Mrs Booth's.[40]

Clearly meat was not an occasional treat. It was, at that time at least, a basic item in the family's diet. Catherine Bramwell-Booth even remembered seeing 'Uncle Herbert' carving meat at the Booth dinner table as late as the mid-1880s, though her grandmother forbade her having any because her parents, Bramwell and Florence, were vegetarians.[41]

'The training of children'

Catherine Booth gave an address on 'The training of children' some years after the period we are considering, possibly in the early or mid-1870s, which was later reproduced in her book *Papers on Practical Religion*. However, while these remarks were made later, they are most relevant to it and show us a great deal about life in the Booths' home.

She, not surprisingly, based her comments clearly and repeatedly upon the Scripture 'Train up a child in the way he should go; and when he is old, he will not depart from it' (Prov 22:6). That echoes throughout her words. She first encouraged her hearers and readers to see their children

---

38 Ibid., p. 300, n. 22; Booth, 'Vegetarianism' in *The Local Officer* and *The Vegetarian Messenger*.

39 Booth, *Letters*, Letters CM7, 12 Dec. 1852; CM93, 13 Sept. 1854; CB143, 11 Sept. 1855, pp. 30, 231, 315 & 316; Booth, *Letters CD*, pp. 33, 230, 313 & 314.

40 'CBLP', Letter P225, 25 Feb. 1862, p. 303; see also Letters P28, probably 29 Nov. 1855; P232, 25 Nov. 1862; P250, probably early October 1863; P261, 2 Feb. 1864, pp. 50, 314, 339, 350; Begbie, *William*, vol. 1, p. 347.

41 Bramwell-Booth, *Catherine*, p. 348.

as 'a heritage from the Lord.' Parents 'are only stewards for God, holding [their] children to nurse them and train them for Him.' She quoted the 'old adage ... "They who rock the cradle rule the world,"' which, Catherine said, 'they certainly do', but 'the world has been very badly ruled', for those who rock the cradle 'have not known how to train the child.' She mourned the lack of 'competent Christian mothers, who realise their responsibility to God and to their children, and who are resolved at all costs and sacrifices to discharge it.' And Catherine knew how to make sacrifices for her own children.

Parents needed, Catherine said, to train their children for God, and inspire them with 'the love of goodness, truth, and righteousness'. Not all parents will be able to educate their children, and 'God does not require of us more than we can do', but 'as far as is possible to us' if we 'train our children ... in the way they should go, they will then go in that way for themselves; God's providence and Spirit and their own bias will guide them on and on.'[42]

Training children was more to Catherine than cramming 'them with religious sentiment and truth'. While that is good, the heart needs to be influenced as well as the head. And the best way to do that is, by example, to 'show' children how to practice the faith, and to guide them in doing so. 'Mothers, if you want your children to walk in the way they should go, you must not only teach, you must be at the trouble to train', and that primarily by example.[43]

A central platform of Catherine Booth's teaching on raising children was the need to secure their obedience. To her it was 'the foundation of all moral excellence'. In addition, a child submitting to its parents is a stepping stone to them submitting to God, but if they do not do the former, they are unlikely to do the latter. And this obedience needs to be taught early. Indeed, the secret of the successful training of children is to begin early, 'not letting Satan get the advantage of us at the start.' While chastising infants is hard, 'There is seldom need for' it if one begins training 'early and wisely ... with the utmost love and tenderness.' Yet, 'Remember, you must conquer in the first battle, whatever it may be about, or you are undone.' Then, as an example, she referred to one of her sons, 'who is now preaching the Gospel', and with whom she fought only one 'decided battle', and that when he was

---

42 Booth, *Practical Religion*, pp. 4–6.

43 Ibid., pp. 8, 10–11.

'ten months old'. He still disobeyed on occasions after that, but, she added, 'I never remember him setting his will in direct antagonism to mine in all the succeeding years of his childhood.'[44] This son was presumably not Willie, for she seems to have had two battles with him when he was about 20 months old.

She protested about encouraging children in lying, by lying to them and allowing them to tell lies. She protested about allowing them to cheat in their games. 'Mothers', she said, 'if you want your child to be truthful and sincere, you must not only teach it to be so, you must be so yourself, and see that your child practices what you teach.'[45]

But we must not stop our training with just these 'qualities and virtues [for] children must be trained in the exercise of devotion and piety towards God.' And 'the Holy Ghost must needs be in the heart of the mother who undertakes to lead her child to God.' When can that take place? 'Why', Catherine asked, 'may they not be led to choose Christ and his yoke at seven or eight years old as well as at seventeen?' After all, Jesus said, 'Suffer the little ones to come unto me'.[46] In all such training, Catherine insisted it is most important 'to make your lessons interesting. If you cannot awaken the interest of your child, you had better give up.' She introduced the Sunday lessons she taught to the children, with a 'short lively tune', followed by a short prayer, which they recited after her and were encouraged to learn. Catherine then taught a lesson, which was followed by another prayer and a 'tune or two'. Then 'they would adjourn to the nursery' and often 'they would go through the whole service again', with Willie preaching.[47]

Catherine also said that children should be taught to seek first God's glory 'and do good to their generation'. Then in what seems to have been a passionate outburst, she declared,

> Oh, mothers, don't be deceived if you want your children to be the Lord's when they grow up, if you want your boy … to come out a man of righteous principle, integrity and honour … you must train him to look upon the world's prizes as dross compared with the joy of a pure conscience and a life of usefulness to his fellow-men. If you want your daughter to be a true woman, willing to sacrifice and to suffer in

---

44 Ibid., pp. 11–13.
45 Ibid., pp. 16–19.
46 Ibid., pp. 20–21.
47 Ibid., pp. 23–24.

the interests of humanity and truth, you must inspire her now with a contempt for the baubles of which so many women barter their lives and their souls. You must teach her that she is an independent, responsible being, whom God will call to as severe a reckoning for the use or abuse of her talents as that of her brother man. Day by day ... you must labour to wake up your children's souls to the realisation of the fact that they belong to God, and that He has sent them into the world ... to devote themselves to the promotion of His [interests], and that, in doing this, they will find happiness, usefulness and glory (Matt 25:14–16).[48]

She closed that address by 'lifting up' her voice against the practice of 'sending children to boarding schools before their principles are formed or their characters developed.'[49]

Finally, the following summary of Catherine Booth as a mother comes from her eldest son. Years later, he said, 'as a mother' she was 'skilled and diligent in household ways, asking no release from any homely duty' despite the many outside demands placed upon her. She was also 'intensely concerned for her children, above all, for their salvation', and 'as a Mother in God' (for her spiritual family) she guided 'with wise counsel, persuading with an eloquence more than words,' yet 'rebuking in a manner which those who came under her displeasure never forgot'.[50]

---

48 Ibid., pp. 27–28.
49 Ibid., pp. 31–32.
50 Booth, *Fifty*, p. 9.

CHAPTER 23

Success in Wales

'If the Lord spares me, I intend to be faithful to the interests of
truth, whoever is faithless. Oh, for more spiritual power!'
Catherine Booth.[1]

Opposition to overseas mission

There is an area in which both Catherine and William Booth can be justly
criticised, at least in their early days. They did not support the work of
overseas mission, and, indeed, at times spoke against it. They, whether they
liked it or not, lived in a missionary age. For example, Hudson Taylor had
gone to China with the Chinese Evangelisation Society in 1853. In 1860
he returned to England to engage new recruits. During that visit, on 25
June 1865, Hudson Taylor received his call to found a new organisation, the
China Inland Mission.[2] This was a week before William Booth began his
work in the East End of London, that later became The Salvation Army. Not
just Taylor, but many others, famous and unknown, were daring to enlist in
a host of missionary organisations to take the gospel of Christ to those in
earth's far flung corners.

In one of her letters in 1863 Catherine said,

I have not patience to read a lot of the twaddle about New Connexion
missions in China and Australia... As I said in a meeting at Cambourne
[sic], '*What* is *that* Christianity which pays missionaries, fits out ships,
& prints Bibles at an immense outlay, to convert *ignorant, idolatrous*
chinamen, and turns its back on a work like [the Booths were doing],
in which its own children, servants, friends & neighbours are being
converted? Is not a cornish miner as much worth converting as a
chineese [sic]? Will he not make as good, & a little better a christian

---
1 'CBLP', Letter P233, probably 18 Feb. 1863, p. 318.
2 Bennett, *Hudson Taylor and China*, pp. 28, 95–98.

on earth & as glorious a saint in heaven? If so, where is the consistency of spending hundreds of pounds to convert *half a dozen* Chinamen & leaving the thousands of our own population destitute of any means adapted to reach them? Ney [sic], of absolutely opposing agencies which God is owning in doing it. Is this Christianity? *Is it?*' I cried, as loud as I could lift my voice. '*No,*' I said, 'it is canting, hypocricy [sic], low, mean, *narrow sectarianism*, & nothing more. It is seeking to exalt my ism, to glorify my *denomination* & not Jesus Xt,' & I felt that my words burnt their way into the consciences of my hearers.[3]

William thought similarly. Their main concern was that the more money and labour was spent on overseas work the less money and labour would be spent on evangelistic work in Britain. Yet both were legitimate and necessary tasks and it was right and important to do both. One can detect too, their regret, even anger, that while the New Connexion and other denominations supported overseas mission, they refused to support the Booths. Later, the Booths were happy for The Salvation Army to send missionaries overseas and even went themselves (Catherine to aid her eldest daughter in France and William around the world). But in their early years it is hard to detect any sympathy for taking the gospel overseas in their early writings, indeed, quite the opposite.

Cardiff

In February 1863 the Booths moved not just to a new county but to a new country, Wales. News about the Booths and their work had travelled, mainly by sea, from coastal Cornwall to the southern coast of Wales, and some Christians in Cardiff liked what they heard and wanted what the Booths had to offer, so they sent them an invitation.

The visit to Wales was to prove important in several ways. There they tried to move beyond their usual Methodist links, they preached in secular locations, they made new contacts and Catherine made a close friend. They began in Cardiff. That was another change, for Cardiff was a much larger town than any they had ministered in, since becoming independent evangelists.

Catherine said, 'the three individuals who were mainly responsible' for them going to Cardiff were 'Mrs Hollier [or Hollyer], Mr Smart & John

---

3 'CBLP', Letter P233, probably 18 Feb. 1863, p. 318.

Cory'[4], and to them can almost certainly be added John Cory's brother Richard. While nothing else is known of Mrs Hollier and Mr Smart, John and Richard Cory were coal merchants and shipowners and, consequently, wealthy. They became keen and generous supporters of the Booths.

Richard Cory was a Baptist[5], as may have been the others who had issued the invitation, and soon after the Booths arrived in Cardiff they began to conduct services in a Baptist chapel. These Baptists must have known about the Booths' Methodist roots and doctrines, but that does not seem to have been a hindrance to them.

It was probably on Wednesday 18 February that Catherine led a morning meeting in that chapel. It was the third occasion that she had preached there. She said that she 'spoke with great liberty for an hour' and 'it was a blessed season.' She 'had 30 or 40 up for full consecration', though whether the Baptists saw that in quite the same way as Catherine is unclear.

But the Booths were 'very unsettled', and William, particularly, did 'not feel at home there'. If they preached at the Baptist chapel, they would attract the Baptists and, presumably, those on the fringes of Baptist work. But the Booths wanted to reach more people, especially those outside the churches, so they began more earnestly considering secular locations, neutral ground, which anyone might feel free to enter. They considered the music hall, but that was an unwieldy, 'ugly, unlikely place'; and the circus was 'not much better.' However, that evening the Booths held a meeting with their hosts and it was decided to rent the circus for a fortnight at '£7 a week, including gass [sic]', with the first service the following Sunday.

William, in fact, was more than 'unsettled' about the work, he was '*very anxious*.' Catherine thought '*unnecessarily* so.' She added, 'I don't know what he would do at these times without me. He forget[s] all his past *success* & goes down into fearful despondency, if he does not swim away at once. Perhaps' she wondered, 'it is needful to keep him from being elated'.

Despite 'all the unsettledness, anxiety & trials' that they encountered in the work, Catherine 'love[d] it as much as ever, nay, more.' She never looked back or had 'a single regret' about taking the step, and believed that in the future they would 'be instrumental in bringing *tens* of *thousands* to the Saviour.'[6] Those were brave words when one considers the uncertainty that they were facing, being unlikely to get support from some denominations,

---

4 Booth, *Reminiscences*, p. 59; *Reminiscences CD*, p. 17.

5 Booth-Tucker, *Catherine*, vol. 1, pp. 361–62.

6 'CBLP', Letter P233, probably 18 Feb. 1863, pp. 316–17.

a limited income and an increasing family. Brave and faithful!

Then she saw the circus.

'The sight of the place almost overwhelmed me at first', she told her parents. 'It looks an immense place.' After her first attempt at speaking at the circus ('for an hour with tolerable liberty') she described the layout of the building:

> We speak from the stage … the ring just before us; the friends have seated, with seats with backs to them, then commences a gallery in the amp[h]itheatre style, rising from the ring to the ceiling, & when full forms a most imposing sight. The side gal[l]eries & those behind the stage were likewise well filled. It was a great effort for me to compass the place with my voice, but I suppose I was heard well, so I shall take it easier next time.[7]

The way the building had been arranged for these meetings it could hold about 2000 people and it 'was usually crowded.' They held their Sunday meetings at the circus and on the weekdays they used Baptist and Wesleyan chapels and various halls. Clearly some of the Welsh Wesleyans did not observe the Conference ban.[8]

The local Wesleyans had, in fact, invited Catherine to speak at their chapel on Wednesday mornings. Coming so soon after the Conference ban on her and William, that invitation greatly delighted her. In a letter to her mother she enthused,

> If the Rev'd gentleman, who talked about the 'Male & female who had been going up & down in Cornwall' in his speech in the conference, hears of it, he will think that said '*Female*' is one too many for him, and his ressolutions [sic] also! I shall glory in being in one of their chapels, *once* at least, after the passing of that wicked ressolution [sic], and if the Lord helps me, I shall give them some warmish truth. My topic is announced as 'The importance of Consistency in Professors.'[9]

Catherine was clearly on the warpath. In a slightly later letter she said, 'prejudice against Female ministry melts away before me like snow in the sun.'[10] Thus she seems to have dealt with that kind of opposition by more peaceful means.

---

7 Ibid., Letter P234, 23 Feb. 1863, p. 319.
8 Booth, *Reminiscences*, p. 59; Booth, *Reminiscences CD*, p. 18.
9 'CBLP', Letter P236, possibly mid-March 1863, p. 322.
10 Ibid., Letter P238, 1 Apr. 1863, p. 326.

Catherine said that there was always a crowd when it was her turn to preach, and she added that she

> seldom spoke with other than pleasure to myself and I think profit to those who heard me. Some of those morning meetings I shall never forget. It was quite a common thing for me to see ministers, local preachers, deacons, elders/leaders of churches, and people in very respectable positions of society, even magistrates, kneeling at the communion rail, bewailing their past unfaithfulness, seeking restoration from backsliding and crying to God to have mercy on their souls and pardon their sins. I believe that God used me to stir up the hearts of many leading Christians and set them to work for Christ after a fashion they had never done before.

Catherine was happier than William about the mission in Cardiff. As was seen above, he went through a period of despondency at this time, and Catherine later said, 'he was very dissatisfied with his work in Cardiff', though this was not unusual for him. But on this occasion Catherine looked on the positive side, adding, 'Still, he toiled on and reaped much fruit, which I have no doubt we shall find again in the great harvest home.'[11]

A summary of the meetings in Cardiff appeared in the *Wesleyan Times*. It said in part

> The special services have been brought to a close during the past week. About 500 have professed to find the blessing of salvation under these servants of the Lord. Many of these were sailors who have left the port. Almost every class of society has been found among the converts, and there is scarcely a church which has not had its numbers increased by the instrumentality of these services. The moral condition of the town is greatly improved, and, at a season of the year when crime is generally on the increase, the magistrates have very little to do.[12]

Pontypridd and Newport

At the end of March, as their Cardiff mission was concluding, some Wesleyans in Pontypridd, just north of Cardiff, invited William to conduct some special services at their church. That is, William was invited, but not Catherine. This is the second example of a group of Wesleyans ignoring the ban on the Booths. As Catherine put it, 'you see, that door is not quite shut

---

11 Booth, *Reminiscences*, pp. 59–60; *Reminiscences CD*, p. 18.
12 Booth, *Reminiscences*, p. 59; *Reminiscences CD*, p. 17, quoting the *Wesleyan Times*, 1863.

after all their pains to shut it.'

Why the initial invitation was not extended to Catherine is unknown. It may have been because she still had some meetings to conduct in Cardiff. She did get a belated invitation and conducted at least two services there in the later part of that mission. According to Catherine, the meetings in Pontypridd were 'real blessed ... and William came back to Cardiff in high spirits.' She added, 'He never could get on without results.'[13]

Next the Free Methodists in Newport, again not far from Cardiff, sent an invitation to both William and Catherine, which they gladly accepted. Their original plan was to hold the weekday services in their chapel and the Sunday meetings in the Drill Hall, which held between 1000 and 1200. However, after one Sunday in the Drill Hall, they decided that, while that building may have been good for drill, it was useless for speaking. For the remainder of their time there they ministered in the Free Methodist Chapel, the Town Hall, which was too small to be ideal, and a large Congregational chapel. While in Newport, Catherine 'had a severe attack of influenza', which limited her activities, and William fell down some stairs and sprained his ankle. Yet, despite these difficulties, Catherine regarded their time in that town as 'a very good work.'[14] Amongst the more than a hundred converts were 'two of the oldest and worst drunkards in the town.'[15]

A new friend and new supporters

Catherine rarely seems to have been able to make close friendships. In Boston she had Jemima 'Eliza' Elsey. In Burnham there was Emma Smith. But the continual travelling and the distance between them, with great busyness and limited communication, meant that these friendships tended to fall away. Catherine employed Miss Newberry, 'a precious friend', as a governess. It was not a wise move. Miss Newberry did not live up to Catherine's expectations and that caused tensions in the friendship.[16]

In April 1863, at the age of 34, Catherine Booth was fast rising in the

---

13 Booth, *Reminiscences*, pp. 62–63; *Reminiscences CD*, p. 21; 'CBLP', Letters P237, possibly 26 March 1863, and P240, 11 Apr. 1863, pp. 323–24, 327.

14 'CBLP', Letters P237, possibly 26 Mar. 1863, & P238, 1 Apr. 1863, pp. 324–25; Booth, *Reminiscences*, p. 64; *Reminiscences CD*, p. 22. William sprained his ankle twice in the space of a couple of months, once in Newport, and later more seriously in Walsall.

15 'CBLP', Letter P242, 20 May 1863, p. 330.

16 Ibid., Letters P107, 17 Dec. 1857, P230, 16 Sept. 1862, & P250, probably early October 1863, pp. 149, 312, 339.

public esteem. She said "*I* have never been so popular any where as' in Cardiff; 'every body treats me with the greatest consideration and affection. I sometimes feel quite overcome.'[17]

One who treated Catherine with especially great 'consideration and affection' was Mrs Billups, and the two women became great friends. Mrs Billups was older than Catherine and, perhaps, her being a little motherly attracted Catherine to her. The strength of the friendship is shown by Catherine remembering her at length in her *Reminiscences*, in which there are ten brief pages dedicated to her.

Catherine spoke of Mrs Billups' 'extravagant love' for her. This mother figure had a 'most retiring disposition, neither calculated for public life, nor desiring it,' but 'in her way, she was a bold, remarkable character and was very useful directly and indirectly I have no doubt to a good many.'

According to Catherine, 'she had a good bodily presence. She was just the sort of woman you would expect a duchess to be, one that could not enter into any room or building without being observed of all observers.' An existing portrait of her does also give that impression. Then, Catherine added, 'she was benevolence itself. She was, I think, the most generous-hearted woman I ever met. I never recollect anyone, either male or female, with such sympathies for human sorrow, so easily excited and so intensely practical and enduring.'

Then, surprisingly, Catherine said, 'When we first knew her, she was a long way from the Kingdom, according to our notions. She and her husband were members of a church, but did not pay much attention to what they would have considered emotional religion.' With that in mind, it seems strange that the two women should have been attracted to each other. Catherine was an ardent devotee of emotional religion, even if her practice of it tended to be quieter than that of many. Yet the two women became deeply attached to each other.[18]

It was also helpful that Mr and Mrs Billups were rich. Their generosity was to be a great relief and comfort to the Booths, who had been facing an uncertain future financially. Not that money was the reason for the friendship.

Other new friends, though not as close, were the Cory brothers, John and Richard. They were also rich and generous. Catherine told the story of

---

17 Ibid., Letter P240, 11 Apr. 1863, p. 328.
18 Booth, *Reminiscences*, pp. 60–62; *Reminiscences CD*, pp. 18–21; Booth-Tucker, *Catherine*, vol. 1, pp. 364–65.

one of their kind gestures in her *Reminiscences*. She said,

> Messrs John and Richard Cory and, I think, Mr Billups, came over to
> spend an hour or two with us. We were sitting over the tea table talking
> over various matters, when one of the company, I think it was Mr John
> Cory, remarked that he had just seen in the papers that a ship named
> the 'William Booth' had just sailed out of Liverpool, and asked William
> if he had seen anything about it. William replied in the negative and
> said that he was not aware of there being a ship with such a name. Mr
> Cory answered back, 'Oh, yes there was', and moreover that it had been
> named after William. Then it was added that it belonged to Messrs Cory
> themselves, and after a little joking they added that they had just bought
> this ship, named it after William, and had set apart a share in it for our
> benefit, expressing the hope at the same time that this small beginning
> of our career as ship owners might be auspicious and lay the foundation
> for future prosperity.
>
> Of course, we expressed our gratitude. It was exceedingly kind of them
> to manifest so much interest in us, who were then comparative strangers.
> They said it was our work that interested them and they were very happy
> to be able to have the power to minister in this small way to what might
> be for our future comfort.

Kind gesture though this was, it did not turn out well. Catherine recalled,

> But, alas, it is well known that there is nothing more uncertain than the
> business of the Seas. The 'William Booth' made two or three voyages,
> was announced to us as being expected home, and that it was hoped
> there would be some sort of profits to remit, when in some gale off the
> East Indies–the island of Bermuda–she was wrecked, and that so near
> to port that it was impossible to obtain the insurance. And so began and
> ended our ship owning experience.[19]

However, Catherine did not get the story quite right. Either her memory
was at fault or she had heard an incorrect account. Recent research has
shown that this vessel was declared unseaworthy on 9 March 1864, and
'condemned at Trinidad' on 30 April.[20]

---

19 Booth, *Reminiscences*, pp. 64–65; *Reminiscences CD*, p. 23.
20 *Lloyd's List*, 30 Mar. and 2 May 1864. (This shipping information has been supplied by
Gordon Taylor.)

CHAPTER 24

Back to England

It was probably in the middle of May that the Booths moved back to England. First, Mr and Mrs Billups took them 'almost by force' for a holiday at Weston-super-Mare in Somerset, south-west of Bristol. This was a welcome rest for the two evangelists and a strengthening of the relationship between the two women. But, as Catherine remembered, 'this little oasis was soon passed and we had to return to the hard and anxious realities of everyday life.'[1]

Walsall

The next sequence of 'hard and anxious realities' was in Walsall a town near Birmingham, with an estimated population of nearly 60,000. The Booths' independent ministry so far had been to small towns and villages, Cardiff excepted. This was a step up and they seem to have known that it might require a new approach.

They began their journey to Walsall on Friday 29 May. The venture did not begin well, and this highlights the difficulties that Catherine was labouring under at this time, as wife, mother and travelling evangelist, a combination that must have been impossible to handle well. She remembered,

Travelling had now become to me especially fatiguing. I could not be relied upon to go the shortest journey without being taken ill on the way. There were five little children, and do as we would there were an increasing number of packages, and the sort of accommodation that we obtained had to be considered not only as having to do with our comfort but with our very existence. However, everything was announced to us as being arranged and we started off for Walsall...

I did the journey with tolerable ease and so did the children, with the

1 Booth, *Reminiscences*, p. 65; *Reminiscences CD*, p. 23.

exception of Emma, who was a very poor traveller then, and on this occasion had to lie on the seat the greater part of the way. But our destination reached, however, we thought the fatigues of the removal were ended, but to our surprise and disappointment instead of taking us to the house which we understood they had taken and furnished and got ready for our use, we were driven to a coffee house, and there informed that the house engaged had been refused by the landlord at the last moment and that another taken only the night before was too dirty for us to enter and at present totally unfurnished.[2]

They seem to have arrived on Saturday, and, despite the housing difficulties, began their mission that Sunday. They were working with a group of Free Methodists, who had been greatly inspired by James Caughey, and thus were sympathetic with the Booths' style of ministry. Attendance at the first morning service, at which William preached, was small. Catherine preached in the afternoon and they had 'a powerful time', at the end of which more than 30 went forward 'to make a full consecration of themselves to the service of God.' That evening William preached again and 17 names 'were recorded as having found the blessing of salvation.'[3]

During the following week attendances were small but the number of responses was higher than expected. By the next Sunday word had clearly travelled about what was going on at the Free Methodist Chapel, for attendances were larger at each of the services. Then events occurred that the Booths would replicate in their Salvation Army days. William Booth recorded in his diary that 'Several rather noted characters had come over from Birmingham to help us, and they went out into the streets singing and exhorting the people. One of them had been a professional horse-racer and gambler. One was a prize-fighter. Another had been a celebrated thief.' Presumably they brought some from the streets into the chapel, and at the end of the service about 20 'professed to find Jesus.'[4]

This account is from William Booth's, now lost, diary, as recorded by Booth-Tucker. It probably contains a few alterations, but there is no reason to doubt the general accuracy of this report. However, it is unknown who initiated the visit of the 'noted characters'. It is unlikely to have been

---

2 Ibid., p. 66; ibid., p. 24.
3 Ibid., p. 67; ibid., p. 25.
4 Booth-Tucker, *Catherine*, vol. 1, pp. 366–67, quoting William Booth's Diary, for 31 May and 6 and 7 June 1863.

Catherine. That was probably not quite her style at that stage in her life. The Walsall Free Methodists may have invited them, or, perhaps, hearing that William and Catherine Booth were in town, they invited themselves. It is also possible, perhaps probable, that William Booth called them over, and they may have been some of the 300 who had 'found peace with God' when the Booths were in Birmingham in 1856.[5] Whichever is true, this was a lesson, clearly remembered, for those who were to form The Salvation Army.

A letter Catherine wrote to her parents a little later, paints a more negative picture of events in Walsall, though this appears to have been because the Free Methodists in that town were 'a small society, *without influence* & awfully poor.'[6] She yearned to be ministering in the larger chapels to the many hundreds, as they had done so successfully in Cornwall. Perhaps inevitably, Walsall proved to be 'a miserable affair temporally'. By as late as mid-July, they had 'not received as much as [their] travelling expenses & house rent' from the church's leaders, and she feared that 'the Tea meeting', a main source of income, 'will be a failure; the people are deadly poor.' Not surprisingly the Booths were 'very unsettled.'[7]

William Booth was never satisfied. He was always stretching for something more. At the end of June, he and Catherine borrowed a trick from the Primitive Methodists and built upon their experience with the 'noted characters'. They organised a camp meeting and arranged for a printer to produce large posters advertising it. The poster declared

Mr & Mrs Booth at Walsall
A United Monster Camp Meeting
will be held in a field near Hatherton Lake
on Sabbath June 28th
Addresses will be given by the Revs. Wm Booth,
T. Whitehouse and other friends of the neighbourhood
Also by converted pugilists, horse racers, poachers and others
from Birmingham, Liverpool and Nottingham
Mrs Booth will preach at Whittimere St Chapel in the evening at 6 o'clock
Services to commence at 9 o'clock in the morning

---

5 *MNCM*, 'Revival at Birmingham', 1856, p. 673.
6 'CBLP', Letter P244, mid-June 1863, p. 331.
7 Ibid., Letter P246, possibly mid-July 1863, p. 335.

Once more a collection of converts with a dubious past were to be used to preach the gospel.

When Catherine preached that Sunday evening, 'the chapel was packed in every corner.' She said, 'The Lord helped me to speak with unusual force and freedom.' While she was speaking in the chapel, 'William held a service in a field close by.' They then 'united in the chapel for the prayer meeting, and although the success was hindered by the great crowd, above 40 persons professed to find salvation, some of whom had not been in a place of worship for many a year gone by.'[8]

While in Walsall, Catherine conducted meetings for children, which were held weekdays in the late afternoon or early evening. Then, health and family commitments permitting, she stayed for the evening services, which William conducted, presumably to help with the post-service counselling.[9] She had carried out similar meetings in Cardiff.

Towards the end of their time in Wales, Catherine had told her parents, 'There is a good work going on in Willie.'[10] In fact, she 'knew that he was deeply convicted at Cardiff, and one night there at the circus [she] had urged upon him very earnestly the importance of his making the decision on which his salvation depended.' For what seemed an age, Willie said nothing. The tension must have been unbearable. But Catherine 'forced him to give [her] an answer as to whether he would accept the offers of salvation or not'. Later she recalled, 'I shall never forget the feeling that thrilled through my soul when my darling boy, only seven years old, about whom I had formed such high expectations with respect to his service for the Master, deliberately looked me in the face and answered, "No!"'

Yet at the close of one of the children's meetings in Walsall, Catherine had found Willie 'squeezed in among the crowd' of those who had moved to the front, 'weeping with a broken heart … confessing his sins and seeking the forgiveness of God.' Catherine said that she 'dealt faithfully with him', and she believed 'that he there and then found salvation and entered into the family of God.'[11]

In the second half of June, while they were in Walsall, Mrs Billups took an unwell Ballington on a holiday by the sea. When this had ended, either

---

8 Booth, *Reminiscences*, p. 71; *Reminiscences CD*, pp. 28–29.

9 Ibid., p. 69; ibid., p. 27.

10 'CBLP', Letter P237, possibly 26 Mar. 1863, p. 324.

11 Booth, *Reminiscences*, pp. 69–70; *Reminiscences CD*, pp. 27–28.

she or her husband took him to London to stay with the Mumfords.[12] One less child to care for took a little of the pressure off Catherine.

It seems to have been right at the beginning of July that William sprained his ankle for a second time. On this occasion it was much worse. 'Some men had been digging outside the door for the laying or repairing of some gas pipes and had left the hole there without any caution.' As Booth was leaving through the back door of the chapel, 'he put his foot in [the hole] and gave his ankle a nasty wrench.' He was 'unable to put his feet to the ground and had to be carried home on the shoulders of some of the friends'. It was two weeks 'before he could get out again.'[13] Catherine described the leg as 'black, blue & yellow almost from the knee to the toes; quite a sight, & the joint very much swol[l]en.' She, ever the willing doctor, adopted a treatment from Smedley's Hydro, 'giving a steam bath to the limb twice & three times per day'. It worked well enough 'to astonish all' who had seen the improvement.[14]

If Catherine had been bearing a slightly lesser load because of Ballington's holiday, that load now became heavier, as she was now 'obliged to take the meetings alone as far as [her] strength would enable' her. Fortunately, 'the Lord sustained [her] wonderfully,' and the work did not seem 'to suffer.' William made his comeback before he had fully recovered, 'preaching standing on one leg and kneeling on the other.' At an 'open-air service he limped round the town singing, "Will you go?"'[15] Though it is unlikely that either of the Booths knew it, in 1751 John Wesley, one of their great heroes, on several occasions preached while kneeling, when he had had injured his ankle slipping on some ice.[16]

By the end of July, 'William's throat was completely done up.' Years later, Catherine said that she had not 'known it as bad, either before or since.'[17] Catherine was also exhausted, so they both went to Smedley's Hydro at Matlock Bank for some much-needed rest and some excessive water treatment. However, Catherine told the Mumfords, 'I seem almost as busy here as at home, tho' in a different way.'

Matlock was in Derbyshire not far from Catherine's birthplace. One day

---

12 'CBLP', Letters P244, mid-June 1863, and P245, 26 June 1863, pp. 332–34.
13 Booth, *Reminiscences*, p. 73; *Reminiscences CD*, p. 31.
14 'CBLP', Letter P246, possibly mid-July 1863, p. 335.
15 Booth, *Reminiscences*, p. 73; *Reminiscences CD*, p. 31.
16 Wesley, *Journal*, 10–18 Feb. 1751, in *Works*, vol. 2, pp. 222–23.
17 Booth, *Reminiscences*, p. 74; *Reminiscences CD*, p. 31.

she and William took a carriage and pair and visited Mr Billups, who was at the time staying at Dove Dale, a local beauty spot. They journeyed to within three kilometres of Ashbourne, but for some unknown reason did not take that final step.[18]

Birmingham and surrounds

Early in September, when they had recovered sufficiently, they moved on to Birmingham. They began at a Methodist New Connexion chapel in the middle of the month, but their time there was not a great success. The chapel was small and 'the Birmingham Fair, in which the town usually runs wild', clashed with their mission and had a negative impact upon it.[19]

While in that area William began a mission at Old Hill, a colliery town about fifteen kilometres away, where he worked with the Primitive Methodists. Once more we have an example of local Methodists ignoring their Conference dictates. This was a very successful campaign, but Catherine does not seem to have been involved in it.[20]

Catherine said that the people at Old Hill wanted her 'to go very much', but it was 'out of the question.'[21] It was out of the question because she was pregnant again. As Catherine told her parents, 'I am very poorly. The *sickness* is commencing! It seems *very hard*; I find it more difficult to submit to this than anything.'[22] They already had five children under the age of eight, so expecting another was a hard thing for her to bear. A little later she wrote, 'I am *wretchedly ill*. The last few days, life has been a burden to me almost intolerable.'[23] In fact, at that time she had felt 'deadly ill' and unable to cope with the demands of the household. The children presented particular problems. They were either 'racing up & down stairs or making an intollerable [sic] noise in the nursery.' Fortunately, her health, and thus her mood, improved a little early in November.[24]

Beginning in the middle of November William conducted a series of missions in Hasbury, Lye and Dudley in the Birmingham area. These seem

---

18 'CBLP', Letter P248, 4 Aug. 1863, pp. 337–38.
19 Booth, *Reminiscences*, p. 74; *Reminiscences CD*, pp. 31–32.
20 Ibid., pp. 74–77; ibid., pp. 32–34.
21 'CBLP', Letter P252, 20 Oct. 1863, p. 341.
22 Ibid., Letter P250, probably early October 1863, p. 339.
23 Ibid., Letter P252, 20 Oct. 1863, p. 341.
24 Ibid., Letter, P254, 12 Nov. 1863, p. 343.

to have continued until the new year. Catherine was not well enough to take much of a part in these, but she appears to have been involved in a small way in Hasbury and Lye. Yet, with William often away, she found it 'a very trying time in every way.'[25]

When Catherine's health had improved further, they began to consider conducting separate campaigns. Up until now they had ministered together in one area, usually amongst a handful of chapels, sharing the workload as circumstances demanded. Now, while the Conference bans were not totally effective, they were making an impact, and at times just one group of Methodists would host them in an area instead of several. This meant fewer opportunities and a lighter workload. It also meant a smaller income, and with a growing family that was a genuine difficulty.

As she had expressed a little earlier,

> I am much tempted to look gloomily towards the future but my 'heart is fixed. I will *trust* and not be afraid.' These words have followed me much of late, '*Do good, dwell in the Land* and verily *thou* shalt be fed.' If I can only fulfill [sic] the first part of the direction, I have no fears about the second, but, Oh, I continually come short... Pray for me! I sometimes feel as tho' I had taken a path which is too hard for me and duties too onerous for me to perform. But it is my privilege to say & to feel, '*I* can do all things through Christ which strengtheneth me'. The Lord help me.[26]

In the months ahead that was to be put to the test.

---

25 Booth, *Reminiscences*, pp. 77–78; *Reminiscences CD*, p. 35; 'CBLP', Letters P256, 17 Nov. 1863, and P258, 8 Dec. 1863, pp. 345, 347.
26 'CBLP', Letter P250, probably early October 1863, p. 340.

CHAPTER 25

Disappointment

Yorkshire

At the beginning of 1864 they moved north to Yorkshire and ministered in the Leeds and Bradford area. Their work there did not prove as successful as in earlier years. In a letter written to her mother at the beginning of February, probably from Farsley, she said,

> We are yet very unsettled. The work here has not been sufficient to warrant our taking a house. We commence at Dudley Hill on Sunday.[1] If we don't see greater things there, I don't think we shall stay in this neighbourhood. If we do, we shall probably stay a long time, as we have already several important spheres open to us. But all depends on the work. The people here seem hardened & stupid to the last degree. Still we have had much good done and we hope for better things.

> Of course, we are much perplexed & often somewhat discouraged, but we must stand still and see the salvation of God. Pray for us... I am but very poorly myself on the whole. Some days I have hard work to keep up and suffer much from that pain in the side of my body that I used to have after Emma was born. My leg is also very bad especially the top part of it. I expect I shall have to lay it up a good deal by & bye, but I have to go on a day at a time leaving the future in the hands of God. Wm is but poorly & low in spirits. Still we are hoping for better things.[2]

The strong note of pessimism in this letter is not hidden by the final hint of optimism.

They went to Dudley Hill, as planned, and were disappointed. Catherine complained to her parents that some churches were inviting them, painting a rosy picture of that church's prospects, and when the Booths arrived, they found it far below what they expected. Catherine thought that they had

---

1 Dudley Hill in Yorkshire is not to be confused with Dudley, where the Booths served when they were staying in Birmingham.

2 'CBLP', Letter P261, 2 Feb. 1864, pp. 350–51.

recently been 'miserably deceived in two or three instances.' However, it was probably a case of the Conference censures taking their effect. It seems that the larger, more successful churches were no longer inviting them, but the smaller churches, which were perhaps more desperate, did. While disappointed, Catherine was not without hope. She said, 'It may be the cloud will break and surround us with sun shine. Any way, God lives above the clouds and He will direct our path.'[3]

They next moved on to Lady Lane Chapel in Leeds, a larger mission field. She described their commencement there as 'very hopeful'. Yet she was cautious, because they had faced 'so much disappointment lately'. One of the problems was that that area had 'been so much worked by almost all the Evangelists in the field', that there remained some uncertainty.[4] This was a problem that presumably all the travelling evangelists faced. People can only be converted once, and in those churches and areas that had been much evangelised in recent times, newly arrived evangelists found themselves preaching mainly to the converted.

This caused Catherine to think once more of preaching in public halls rather than chapels. She said,

> If this place disappoints us I shall be quite tired of tugging with Churches, & insist on Wm taking some Hall or Theatre somewhere and trying that. I believe the Lord will thrust him into that sphere yet. We *carn't* [sic] *get at the masses* in the *chapels*. They are so awfully prejudiced against all connected with the *sects*, that they won't come unless under some mighty excitement.[5]

Here there seems to have been a development in Catherine's thinking, even an about-turn. In this instance she is advocating 'some mighty excitement' to attract people to hear the gospel. Eleven years earlier she had praised the controlled and thoughtful preaching of David Thomas and criticised the 'exceeding injudicious and violent' preaching of Isaac Marsden, whom her husband admired.[6] Had Catherine learned this from William, or was it a change of opinion based on wider experience and knowledge, or both? According to Catherine, the desire to preach in secular halls rather the

---

3 Ibid., Letter P262, 8 Feb. 1864, p. 351.
4 Ibid., Letter P263, 29 Feb. 1864, p. 352.
5 Ibid., Letter P263, 29 Feb. 1864, p. 352.
6 Booth, *Letters*, Letter CM29, 20 Mar. 1853, p. 87; Booth, *Letters CD*, p. 90.

chapels 'was especially William's feeling'.[7]

Catherine had said, 'If this place disappoints us...' Sadly, their mission at Lady Lane Chapel did disappoint them. Early in March Catherine reported to her parents,

> Wm had a hard night last night & much to discourage him. After a deputation waiting on us at Farsley of a minister & 2 lay gentleman [sic] and representing Lady Lane as ripe and ready with a Society of 700 members, etc., etc., etc., all glowing & glorious, we find now we get here that the Society is split up into two parties: Associationists & Reformers.[8] A *few Revivalists*, & the great bulk anti-*revivalists* standing aloof altogether from special services. One of the very men who came to Farsley to invite us said to Wm at the noon day prayer-meeting today 'If you can get a Revival at Lady Lane you can get one any where!!' So much for Methodist truthfulness & sincerity.[9]

Once more Catherine believed that they had been deceived.

Nottingham

For their visit to Leeds the Booths had sent the children with Mary Kirton to stay with William's mother and sisters in Nottingham. By this time Catherine was about seven months pregnant. Then the news came that Willie and Emma had scarlet fever. The Booths brought the mission at Lady Lane to what seems to have been an earlier than intended ending, Catherine went to join the children in Nottingham and William began a campaign in a Free Methodist chapel in another part of Leeds.[10]

Catherine arrived in Nottingham probably in the middle of March and the chaos unleashed made her feel worse than she already was. Catherine described the experience graphically, with the expected birth dominant.

> I came here on Tuesday and have scarce been able to move out of the Nursery since. I have a bed in the Nursery where I mostly lay & overlook the children. I never was in such a muddle in my life, but I suppose it

---

7 Booth, *Reminiscences*, p. 79; *Reminiscences CD*, p. 36.

8 Many groups of the Wesleyan Association and the Wesleyan (or Methodist) Reformers did amalgamate, but, it seems, not all did so happily.

9 'CBLP', Letter P264, 1 or 8 Mar. 1864, p. 353.

10 Booth, *Reminiscences*, p. 78; *Reminiscences CD*, p. 36.

is amongst the 'all things', and the Lord knows all about it. I don't know what makes me so helpless, but I am just as bad as I was within two or three days of my time last time. Willie continues to improve; Emma also is getting better. I fully expect they will all have it. If we were only in our own home I should not mind so much, but I do dread anything happening me here amongst all the children. Grandma is poorly & Aunt Emma is all but laid aside, which makes matters worse. However, we shall be brought through some way. I have had much anxiety lately & a deal of relaxation of bowels, which perhaps has made me worse. I don't think I can possibly go to the time. William will get a house as soon as he possibly can.[11]

A few weeks later she reported that Katy and Herbert were 'improving nicely', having presumably also been struck by the fever, though 'Ballington continues very poorly indeed.' The doctor confirmed that he was 'in a very unsatisfactory state indeed.' She feared consumption, as did the doctor. 'He has a cough & complains much of pain in his side when he coughs. He sweats at nights very bad and is very weak. The Dr orders him all the nourishment we can get down, which I don't fail to give him.'[12]

But there was good news too. William sent her a letter from Leeds telling her that at the evening service the previous Sunday he had 'between 30 & 40 cases' of people seeking salvation. He also appeared optimistic about finding a house in which the family could be reunited.[13]

Early in April her health was still poor, some days she was so ill she was 'little off the bed'. At other times she was well enough, she said, 'to do a little at the children's clothes, which I found much needing my attention.' She was considering visiting Cardiff, though presumably for Mrs Billups's nursing rather than ministry, and 'then go to a home', assuming William had found one, 'in time for first week in June.[14] However, she soon gave up the plan to go to Cardiff.[15]

Leeds

The reason for the proposed return to 'a home' early in June was because that was when she believed the baby was due, though she often felt that it

---

11 'CBLP', Letter P265, mid- or late March 1864, pp. 354–55.

12 Ibid., Letter P268, 12 Apr. 1864, p. 358.

13 Ibid., Letter P266, 28 Mar. 1864, p. 356. William's letter no longer exists.

14 Ibid., Letter P267, 6 Apr. 1864, p. 357.

15 Ibid., Letter P268, 12 Apr. 1864, p. 358.

might come earlier.[16] It did. Marian (or Miriam) Billups Booth was born, according to her birth certificate, on 19 May, in the new home that William had found for them in Leeds. Some sources say that she was born on 4 May, but this must be incorrect.[17] Now there were six children. And Mrs Billups had been rewarded for her friendship.

The move to their new home went well, except for one near disaster. When preparing to leave Nottingham, Catherine went downstairs and fell over a box at the bottom and landed heavily. It 'did not tend to improve' her. They then travelled by train to Leeds and took a cab to their new home, but Catherine, badly bruised, found it difficult to walk from the station to the cab. On the Saturday after their arrival, she 'lay on the Bed ... looking at the confusion around' her and longed for her mother to come and help her.[18]

However, Catherine was delighted to be once more in a home of her own. Living in other people's homes was not always pleasant, particularly with young children in tow. As she later said,

The torture I had endured through always treading on other people's carpets and using other people's furniture, I see now was foolish in the extreme, seeing that we always paid a good price and rarely left things any worse than we found them, but so it was, and therefore the comfort of having the children in our own home, though most humbly and scantily furnished, made all other sacrifices and privations insignificant. We always carried a nursery carpet and when I took a furnished house, we chose a room for a nursery, put some common chairs and some plain furniture in and turned them in with their nurse. Then when these had got settled, we could go on with the other things.[19]

Catherine did not only like being in a house of their own once more, she also liked the house itself. It had

Low Kitchens, at least *half* under, but the front one is a real nice room, quite suitable to take meals in, etc., etc. The back one is a good room, fitted up with a first rate cooking range, sink, Copper & *every* convenience. A capital Water closet & coal & Wine cellar, all under cover. It is by far the best house we have had; the great draw back is that what furniture we can afford to buy looks almost lost in it. However, I would rather have a good house half empty than a poor one ever so grand.

16 Ibid., Letter P266, 28 Mar. 1864, pp. 355–56.
17 See 'CBLP', p. 354, fn. 656. Birth certificate details provided by Gordon Taylor.
18 'CBLP', Letter P271, probably early May 1864, p. 361.
19 Booth, *Reminiscences*, p. 79; *Reminiscences CD*, p. 36.

William, as always, was madly busy. On their reunion she found him 'looking ill in the extreme.' She said, 'He has gone through untold anxiety & fatigue with one thing or another,' but her presence improved his spirits. Catherine said, 'we feel as tho' we were litterally [sic] walking on the *waters* with nothing but the promises of God to depend on. Faith says, "Well, is that not *enough*?" The Lord help us to feel it so.'[20]

William had preached for the Free Methodists at the Meadow Lane Chapel and then branched out. According to Catherine's *Reminiscences*, William, 'In conjunction … with six earnest people, most of them Methodists,' began to preach 'in the markets, streets, squares and in concert halls, old chapels, or any other buildings that could be obtained.' This earnest group also held all-nights of prayer. Catherine said that she assisted with this 'so far as my health would allow', which, one suspects, was not often.

It seems to have been at around this time that Catherine 'suffered one of those serious attacks after preaching, which [she] sometimes had'. This she thought was caused by 'over-exertion in the heated atmosphere… The chapel,' she said, 'had been packed and I had lost all realization of myself from beginning to end of the service. After it was over, I was so prostrated that I had to be laid on forms, on which were laid some cushions, which friends procured in the vestry.'[21] Catherine gave her all when she preached, and she usually spoke for more than an hour. In her physical condition this was bound to take its toll. When she returned home that night, she was unable to climb the stairs to the bedroom and they had to fit up a bed for her downstairs.[22]

Apart again

When Catherine had fully recovered from the birth of Marian and that 'attack', probably in the second half of August, she began a series of meetings in nearby Batley. She held the weeknight meetings in the Free Methodist's Providence Chapel and Sunday services in the Town Hall. She described it 'as wonderful a work as ever I had experienced. The whole town was moved. They used to troop to the chapel as if they were going to a fair.'

A report on this mission in the *Wesleyan Times* said, 'Mrs Booth devotes

---

20 'CBLP', Letter P271, probably early May 1864, p. 361.
21 Booth, *Reminiscences*, pp. 79–80; *Reminiscences CD*, pp. 36–37.
22 Ibid., p. 81; ibid., p. 39.

much attention to the members of the church. Her cogent reasonings, pungent appeals and winning entreaties told powerfully on this class, often melting the audience to tears and inducing the whole society to come out to the penitent form, acknowledging its worldliness and indifference and to consecrate itself to Christ and duty.'[23]

William, meanwhile, was preaching in Hyde, near Manchester. She then held a highly successful mission in Pudsey from mid-September to late October. Writing to her parents at the end of September she said,

> I had a *very good* week; chapel, which seats about 800, nearly full every night, & 20 & 30 per night for full consecration, as well as a few penitents. On Sunday night chapel crowded, but so hot & myself so poorly I could not command my usual power in speaking, & consequently only a few cases, whereas I had hoped for 20 or 30 sinners. Nevertheless, it was a good service and I am hoping for a break down to night.
>
> Oh, for more Divine unction. They say the Pudsey sinners will '*bide* some bringing down.' Well, the Lord can do it, I suppose. I am immensely popular with the people, but that is no comfort unless they will be saved by me. There has been a *precious* work amongst the members. There are few who have not been forward for full consecration.

However, she had 'been terribly prostrate with one thing or other,' but she hoped her health would improve.[24]

A week later she said,

> I had a splendid service on Thursday night, 29 adults, real good cases, & near 20 children, many of them 12 & 14 years of age. Sunday night chapel crowded, but not such a good prayer-meeting. The heat of the place mititates [sic] against the success on a Sunday night. We had 7 or 8 good cases, however, & scores deeply convicted. Last night another good service, 17 adults and a good, solemn influence. I am hoping for still greater things to night.

While in Pudsey she had bad toothache, which makes all her efforts in the pulpit seem even more remarkable. She said, 'I have suffered a good deal with my teeth, & after going backwards & forwards to the Dentist's four or five times, I was obliged to go & have one extracted on friday night. It was a heavy pull but a great relief to get rid of it. There is another will have to share the same fate, I fear.' She then added the note that so many have sung,

---

23 Booth, *Reminiscences*, p. 80; *Reminiscences CD*, p. 37, quoting the *Wesleyan Times*.
24 'CBLP', Letter P276, 27 Sept. 1864, p. 367.

'I neglected them too long before I had them attended to.'[25]

In the mission at Pudsey 'Two hundred and thirty adults and a large number of children professed to find salvation.'[26] Catherine Booth seemed to have the Spirit's blessing to bring the Pudsey sinners down.

But her missions at Batley and Pudsey were not her only concern at that time. She still had little Marian to care for and the rest of the children. It appears to have been while ministering in one of those towns, probably both, that she 'used to nurse the baby, Marian, the last thing on Saturday night, and leave her about 6 or 7 o'clock, catching the last train for' her destination. Marian 'used to be fed with the bottle on Sundays and I used to get back to her as soon as I could on the Monday morning.'[27] When it is remembered that Catherine also had to prepare for the services she conducted, and organise the servants, it is hard to imagine how this 'frail thing, soon exhausted' managed to cope.

While Catherine was doing so well, William, in Hyde, was in the pit of despair. He told her,

> I wish I were in a more satisfactory state spiritually. I feel almost dead–powerless. Consequently, my preaching and praying in public has but little effect on the people. But wishing produces no improvement. O, that God would come and give me some new light or some new power. Will you pray for me? I never felt less emotion and power in prayer in my life. And I am sure I don't know what to do...

> It is no use me talking about my rebellion of heart against this separation. I must submit and say, 'Thy will be done.' I wish I was sure that it was His will. As I turned into my lonely lodgings last night a young gentleman with a lady on his arm knocked at the door of the house opposite mine, [and] I could not help asking why I was parted from my young and precious wife. I know why, and for a season it must be so. Perhaps we shall grow accustomed to it and not feel it so much. I do feel a measure of comfort from the thought that we are securing our own livelihood by it and not hanging on to any one. That thought has been like a canker at my heart of late. It must not be after that fashion. We will work and then rest together and then work again.[28]

25 Ibid., Letter P277, 4 Oct. 1864, p. 369.
26 Booth, *Reminiscences*, pp. 80–81; *Reminiscences CD*, p. 37.
27 Ibid., p. 82; ibid., p. 39.
28 Booth, *Letters*, Letter (WB132), mid-September 1864, p. 346; *Letters CD*, p. 343.

That separation was most painful to each of them. In one letter he addressed her as 'My dear little disconsolate wife', which suggests that Catherine had expressed her sadness at that separation (in a letter now lost). In that same letter of William's, possibly written from Sheffield, he said that he was meeting with more success and he was consequently in better spirits. He cheerfully told her that the people he was ministering to had 'a great spirit of enquiry and reconsecration.'[29]

Yet he was soon down again and begged Catherine to send him 'a little love talk', for he feared that there might be 'gloomy hours' of separation 'in the future.' He added, perhaps to comfort himself as well as her, 'I am feasting on you and on the hour when again I hold you, and look at you, and kiss you, and have the delicious rapture of hearing you say you love and reciprocate all my feelings.'[30]

The frequent separations and growing uncertainty about the future were affecting them both. William was often depressed and Catherine went through at least one bout of insomnia in the later months of 1864. When he heard about her being unable to sleep, he urged her to 'rest next week' and not to 'let little things put [her] about.' But with her preaching commitments, the children and household issues, including problems with at least one servant, she faced a lot of 'little things', and some not so small.

On the positive side, William suddenly seemed more confident about getting work, as the way was, he said, now 'wide open', and he seems to have been having discussions about a mission for the Congregationalists. However, that optimism may have been expressed just to cheer Catherine. Yet, also on the positive side, William reminded her, 'Our children are in health. We are saved, so far, from those gloomy visits to the churchyard which so many other families have to pay.' Sadly, many families did have to make those 'gloomy visits' in the Victorian era, but despite various illnesses their six children were alive and, for the most part, well. He added, 'And we have many, many, many other mercies. And we have that which is most precious of all that is human, our own *warm, sympathetic, thorough, intelligent, well-grounded confidence in and affection for each other.*'[31] That was the greatest of temporal blessings.

After Christmas, while the family was still living in Leeds, Catherine

---

29 Ibid., Letter (WB138), possibly early October 1864, p. 349; ibid., p. 345.
30 Ibid., Letter (WB140), October 1864, p. 349; ibid., p. 346.
31 Ibid., Letter (WB145), November 1864, p. 351; ibid., pp. 347–48.

began a campaign in Rotherham, more than 40 kilometres to the south. It continued until early in February, but it was close enough to Leeds for her to return home frequently. She described it as 'one of the most wonderful times' that she 'ever experienced', though she was 'in great bodily weakness' at the time. It is said 'that 300 people professed conversion' during her five weeks there.[32]

As the year drew to a close, the Booths considered future places for their evangelism. Catherine told her parents, 'I wish it may be London.'[33] Apart from anything else, that would place her much closer to the Mumfords. Another reason for choosing London was to fix the problem of her having to leave the children so often and for so long, for there were likely to be more opportunities to minister within easy reach of wherever they chose to live.[34] It also meant that even if she and William were preaching in different places, they would probably not be apart much. However, when they did make the move, it did not work out that way at first.

War and slavery

At the close of 1864 she stated her feelings very clearly about the Civil War in America, which was then coming to an end. She said,

> The tide seems to be turned in favour of the North, the day of vengeance of 'inquisition for blood' (Ps 9:12), which Mrs Stowe foretold, has surely come, and America is receiving at the hand of the Lord double for her sins. Well, if it only ends the hel[l]ish system of slavery, it is well. Oh, for the reign of righteousness & truth, but alas, alas, it seems afar off, and in all lands the wicked triumph. Well, let us do our part towards it & then we 'shall stand in [our] lot at the end of the days' (Dan 12:13).[35]

This contains hints of her future involvement in social issues.

---

32 Booth, *Reminiscences*, p. 82; *Reminiscences CD*, p. 39.
33 'CBLP', Letter P282, 30 or 31 Dec. 1864, p. 374.
34 Booth, *Reminiscences*, pp. 82–83; *Reminiscences CD*, p. 40.
35 'CBLP', Letter P282, 30 or 31 Dec. 1864, p. 374.

CHAPTER 26

London

The people's call to the Booths was 'Come to London'; some were always saying, 'London is the sphere. Anyway, get somewhere within our reach.'[1]

Rotherhithe

The year 1865 probably should be regarded as the most important year in the lives of Catherine and William Booth. But when it began, they had no idea that it would see the birth of a movement, directed by them, that would challenge Britain and, eventually, travel the world. But they moved to Britain's capital at a low point in William Booth's career as an evangelist, though at a promising time for Catherine. In one letter early that year, William had said despairingly to Catherine, 'You heard how they pitched into my writing and praised yours. There, as elsewhere, I must decrease and you increase!'[2]

Yet he need not have worried. Catherine, despite her poor spelling and almost non-existent punctuation, was always the better writer of the two, but there were very few superior evangelists and inspirers of men in Britain than William Booth. His time would come.

At the beginning of the year the Booths were apart again, and Catherine found 'This mode of life … any thing but congenial,' as, no doubt, did William. She added, philosophically, 'but there is no help for it at present.' Ballington's health was also an ongoing worry in this period, with deafness being one of his problems.[3] Catherine and the children seem to have moved to London late in January.

1 Booth, *Reminiscences*, p. 58; *Reminiscences CD*, p. 17.
2 Booth, *Letters*, Letter (WB151), late February 1865, p. 353; *Letters CD*, p. 350.
3 'CBLP', Letter P283, probably 2 Jan. 1865, pp. 374–75.

At about that time William accepted an invitation to minister in Louth in Lincolnshire, beginning on 12 February, and Catherine accepted one, scheduled a little later, from Rotherhithe in London. William had a successful ministry in Louth, with '150 names being registered.'[4]

Catherine then conducted three successive missions in Rotherhithe, Bermondsey and Deptford all in south-east London. She began her meetings at the United Methodist Free Church in Rotherhithe at the end of February.

William had preached at that same chapel in Rotherhithe, probably in 1852, and had seen 'much good done.'[5] Now it was Catherine's turn. A writer in the *Wesleyan Times* said that during her first two weeks there her subjects included 'The judgment day and its consequences', 'Heart hardening', and 'Almost persuaded'. The writer then added, 'She reminds us more of Finney than of any other evangelist.' However, it is a pity that writer did not elaborate on why she was like Charles Finney. She concluded at Rotherhithe on 19 March.[6]

Booth-Tucker gave an account of these meetings, which had been remembered by one of the converts. A friend had given this lady a handbill, which said, 'Come and hear a woman preach.' So she accepted the invitation. That night Catherine preached on, 'Now advise and see what answer I shall return to him that sent me' (2 Sam 24:13). In applying it, Catherine asked if any among her hearers had promised on a bed of sickness to give their hearts to God, and when they had recovered had failed to do so. That message struck home to this woman and she 'resolved to redeem [her] vows that very night.'

That woman said that amongst the converts in that campaign was a daughter of the landlord of the Europa public house. When that new convert's sister heard about her conversion, she went to the Free Church to ridicule the services. She sat in the gallery, but instead of mocking she was so overcome by Catherine Booth's words, that at the end of the service she rushed down to the communion rail, crying, 'I must come! I must come!'

---

4 Booth, *Reminiscences*, p. 83; *Reminiscences CD*, p. 40.

5 Booth, *Letters*, Letter (WB152), probably late February 1865, p. 353; *Letters CD*, p. 350. Booth-Tucker, *Catherine*, vol. 1, p. 382, says that it was 12 years before Catherine's visit in 1865, but as William was in Lincolnshire in 1853, it was presumably in 1852.

6 The available extract from the *Wesleyan Times* of 13 Mar. 1865, is brief, and the writer may have given more details in the original, see Booth, *Reminiscences*, p. 83; *Reminiscences CD*, p. 40.

Later their father was also converted, gave up the public house and they became members of Spurgeon's Tabernacle.

This woman said that she had seen as many as 30 people 'seeking salvation' at one of these meetings. Remarkably, this woman also claimed that when she examined the Free Church's roll some years later, she found 100 names of people who professed to have been converted during Catherine's campaign.[7]

An article in the *Wesleyan Times*, commenting on Catherine's preaching at this time, said,

> many persons whose scruples would lead them to condemn female ministry have been forced to admit that they would hesitate long before bidding this devoted lady hold her peace. All that we say is, we only venture to think that that if all our ministers and preachers were to speak as she does, pressing the truth in the same forcible and telling manner, our success would be such as we have never yet seen.[8]

Similarly, that March, R.C. Morgan and Samuel Chase, publishers of *Revival* (later *The Christian*), wrote a letter for that publication questioning whether it was right for women to preach. Their objections were drawn from Scripture and also expressed the concern that while a mother was preaching, she was neglecting her children. It says much for the force of Catherine Booth's ministry that Messrs Morgan and Chase later changed their minds.[9]

Though the order of these events is not entirely clear, William came south, probably during or at the end of Catherine's Rotherhithe campaign, and established the family in a home in Hammersmith in the west of London.

Bermondsey

After Rotherhithe, Catherine took a few days' rest, and then began another series at Grange Road, Bermondsey, once more, it seems, for the Free Methodists. At about that time, William went north again to conduct a mission in Ripon in Yorkshire.[10]

---

7 Booth-Tucker, *Catherine*, vol. 1, p. 382.

8 Booth, *Reminiscences*, p. 83; *Reminiscences CD*, p. 40, quoting the *Wesleyan Times*.

9 Bennett, *General*, vol. 1, p. 342.

10 Booth, *Reminiscences*, pp. 83–84; *Reminiscences CD*, pp. 40–41; Booth-Tucker, *Catherine*, vol. 1, p. 386.

A report of Catherine's meetings at Grange Road appeared in the *Gospel Guide*, which beautifully describes her in action. It said,

> In dress nothing could be neater. A plain, black, straw bonnet, slightly relieved with a pair of dark violet strings, a black velvet loose-fitting jacket, with light sleeves, which appeared exceedingly suitable to her while preaching, and a black silk gown constituted the plain dress of this female preacher. [She has] a prepossessing countenance, with at first an exceedingly quiet manner, enlisting the sympathies and riveting the attention of her audience.
>
> Mrs Booth is a woman of no ordinary mind, and her powers of argument are of a superior order. Her delivery is calm, precise and clear, without the least approach to formality or tediousness. Her language is plain and well chosen, and her ability for public speaking is above the ordinary general order of the opposite sex who occupy a similar position. Not the least appearance of anything approaching nervousness or timidity was observable in her, still there was an entire absence of unbecoming confidence or assumed authority over her audience.

That she did not have, in the writer's opinion, 'the least appearance of anything approaching nervousness or timidity' is significant when one is aware of her earlier struggles. Yet, if she was now bold, she did not assume 'authority over her audience.'

The *Gospel Guide* article added, 'May we say that many of the ministers, deacons, elders and members would do well to hear Mrs Booth. They might learn a lesson from her devotedness, her evident sincerity for the good of souls, her intense earnestness, her affectionate words, her perpetual and heavy labours for the cause to which she appears so warmly attached.' The writer of the article seems to have had no problem with a woman preaching.

She preached her last sermon at Grange Road on Sunday 30 April to a packed chapel. They closed with a farewell tea later that week, at which 'William and several other ministers ... spoke.'[11]

While in Bermondsey, Catherine also 'addressed the parents and scholars of the Cherry Gardens Ragged School.'[12] Ragged schools were, as their name implies, schools for poor children. On the last day of March, she had also addressed a meeting at the Southwark Temperance Institute.

---

11 Booth, *Reminiscences*, pp. 85-86; *Reminiscences CD*, pp. 42–43, quoting the *Gospel Guide*.

12 Ibid., p. 83; ibid., p. 40, quoting the *Wesleyan Times*.

At that she said, 'Of all questions of importance next to the Gospel, which contributed to the well being of the human race it was that of temperance.'[13]

Now that they were living in Hammersmith, their home was about ten kilometres away from Bermondsey and, later, Deptford, which created problems. Catherine 'did not feel justified in being away from [her] children' longer than could be helped, so she travelled to south-east London 'on Saturday night ... returning on Monday morning, and then travelling to and fro during the week.'

In her *Reminiscences* she described her journey from Hammersmith to Deptford, and this presumably would have been similar for Bermondsey. She said,

> Although the journey was not a long one, it was a tedious one, and in my state of health especially trying. I had first to journey from my own house to the station, then the underground journey to Moorgate St, lasting at that time three-quarters of an hour. I had then to take a cab across to London Bridge, where I again took the train to Deptford station, from whence I had to get to the hall, which I often did in a most exhausted condition, sometimes feeling it utterly impossible to go through with the service.[14]

Despite how she felt, she still nearly always did 'go through with the service.' Usually, the resident minister or some other person would lead the service through, and Catherine would preach. On one occasion, while the earlier parts of the service were proceeding, Catherine felt so ill that she feared that she would not be able to stand, let alone preach. She 'whispered to a young minister, sitting near [her], "You will have to preach."' Acting as a replacement for Catherine Booth was not an attractive prospect for any minister, young or old, and 'The poor fellow turned as white as death.' Catherine thought that he now looked 'almost as bad as' she felt. So, 'Seeing this, I strung myself up for the effort, casting myself on the Lord for the moment, who wonderfully brought me through, and we had a blessed meeting.'[15]

That 'frail thing, soon exhausted' often showed a remarkable degree of stamina and courage.

---

13 *The South London Chronicle,* 'Opening of the New Southwark Temperance Institute', 8 Apr. 1865, p. 5, col.6.
14 Booth, *Reminiscences,* p. 87; *Reminiscences CD,* pp. 43–44.
15 Ibid., p. 87; ibid., p. 44.

The Midnight Movement

Her mission in Deptford began on 7 May in a chapel, which was soon over-crowded. So, while they decided to continue the weeknight meetings in the chapel, they held the Sunday services in a large public hall. She believed that 'a real work for eternity was done' in Deptford. She also said that during that time she was 'never ... more conscious of the Master with [her] and in which the results seemed to give more ungainsayable evidence to the fact.'[16]

William, meanwhile, had concluded his meetings in Ripon and returned home to Hammersmith. After a few days rest he went to Launceston in Cornwall to begin another mission.[17]

That April Catherine was invited to speak for the Midnight Movement, a ministry to prostitutes, and she did so on two occasions. She later described her thoughts on receiving that invitation in her *Reminiscences*,

> I had from my first knowledge of the condition of society, which involved the existence, employment, misery and utter ruin of a large number of my sex for the gratification of the lusts of men, looked upon the class so degraded with feelings of the deepest pity, yearning over them and regretting my inability to help them. Consequently, when an invitation came to me to address a meeting of girls of this class, especially convened, I embraced it I might say with gladness.

At the first meeting, 'The girls had been invited to tea, which had been provided and spread before them with a liberal hand. [Catherine] sat and watched them eat.'[18] One account says that there were 'two to three hundred' prostitutes present and that the gathering was held in 'one of the very worst localities in London.'[19]

In the notes for the *Reminiscences*, there is an exchange of comments possibly between Catherine and William, which might suggest that he was at one of these meetings, most probably the first. Catherine was the guest speaker, but it seems that some involved in the movement made a few 'cold, perfunctory speeches' before it was Catherine's turn. When Catherine spoke, 'how they listened, [and] the marks of levity' disappeared from their faces. A writer from the *Wesleyan Times*, who was present, reported,

---

16 Ibid., p. 86; ibid., p. 43.
17 Ibid., p. 87; ibid., p. 44.
18 Ibid., p. 84; ibid., p. 41.
19 Unsworth, *Maiden Tribute*, pp. 2–3.

The address of Mrs Booth was inimitable, pointed, evangelical, impressive and delivered in a most earnest and sympathetic manner, bringing tears from many of those present and securing the closest attention from all. She identified herself with them as a fellow sinner, showing that if they supposed her better than themselves it was a mistake. All were sinners against God. This being the main point and not the particular sin which they might be guilty of. Then the Saviour was exhibited as waiting to save all alike, urging them by a variety of reasons to decision. Then the consequences of neglecting or accepting were set before them, encouraging them by relating details of the conversion of some of the most degraded characters she and her husband had been instrumental in bringing to Christ.

It was probably at the second meeting that '15 girls presented themselves to be taken away to the different homes provided.'[20]

Step by step, Catherine Booth was expanding her ministry and helping to establish a foundation for an Army not yet imagined, of which her husband would be the undisputed General. He was the one who could command.

---

20 Booth, *Reminiscences*, 84–85; *Reminiscences CD*, 41–42.

CHAPTER 27

The crucial decision

Catherine Booth 'was a warrior; of compromise
she would have none',

William Bramwell Booth.[1]

The call of London's East End

We now come to the most crucial moment in their lives, the vital decision, which was influenced by a host of experiences. It is best to let Catherine describe these events, as she did in her *Reminiscences*. It was late in June

> that events were shaping themselves for another new departure, one that was to lead to results more remarkable than any that had preceded it. When we look back now, we can see how God had been preparing us for it, gradually training our minds and hearts for the great work He had for us to do, and then leading us out step by step to its performance.

> It was, I think, just as I was closing the Deptford meetings that William came home from the City, where he had been about some business, with the information that he had promised two friends, who were much interested in the work outside the churches, to hold a week's meetings in a tent in Whitechapel.[2]

These two friends appear to have been John Stabb and Samuel Chase, Christian publishers. Some sources say that it was R.C. Morgan and Chase who made the invitation, but Booth, himself, writing six weeks into the campaign, said that it was Stabb and Chase[3], though Morgan may also have been involved in this work.

Catherine continued,

---

[1] Booth, *Echoes*, p. 7.

[2] Booth, *Reminiscences*, p. 88; *Reminiscences CD*, p. 44.

[3] Booth-Tucker quotes an article by William Booth from *The Christian*, which says that Stabb and Chase issued the invitation, *Catherine*, vol. 1, p. 389. See also Ervine, *Soldier*, vol. 1, p. 281; Green, *Catherine*, pp. 153–54.

Arrangements were ... being made for him to conduct some meetings in South Wales, but these were not completed, consequently he had a few days on his hands.

He was not at all taken with the idea [of preaching in London's East End] from a fear, very foolish I thought, that he was not cut out for talking to the poor people. Still, the longing he felt to do something for their benefit, which had never flagged from the days when he went down to the lowest purlieus of his native town and talked to the very poorest and worst, was still strong in him, and this together with the fact that he had no other engagement had led him to consent to the importunate request of these friends.

I don't know that I thought much about the matter. I was very glad for him to carry the news of salvation anywhere. I saw no particular opening for anything remarkable, neither did he. It was just a passing opportunity in our estimation for doing good and nothing more, so we took it up.

The mighty results that that have sprung from that week's services I have often used as an illustration of the value of importunity in a good cause. But for the determined arguments and entreaties of these two friends, humanly speaking, William would never have gone to the East of London, and consequently the first step towards the foundation of The Salvation Army would never have been taken, at any rate at that time.[4]

While Catherine says here '*we* took it up', it was, in fact, William who took it up.[5]

There are some other points in what Catherine says that need noting here. First, William seemed to doubt his ability to minister successfully to the poor, even though he cared about them. Though Catherine does not say it, he also seems to have been trying to avoid ministering in London. He had already tried that years before and had not met with the success that he had had in the towns and villages of Cornwall, Wales and Yorkshire. So, Wales, again, seemed more attractive, and he was making arrangements to conduct another mission there. But while waiting, he received this invitation to minister for a week in a tent and in the open-air in London's East End. He knew enough about the East End to know that it would be tough going. Fortunately, Stabb and Chase were very persistent, and Catherine says that

---

4 Booth, *Reminiscences*, p. 88; *Reminiscences CD*, pp. 44–45.
5 The original text of the *Reminiscences* does say 'we took it up.'

if they had not been, her husband would not have gone there. But he did, though this tent-mission was initially only intended as a fill-in until he could go to Wales. Neither Catherine nor William expected 'anything remarkable'.

On Sunday 2 July, William Booth began 'his week's meetings at the East, during which time his heart grew so much interested in the dense masses of misery, sin and vice around him,' that when his hosts asked him to stay another week, 'he cheerfully' agreed to do so. At the end of the second week, 'the interest he felt was greater still, and the question sprung up within him to as to whether he ought not to settle down there and devote his life to what appeared to him to be to the most destitute and deserted people he had ever seen.'

Catherine's *Reminiscences* become a little unclear at this point. It seems to have been during these two weeks that William was asking himself,

> 'Why go so far afield? Open your eyes and see. Can any people be more needy of the salvation of God than these tens of thousands who are all about you? Who needs the Saviour whom you preach more than they do and to whom could he possibly bring a greater blessedness for this world and the next? Why not stay here and spend your days in endeavouring to lift them out of the paths of their wretchedness by bringing them to God?' This feeling was ever present with me/him and with prayer and much deliberation he decided on giving up the evangelistic life after the fashion he had followed it for the last two years and a half, and to settle down and strive to benefit the masses in the East of London.[6]

The *Reminiscences* say, 'This feeling was ever present with me/him'. Which is correct, 'me' or 'him'? Catherine or William? The *Reminiscences* were dictated on Catherine's deathbed, taken down in shorthand, written up and then corrected by Catherine or anyone else available who might know about a particular issue. (There are many additional notes on the manuscript written by people known and unknown.) Here the manuscript has 'me', which has been crossed out and 'him' added in its place. The alteration seems to have been made at the time and not by a later researcher, so, presumably with Catherine's approval. 'Him' also fits the context better, as the text continues 'he decided...'. If that is correct, these thoughts were developing in William Booth's mind during those first two weeks in the East End.

---

6 Booth, *Reminiscences*, p. 88; *Reminiscences CD*, p. 45.

The decisive night

Then came the key night, the time of decision. This account again comes from the *Reminiscences*, though it is an addition, but one clearly made early, so presumably at Catherine's request. She said,

> I distinctly remember the occasion on which I believe we decided the question. He came home one night from one of the meetings, worn out, between 11 and 12 o'clock. Throwing himself into an easy chair, he said to me, 'Oh, Katie, as I passed the flaming gin palaces and the doors of the public houses tonight I seemed to hear a voice sounding in my soul, "Where can you go where there are such heathen as these and where there is so great a need for your labours?" And I felt as if I ought to stop and preach to these East End multitudes.'
>
> I remember the emotion this produced in my soul. I sat looking into the fire and the devil said to me 'This means another new departure, another new start in life.' But I did not answer discouragingly, but after a moment or two's pause for thought and prayer I said, 'Well, if you feel you ought to stay, stay. We have trusted the Lord once and we can trust Him again.'

That final comment referred to the matter of their financial support. When they had launched out as independent, travelling evangelists, they had no guaranteed income, yet the money had come. It was not always as much as they wanted, but they managed, and sometimes they had extra to help both the Mumfords and Mary Booth.

Catherine continued,

> I believe that night the resolution was formed to go on, at any rate until the Lord made his mind clear to us on the question.
>
> He had no idea himself of what he was going to do and no plan of how he was going to work, much less had he any notion of what was going to follow. He saw the people, he believed that the salvation of God was the remedy for all their miseries, temporal and spiritual. He knew they neglected it, because they were ignorant of it. They had trodden the broad way which led to destruction, because they were thoughtless. He set to work to make them think and hear and think[7] that so they might seek salvation and find it.[8]

---

[7] The duplication of 'think' may have been deliberate.
[8] Booth, *Reminiscences*, p. 89; *Reminiscences CD*, pp. 45–46.

It needs to be noted that it appears that at this time both Catherine and William 'believed that the salvation of God was the remedy for *all*' the miseries of the poor, '*temporal* and spiritual.' They assumed, and it was often proved correct, that if a man who spent much of his time and money in the local pub became a Christian, he would then spend more of his time and money on his family, and thus they could be lifted out of their poverty. However, there were still grim spectres such as unemployment and bad housing. Becoming a Christian did not necessarily help with those. Later the Booths came to realise that some temporal miseries required social, even political action.

The Founders?

We now come to the question, 'Who founded The Salvation Army?' Was it William Booth or William and Catherine Booth? Immediately after the above, Catherine added, 'I knew nothing of the beginning of the work, but from the descriptions that he gave me and some of the members of the household who went down to see it. Every moment of my time and all the strength I possessed was fully taken up by my own work and by the meetings at Islington.'[9] In other words, she says that she was not involved in the beginning of the mission that became The Salvation Army.

Booth's mission appears to have been originally called the East London Christian Revival Union[10], and it was William Booth's baby. Catherine Booth says that she 'knew nothing of the beginning of the work'. Yet it must be remembered that William had received an invitation from other people to participate in *their* mission. It appears that another man had been asked to lead it, but had been taken ill, so Stabb and Chase chose Booth as his replacement.[11] If this is correct, it suggests that the mission was just beginning and may not have been thought of as a long-term prospect. Rather, until Booth came along, it may have been viewed as only a short-term campaign and it seems to have been organised by more than one existing mission.[12]

But once William Booth became involved it appears to have begun to develop into something distinct and more permanent. Catherine said

---

9 Ibid., p. 89; ibid., p. 46.

10 Bennett, *General*, vol. 2, pp. 13, 39, fn. 1; Green, *Catherine*, pp. 154, 310, fn. 7.

11 Cyril Barnes, *With Booth in London*, p. 14.

12 Bennett, *General*, vol. 1, pp. 352–53.

that 'the helpers were very few' initially, and even some of those who were involved soon left because of disagreements with Booth over doctrine and methods.[13] All this suggests that William Booth quickly assumed command over this new and now ongoing mission.

Catherine dictated her *Reminiscences* in the late 1880s, that is, more than 20 years after these events, so the questions must be asked: 'How accurate was her memory? Did she really know "nothing of the beginning of the work"?' When one compares this dictated document on other issues with the letters written during the relevant years, one finds that her memory was generally accurate on major events, but sometimes faulty concerning details. (She did also use old publications and the memories of others to assist her in producing the *Reminiscences*.) So, was her memory playing tricks here?

One test is that she said that the summer of 1865 was very hot.[14] Was she correct? When the British newspapers of that summer are consulted, they clearly show that May, June, July and late August were hot, often unusually so, which led to an early harvest.

When her activities that summer and autumn are examined, she said she began a mission in Kensington at the end of July that lasted about three weeks. At Kensington her listeners would have been rich, very different from those that her husband was ministering to in the East End. She then conducted another in Islington, which was organised by three men including Samuel Chase, who had earlier questioned her right to preach. This presumably began early in September and seems to have ended mid-November. She described this mission as 'one of the most useful series of meetings I held in London. Christians of all denominations flocked to the services. We were packed and some hundreds of people professed salvation... Some half dozen prominent men from the different denominations helped me in opening the meetings and taking the oversight of the arrangements.'

It appears to have been while the mission was proceeding in Islington that there was a major problem at home. One morning Catherine was called to the nursery where Marian, about fifteen months old, was convulsing. The nurse thought the child 'had swallowed something and was choking, but it proved to be a fit.' Sadly, 'The attacks were continued with increased rapidity and virulence and did not leave her until her body and mind had

---

13 Booth, *Reminiscences*, p. 90; *Reminiscences CD*, p. 46.
14 Ibid., pp. 89–90; ibid., p. 46.

been permanently injured by them.' In addition, the usually-loyal Mary Kirton was causing Catherine some unease.[15]

Booth-Tucker says that Catherine then conducted a mission in the Horns Assembly Rooms in Kennington (not Kensington), near where William lived when he first moved to London. However, in her *Reminiscences*, Catherine says that the Kennington meetings were not held until the spring of 1866.[16] Booth-Tucker must be wrong, for Catherine also says that she did not end her campaign in Islington until mid-November 1865, which seems to have ended her campaigning for that year.

Late that summer and well into autumn, Catherine was heavily involved in missions in Kensington and Islington. She had problems at home, and she was also soon to give birth to her seventh child. Their home in Hammersmith was about 17 kilometres from where her husband was ministering in the East End. Islington was a bit closer, Kensington much closer.

In 'the middle of November' 1865, the Booth family moved from Hammersmith to Hackney in the East End[17], so that William could be near his work. That, at least, put her in the right place, but by then she was about eight months pregnant. When all this evidence is considered, it means that Catherine almost certainly had nothing to do with this new mission in the first six or seven months of its existence. In other words, she cannot be considered a founder of the East London Christian Revival Union. However, by the time that mission had gone through its various phases and name changes and become The Salvation Army, she had been heavily involved in it and was playing a major part in shaping its identity. She can, therefore, be fairly and rightly considered joint-founder with her husband of The Salvation Army.

Catherine also later recalled that for the 'next few weeks' after the move to Hackney that November, she 'was shut out from public work' as her pregnancy reached its later stages. So, she 'endeavoured to redeem the moments by attending to home duties.' On Christmas Day she gave birth to their fourth daughter. They called her Evaline Cory Booth, and Catherine always thought of her as 'A Christmas Box', a bonus.[18] Once more the

---

15 Ibid., pp. 91–94; ibid., pp. 47–50.

16 Booth-Tucker, *Catherine*, vol. 1, p. 399; Booth, *Reminiscences*, pp. 99–100; *Reminiscences CD*, p. 55.

17 Booth, *Reminiscences*, 96; *Reminiscences CD*, 52.

18 Ibid., 96–97; ibid., 52–53. Evaline's name is spelled in a bewildering variety of ways in books and articles, but this was probably the original spelling.

Booths paid tribute to their financial supporters in naming their child after the Cory brothers. Eva, as she became known in the family, proved to be the most formidable of the Booth children, and, as Evangeline Booth, was to be the fourth General of The Salvation Army.

Concentrating on this mission to the poverty-stricken East Enders was financially risky. Catherine, when well, earned some money from preaching to richer congregations. The Cory brothers and Mr and Mrs Billups also continued to support them. But they now had a family of two adults, seven children and, usually, two servants to feed and clothe. This departure into poor territory, amongst people who could not support them financially, was a great step of faith in God. However, it was rewarded early in 1866, as another financial supporter unexpectedly stepped in, a rich Liberal MP named Samuel Morley. Morley invited William to meet him, which Booth did. After a discussion about Booth's activities, Morley gave him a cheque there and then and a promise that there would be more to follow.[19]

The East London Christian Revival Union had begun. It had a talented and dedicated man at the helm. His equally, though differently, talented wife would soon become heavily involved in it. They had financial support, and soon would appear an army of converts intent on taking the gospel of Jesus Christ to the world.

---

19 Ibid., 97–99; ibid., 53–55.

APPENDIX

The Reminiscences

Catherine Booth dictated her Reminiscences on her death-bed, and they were recorded on more than 1,100 handwritten pages. However, the subsequent history of the Reminiscences is highly confused. Put simply, numerous newspapers reported in July 1891, the year after she died, that 600 pages of these Reminiscences had been lost. The existing collection of these papers begins at page 617, at August 1862. In other words, the existing pages have nothing about Catherine's life before 1862. One would also automatically assume that the missing 616 pages were the same as the 600 pages lost in 1891, 600 being a rounded down figure for the whole.

However, in Harold Begbie's biography of William Booth (1920) he quotes pre-1862 material from Catherine's 'Reminiscences.' In Catherine Bramwell-Booth's biography of her grandmother (1970), she also quotes pre-1862 material from Catherine Booth's 'Reminiscences.'

How can this be? There seems to be three possibilities. Firstly, the lost early pages were found in time for Begbie to use them, so not later than the second decade of the twentieth century, then lost again after Bramwell-Booth had used them. Secondly, the 600 pages originally lost were not the early pages. This would mean that 600 pages about a later period were lost in 1891 and found again, and then 616 pages of the early section were lost after 1970. These two alternatives seem extraordinarily unlikely, and, it must be added, rather careless. The third possibility is that there were two editions of the Reminiscences, but the second edition no longer exists or, at least, its location is unknown. While this third possibility is more likely than the first two, it would mean that not only have 600 pages of one edition of the Reminiscences been lost, but the whole of the other edition has either been lost, destroyed, or housed in some unknown place.

I deal with the issue of the lost pages in more detail in the *Australasian Journal of Salvation Army History*, vol.2, iss.2, pp.151–63. But it is a problem which still has not been solved.

In this work I use the existing edition of the Reminiscences (the original of which is in the International Heritage Centre of The Salvation Army) and the quotations in Begbie and Bramwell-Booth from the missing material.

David Malcolm Bennett (2019)

BIBLIOGRAPHY

The Booth Collection

Books

Booth, Catherine (Mumford), *The Diary and Reminiscences of Catherine Booth*, David Malcolm Bennett (ed), Camp Hill Publications, Brisbane, 2005.

Booth, William and Catherine, *The Letters of William and Catherine Booth*, David Malcolm Bennett (ed), Camp Hill Publications, Brisbane, 2003.

PDF

Booth, Catherine, 'Catherine Booth's Letters to her Parents' PDF, David Malcolm Bennett (ed), Camp Hill Publications, Brisbane, 2018.

The Booth Letters CD

Booth, Catherine (Mumford), *Catherine Booth's Diary*, in *The Booth Letters CD*, David Malcolm Bennett (ed), Camp Hill Publications, Brisbane, 2011.

Booth, Catherine, *Catherine Booth's Reminiscences*, in *The Booth Letters CD*, David Malcolm Bennett (ed), Camp Hill Publications, Brisbane, 2011. (The original is in the International Heritage Centre of The Salvation Army, CBB/8/2/1).

Booth, William and Catherine, *The Letters of William and Catherine Booth*, in *The Booth Letters CD*, David Malcolm Bennett (ed), Camp Hill Publications, Brisbane, 2011.

Other sources

'1851 England, Wales & Scotland Census Image, 35 Duke Street, Brighton, Sussex, England', https://search.findmypast.com.au/record?id=GBC/1851/4297812/00196&parentid=GBC/1851/0006 189741, '1851 England, Wales & Scotland Census: 7 Russell

Street, Lambeth, London', https://www.findmypast.com.au/transcript?id=GBC/1851/0004980388

'Age at last birthday', see Search Ancestry article on the '1851 England, Wales & Scotland Census,' https://search.ancestry.com.au/search/db.aspx?dbid=8860.

Amos, Denise, 'General William Booth', in The Nottingham Heritage Gateway, https://www.nottsheritagegateway.org.uk/people/generalbooth/structural.htm.

Arnett, William M. 'What Happened to Wesley at Aldersgate?' https://place.asburyseminary.edu/cgi/viewcontent.cgi?referer=https://www.google.com/&httpsredir=1&article=2041&context=asburyjournal.

'Ashbourne's Chapels and Ministers', <http://www.ashbournmethodist.org.uk/places/ashbourne-history/ashbournes-chapels-and-ministers.php.

'Ashbourne Methodist Society', www.ourashbourne.co.uk/event/the-ashbourne-methodist-society?rt=place%2Fthe-methodist-chapel.

Baptismal Register, St Botolph's Church of England, Boston, https://www.findmypast.com.au/transcript?id=GBPRS/LINCS/BAP/00201292.

Barnes, Cyril, *With Booth in London*, Salvation Army, London, 1986.

Begbie, Harold, *Life of William Booth*, 2 vols. MacMillan, London, 1920.

Bennett, David Malcolm, 'Catherine Booth's letters to her parents, John and Sarah Mumford', *AJSAH*, vol. 3, iss. 2, 2018, p. 51.

———, 'Catherine Booth's *Reminiscences* and the lost pages', *AJSAH*, vol. 2, iss. 2, 2017, pp. 154-55.

———, 'William Booth's resignation from the Methodist New Connexion', *AJSAH*, vol. 4, iss. 1, 2019, pp. 25-39.

———, *Catherine Booth on Women's Place and Ministry*, Camp Hill Publications, Brisbane, 2004.

———, *Hudson Taylor and China*, Rhiza Press, Brisbane, 2018.

———, *The General: William Booth*, 2 vols. Xulon Press, FL. 2003.

Bennett, David, *The Altar Call: Its Origins and Present Usage*, University Press of America, Lanham, 2000.

Best, Geoffrey, *Mid-Victorian Britain 1851–75*, Weidenfeld & Nicolson, London, 1971.

Book of Common Prayer, Cambridge University Press, London [1662], 1968.

Booth-Tucker, Frederick de L. *Catherine Booth*, 2 vols. Salvation Army, London, 1892.

Booth, (William) Bramwell, 'Vegetarianism' in *The Local Officer* and *The Vegetarian Messenger*, http://christianvegetarianarchive.blogspot.com/2010/09/vegetarianism-by-bramwell-booth.html.

———, *Echoes and Memories*, Hodder, London, 1926.

———, *These Fifty Years*, Cassell, London,1929.

Booth, Catherine Bramwell, *Bramwell Booth*, Rich & Cowan, London, 1933.

Booth, Catherine Mumford, *Female Teaching: or The Rev. A. A. Rees versus Mrs Palmer*, 2nd edition enlarged, G. J. Stevenson, London, 1861. This was downloaded from the 'Victorian Women Writer's Project: an Electronic Collection', Indiana University.

Booth, Catherine, *Female Ministry: Woman's Right to Preach the Gospel*, Salvation Army, NY (1870) 1975.

———, *Terms of Empowerment: Salvation Army Women in Ministry*, Salvation Army, NY, 2001.

Booth, Mrs (Catherine), 'Some Objections to the Salvation Army Answered', *The War Cry*, 23 Dec. 1880, p. 2, col. 1.

———, *Papers on Aggressive Christianity*, Salvation Army, London, 1891.

———, *Papers on Practical Religion*, 4th ed. Salvation Army, London, 1891.

———, *Popular Christianity*, 3rd ed. Salvation Army, London, 1888.

Booth, William, 'Resignation of The Rev. W. Booth', (privately printed, 1861); photocopy supplied by the International Heritage Centre of The Salvation Army, London.

Bramwell-Booth, Catherine, *Catherine Booth: The Story of her Loves*, Hodder, London, 1970.

Brooks, Alan, *West End Methodism: The Story of Hinde Street*, Northway, London, 2010.

Carlisle Journal, 'Irish Revivals, The', 7 October 1859, p. 5.

Cartledge, Charles, 'The Great American Revival', *MNCM*, 1858, pp. 295–318.

Carwardine, Richard, *Transatlantic Revivalism*, Greenwood, Westport, 1978.

'Catherine Booth', in Experience Ashbourne History, http://www. ourashbourne.co.uk/place/the-methodist-chapel.

Chester Chronicle, 'Pepper Street Chapel', 14 Feb. 1857, p. 8, col. 3.

Chilcote, Paul W. *The Methodist Defense of Women in Ministry: A Documentary History*, Cascade, Eugene (OR), 2017.

Christian Mission Magazine, 1 Feb. 1870.

Clarke, Major Douglas, 'Female Ministry in the Salvation Army', *The Expository Times*, 95, May 1984, pp. 232–33.

'Clifton Suspension Bridge', https://visitbristol.co.uk/things-to-do/Clifton-suspension-bridge-p24661.

'Constitution of the Christian Mission, The', Section 'XII, Female Preachers', from the Mission's Minutes of Conference, 1870, courtesy of the Heritage Centre of The Salvation Army, Sydney.

Cornish Telegraph, 'Farewell Tea Meeting to Rev. W. Booth', 22 Jan. 1862, p. 2, col. 4.

Crisp, Frederick Arthur (ed.) *Visitation of England and Wales*, vol. 10 (1902), pp. 81–83; https://en.wikipedia.org/wiki/List_of_mayors_Nottingham

Derby Mercury, 'Deaths', 9 Sept. 1829, p. 3, col. 1.

———, 'H. S. Milward's Academy', 29 Dec. 1808, p. 3, col. 4.

———, 'Ladies Seminary', 14 Nov. 1805, p. 3, col. 4.

———, 'To be sold by auction', 29 Aug. 1805, p. 2, col. 4.

———, 'Wanted', 18 Aug. 1808, p. 3, col. 4.

Eason, Andrew Mark, *Women in God's Army*, Wilfred Laurier UP., Waterloo, 2003.

Edwards, Maldwyn, *Methodism and England: A Study of Methodism and its Social and Political Aspects during the period 1850–1932*, Epworth, London, 1943.

Ervine, St. John, *God's Soldier*, 2 vols. Heinemann, London, 1934.

'Extracts from the Minutes of the Methodist New Connexion Newcastle District meeting, 6 and 7 May 1861, Part 15, 2nd and 3rd sections,' kindly supplied by the Tyne & Wear Archives & Museums, Newcastle upon Tyne.

Firbank, John, 'Revival in Gateshead', *MNCM*, 1859, p. 224.

Green, Roger J. *Catherine Booth*, Monarch, Crowborough, 1997.

Hardman, K.J. *Charles Grandison Finney: 1792–1875*, Evangelical Press, Darlington, 1987.

Harker, J., A Letter, 11 Nov. 1862, *MNCM*, 1862, pp. 755–76.

Hattersley, Roy, *Blood and Fire: William and Catherine Booth and their Salvation Army*, Little, Brown & Co., London, 1999.

Hentzschel, Garth R. 'A recitation to romance: a study on the poem and event which led to the romance of William Booth and Catherine Mumford', *AJSAH*, vol. 1, iss. 1, 2016, pp. 32–49.

———, 'A new look at an old poem: The poem that changed William Booth's life', *AJSAH*, vol. 1, iss. 1, 2016, pp. 50–71.

'Introduction: The Ashbourne Methodist Society, The', www.ourashbourne.co.uk/event/the-ashbourne-methodist-society?rt=place%2Fthe-methodist-chapel.

John Mumford, Derbyshire Burial Index 1538–1910, https://www.findmypast.com.au/transcript?id=R_22562224309.

Jones, W. Harold and G. A. M., *One is Your Master: The Story of One Hundred Years of the Wesleyan Reform Union*, WRU., Sheffield, Yorks., revision of 1949 ed.

Kendall, H. B. *The Origin and History of the Primitive Methodist Church*, 2 vols. Dalton, London, n.d.

Kent, John, *Holding the Fort: Studies in Victorian Revivalism*, Epworth, London, 1978.

'King Street Wesleyan Chapel Church Register, England & Wales Non-comformist births and baptisms', https://search.findmypast.com.au/record?id=TNA/RG4/0697/0/0030&parentid=TNA/RG4/BAP/337389

Lloyd's List, 30 Mar. and 2 May 1864. (Supplied by Gordon Taylor.)

London Daily News, 'Expelled Wesleyan Ministers, The', 1 Sept. 1849, p. 5, col. 5.

Longford, Elizabeth, *Victoria R. I.*, Weidenfeld & Nicholson, London, 1964.

M[umford], C[atherine], 'How to Train New Converts', *MNCM* 1855, pp. 319-21.

Minutes of the Methodist Conferences, 1765-98, vol. 1, pp. 282, 303-304, 325, 354, 389, 424. https://archive.org/details/ minutesofmethodi00wesl

MNCM, 'Brighouse Chapel', 1856, p. 102.

———, 'Connexional Progress', 1862, p. 40.

———, 'Dudley Conference, The', 1862, p. 451.

———, 'Extracts from the Minutes of the Methodist New Connexion Conference of 1854' 1854, pp. 664-70.

———, 'Extracts from the Minutes of the Methodist New Connexion Conference of 1857', 1857, p. 662, fn.

———, 'Extracts from the Minutes of the Methodist New Connexion Conference of 1858', 1858, pp. 666, 669.

———, 'Hartlepool', 1861, pp. 261-62.

———, 'Memoir of the Prince Consort', 1862, pp. 33-40.

———, 'Presentation to the Rev. W. Booth', 1857, pp. 102-103.

———, 'Presentation to the Rev. W. Dunkerley', 1858, p. 394.

———, 'Recent Conference at Liverpool, The', 1861, pp. 324-25.

———, 'Revival at Birmingham', 1856, p. 673.

———, 'Revival services, Macclesfield Circuit', 1856, p. 395.

———, 'Sheffield North Circuit', 1856, p. 549.

———, 'Stafford', 1857, p. 401.

———, 'Truro Circuit Revival Services', 1857, p. 400.

———, Firbank, John, 'Revival in Gateshead', 1859, p. 224.

———, Ridgway, John, 'Revival at Hanley', 1855, p. 96.

'Methodist Church in Cornwall', https://www.cornwall-calling.co.uk/churches/methodism-cornwall.htm.

Murdoch, Norman, 'Female Ministry in the Thought and Work of Catherine Booth', *Church History*, Fall 1984, p. 349.

———, *The Origins of The Salvation Army*, University of Tennessee, Knoxville, 1996.

Newcastle Guardian and Tyne Mercury, 'Lady Preachers', 8 Sept. 1860, p. 5, col. 6.

Oden, Thomas C. (ed.), *Phoebe Palmer: Selected Writings*, Sources of American Spirituality, Paulist, Mahwah (NJ), 1988.

Page from Church Register, England & Wales Non-conformist births and baptisms, https://search.findmypast.com.au/record?id=TNA/RG4/0697/0/0030&parentid=TNA/RG4/BAP/337389.

Petty, John, *The History of the Primitive Methodist Connexion*, Davies, London, 1864.

'Primitive Methodist Magazine', 1834, New Series, vol. IV, p. 359. (Courtesy of British Online Archives.)

Read, John, *Catherine Booth: Laying the Theological Foundations of a Radical Movement*, Pickwick, Eugene (OR), 2013, Kindle.

'Record Transcriptions, England Marriages 1538-1973, John Mumford and Sarah Milward', https://www.findmypast.com.au/transcript?id=R_22671016506/1

'Richard Burt's Household Members' and 'Maria Numford's Household Members', 1851 England, Wales & Scotland Census, Duke Street, Brighton, Sussex, England; and 1851 England, Wales & Scotland Census Image, 35 Duke Street, Brighton, Sussex, England. (This link to the 1851 Census was kindly provided by Gordon Taylor.)

Rochdale Observer, 'Review of the Year', 31 December 1859, p. 2.

Rowe, Mrs Elizabeth, *Devout Exercises of the Heart*, C. Cooke, London, 1737.

'*Royal Cornwall Gazette*, 'Penzance and its Western Villages', 21 Nov. 1862, p. 6, col. 1.

'Ryde Congregational Church', http://rshg.org.uk/ryde-churches/ryde-congregational-church-history.

Shade, JoAnn, 'Let the women speak', *The Officer*, May/June 2010.

Sheffield and Rotherham Independent, 'Metropolitan Gossip', 1 October 1859, p. 7.

'Slums in Southwark: Bradshaw's Handbook to London (No.85)', see Fig. 18, 'Duke-street, Southwark', https://londontraveller. org/2015/01/03/slums-in-southwark-bradshaws-hand-book-to-london-no-85.

Smith, George, *History of Wesleyan Methodism*, 3 vols. 3rd ed. Longman, Green, London, 1862.

'Staffordshire, Dioceses of Lichfield & Coventry Marriage Allegations And Bonds, 1636–1893', https://www.findmypast.com.au/ transcript?id=GBPRS/STAFF/MARRLICENCE/130289/1

Staffordshire Advertiser, 'Methodist New Connexion Annual Conference, The', 1 June 1861, p. 5, col. 5.

Staffordshire Advertiser, 'Mrs. Milward's Seminary', 7 Dec. 1805, p. 4, col. 5.

Stead, W.T. *Catherine Booth*, Nisbet, London, (1900) r.p. 1979.

Stead, W.T. *General Booth*, Isbister, London 1891.

The Argus, 'Wesleyan Conference: Recent Expulsion of Ministers, Official Statement, The', Melbourne, Australia: 1848-1954, Wednesday, 19 Dec. 1849, p. 4, http://newspapers.nla.gov.au/ndp/del/ printArticleJpg/4764941/3?print=y

The South London Chronicle, 'Opening of the New Southwark Temperance Institute', 8 April 1865, p. 5, col. 6.

Unsworth, Madge, *Maiden Tribute*, Salvationist, London, 1954.

Vickers, John A. (ed.), *A Dictionary of Methodism in Britain and Ireland*, Epworth, Peterborough, 2000.

Walker, Pamela J. *Pulling the Devil's Kingdom Down: The Salvation Army in Victorian Britain*, University of California Press, Berkeley, 2001.

Werner, Julia Stewart, *The Primitive Methodist Connexion: Its Background and Early History*, University of Wisconsin Press, Madison, 1984.

Wesley, John, *The Works of John Wesley*, 14 vols. 3rd ed. Thomas Jackson, Baker, Grand Rapids, (1872), 1991.

Western Times, 'Wesleyan Conference at Camborne, The', 16 Aug. 1862, p. 8, col. 1.

Wickham, E.R. *Church and People in an Industrial City*, Lutterworth, London, 1957.

Williamson, Andy, 'William Booth and Revival on Tyneside', www.vision.pwp.blueyonder.co.uk/revival/booth.html.

Wilson, A.N. *The Victorians*, Hutchinson, London, 2002.

Wilson, P.W. *General Evangeline Booth of The Salvation Army*, Scribner's, NY, 1948.

Youssef, Belinda (with Garth Hentzschel), 'An Overview and History of Toys Relating to The Salvation Army', *AJSAH*, vol. 3, iss. 1, 2018, pp. 21-44.

INDEX

Printed in Australia
AUHW011055101120
336786AU00014B/14

9 780647 530726